JUST IS

in the Art of SAMUEL BAK

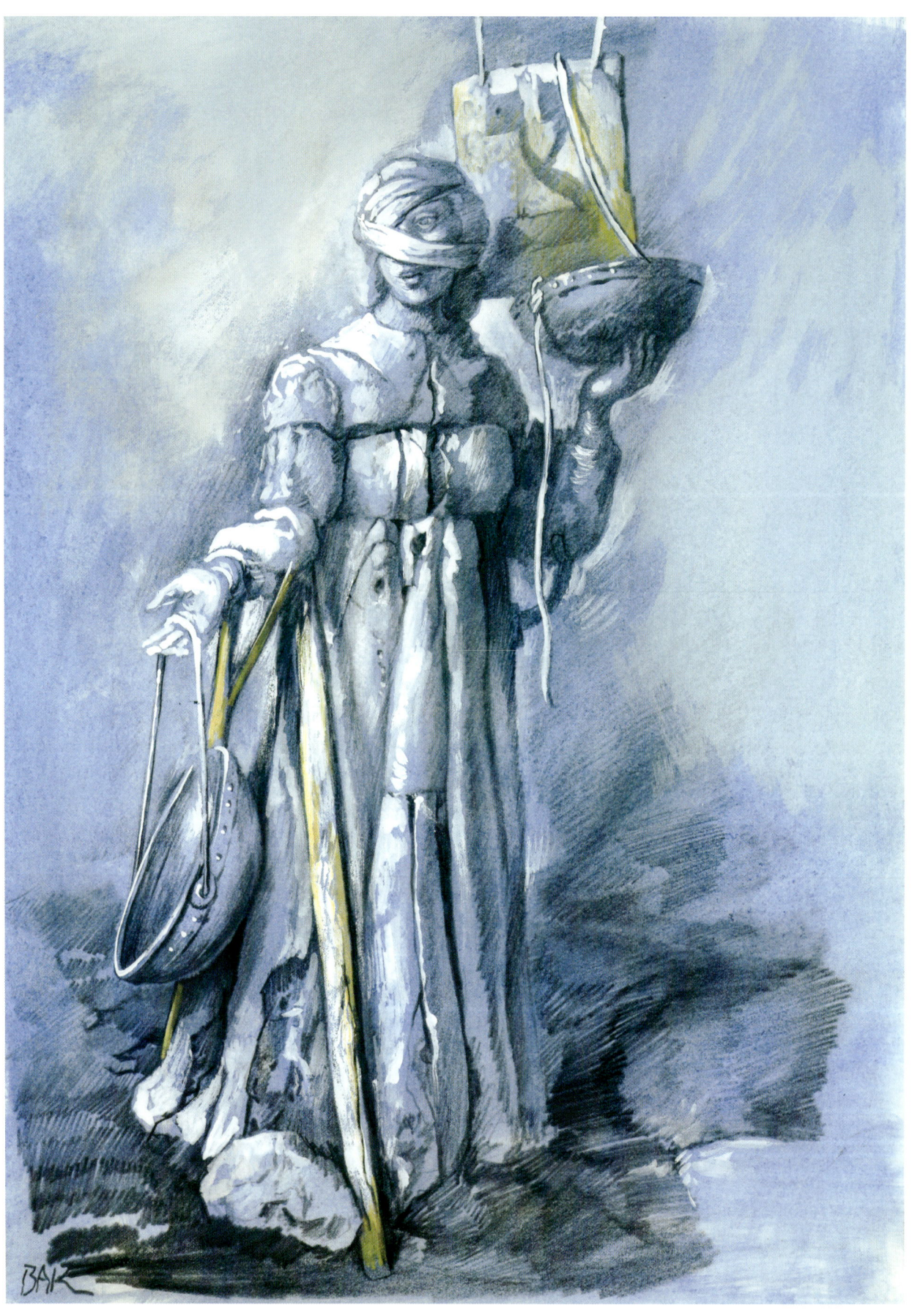

JUST IS

in the Art of SAMUEL BAK

BY GARY A. PHILLIPS

FOREWORD BY JOHN K. ROTH

PUBLISHED BY PUCKER ART PUBLICATIONS

DISTRIBUTED BY SYRACUSE UNIVERSITY PRESS

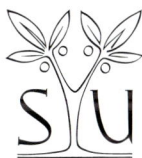

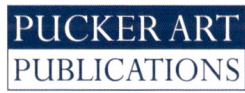

JUST IS

in the Art of SAMUEL BAK

© Pucker Art Publications, 2018

Published by Pucker Art Publications
Boston, Massachusetts 02116

Distributed by Syracuse University Press
Syracuse, New York 13244-5160

Design by Leslie Anne Feagley
Editing by Jeanne Koles and Paige Johnson
Printed in Canada by Friesens Corporation

ISBN: 978-1-879985-33-9

Library of Congress Cataloging-in-Publication Data

Names: Phillips, Gary Allen, author. | Roth, John K., writer of foreword. |
Pucker, Bernie, writer of supplementary textual content. | Bak, Samuel.
Paintings. Selections.
Title: Just Is in the art of Samuel Bak / Gary A. Phillips ; foreword by John
K. Roth.
Description: Boston, Massachusetts : Pucker Art Publications, 2018. |
Includes bibliographical references.
Identifiers: LCCN 2018002239 | ISBN 9781879985339
Subjects: LCSH: Bak, Samuel--Themes, motives. | Justice in art.
Classification: LCC ND979.B27 P49 2018 | DDC 759.95694--dc23 LC record available at
https://lccn.loc.gov/2018002239

FRONTISPIECE:
Study for "Tsedek"
Watercolor, gouache, and crayon on paper
14.25 x 10.25"
BK1988

For Sue and Bernie

Sam

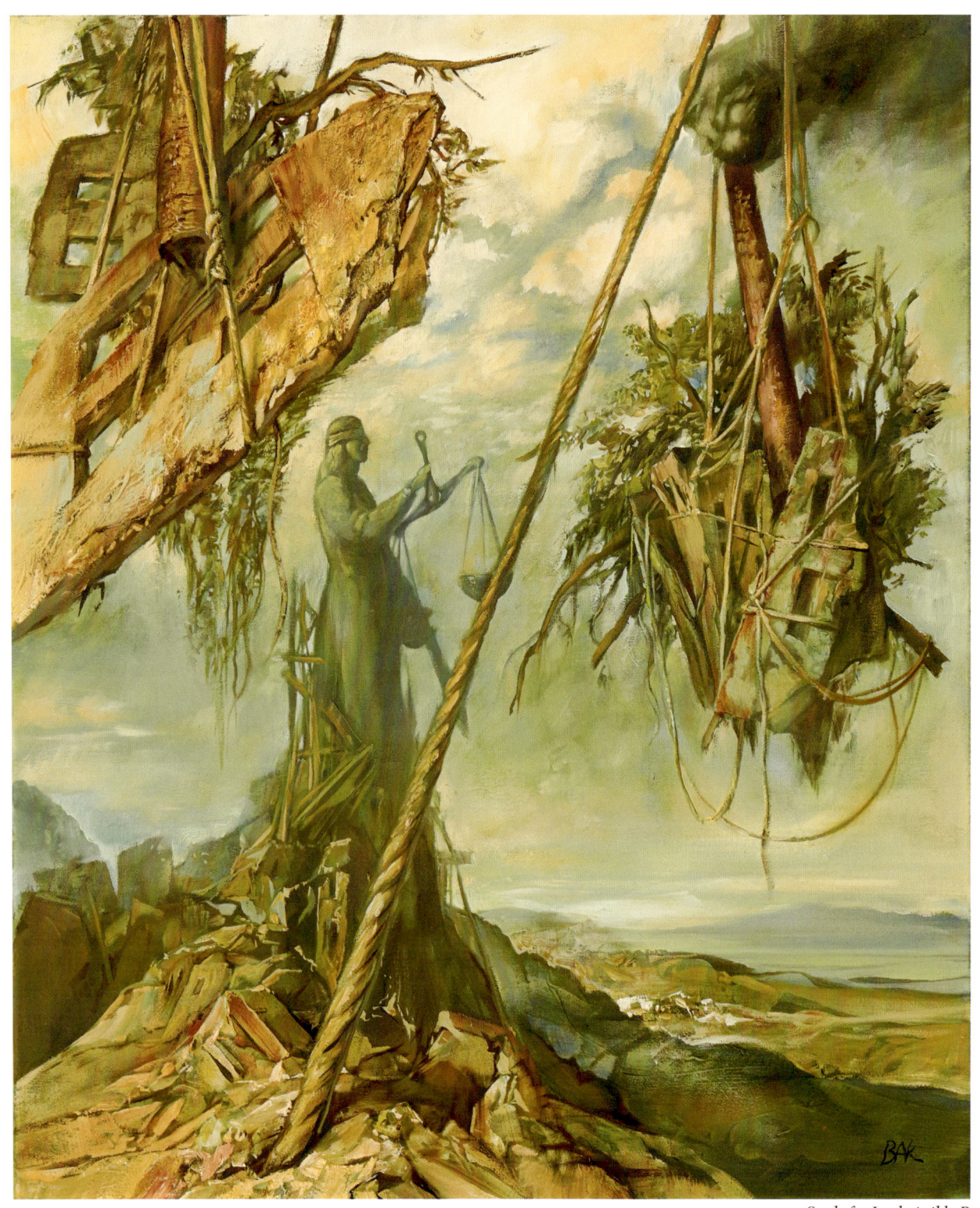

Study for Inadmissible B
Oil on canvas
24 x 20"
BK1961

FOREWORD

By JOHN K. ROTH

During his prolific and magisterial career, the Jewish artist Samuel Bak has drawn profoundly on his experience as a survivor of the Holocaust to assess the damage done by that catastrophe and to weigh how best to live in what Gary A. Phillips aptly calls "the atrocity universe." Brilliantly interpreted by Phillips, the paintings cataloged in *Just Is* are emblematic of Bak's challenging struggle with that dilemma.

In the murderous and monstrous world that Bak depicts, violence and suffering have laid waste to life and landscape. No casualty of the onslaught is more forlorn than *justice*. Bak's art limns how the Holocaust and other mass atrocity crimes wreck trust that right can withstand wrong, blast hope that goodness will prevail over evil, and scorn faith that someday justice will, as the biblical prophet Amos implores, "roll down like waters, and righteousness like an everflowing stream."

Intensifying his disorienting images, Bak's mastery includes the tersely tense word-play titles that identify his works. *Just Is,* for example, can sound like justice, seemingly affirming that what is good and right prevails or someday will. Unfortunately, the atrocity universe shatters that benign conjunction. Its wrack and ruin are compounded by indifference that gazes at our battered world—and perhaps even at Bak's artistic portrayals of a cratered existence bereft of justice—and settles for "just is," as in "that's just the way things are." Bak resists that despairing outcome, but his art also insists that one must discern deep down how desperately fraught things are before it can be even remotely credible to affirm justice/ just is.

If your experience is like mine, it may be that when you explore the paintings in *Just Is,* your eye—helpfully focused by one of his word-play titles—becomes a mind's eye that keeps pondering just a few of the many possibilities he puts before us. Otherwise, an encounter with Bak's atrocity universe can be unrelieved, overwhelming, and exhausting. Those experiences should be part of any journey—unavoidably somber and sobering—through desolation. But stopping places to ponder and reflect along the way show that if despair wins, injustice is needlessly compounded.

So, *Just Is* makes me pause to consider the drawing called *After the Before* (page 112). Reminded that destruction is the *after* of what

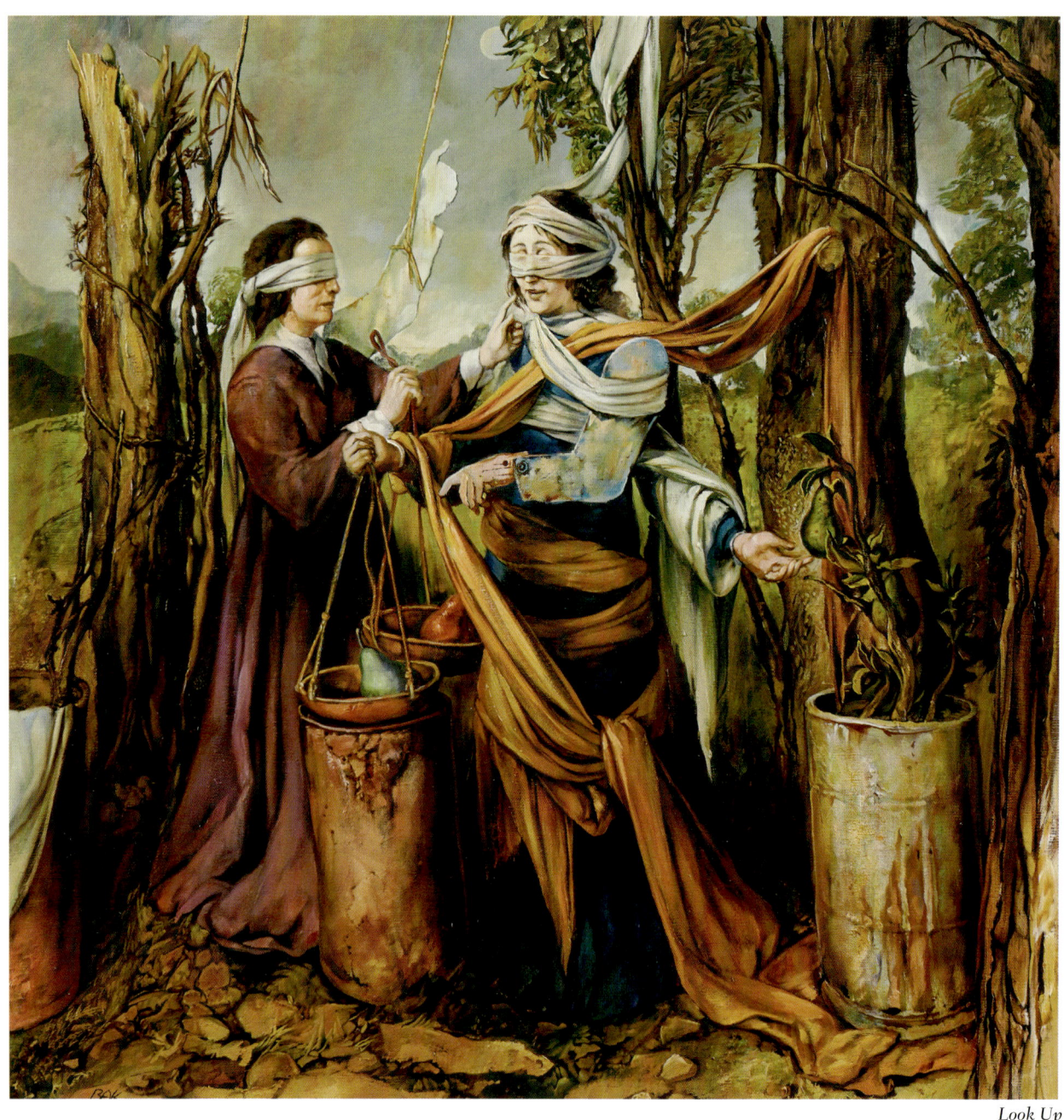

Look Up
Oil on canvas
36 x 36"
BK1933

2

stood *before,* I see three people who are present after the wreckage before them. Who are they? What are they trying to do? Can they do anything significant to restore justice after the before? Are they the scouts for a salvage team that will try to pick up the pieces and mend the fragments together again?

Bak paints questions. They teach that *justice* is an after-word. Cries for it and appeals to it are usually pronounced when something already has gone badly wrong. If life were fair, unscarred by greed, terror, war, genocide, to name but a few of the follies and failures, debacles and disasters that infect it, there would be little need to give justice a second thought. But justice deserves and requires much more than that. It does so because *justice* also remains an after-word in the sense that it is something still worth pursuing—going *after*—even though it is too rarely achieved despite claims that we pursue "justice for all."

Bak's question-painting insists on accountability as we live after the before. Easy to say, but another of his *Just Is* works, one called *In Vain* (page 80), suggests that such responsibility is too hard. A lone traveler in this painting appears fated to draw that conclusion: the way forward seems blocked by obstruction that contains shattered scales and a blurred figure of Justice, all obscured with barely traces remaining. What destination was the traveler after before the obstruction of justice? What will happen next? Was the traveler surprised, dismayed, indifferent, or moved to confront the obstruction with determination to try to set things right? If the latter, was the trip in vain? Will matters always be that way because that's just the way things are? *In Vain* may say "perhaps" or even "probably" but also "maybe not."

In spite of its bleakness, *Just Is* insists that we should bet our lives on *maybe not,* failing to do so at humanity's peril. That's what I see two women doing as they drag broken scales of justice on their way in the drawing called *Unrelented* (page 109). They may seem forlorn and in mourning, but Bak's title hints defiantly instead that the women refuse despair and thereby resist injustice no matter what. At the end of the day, and at every day's beginning too, *Just Is* says: Try to be unrelented. Like those women, relentlessly salvage and restore justice as well and as long as we can.

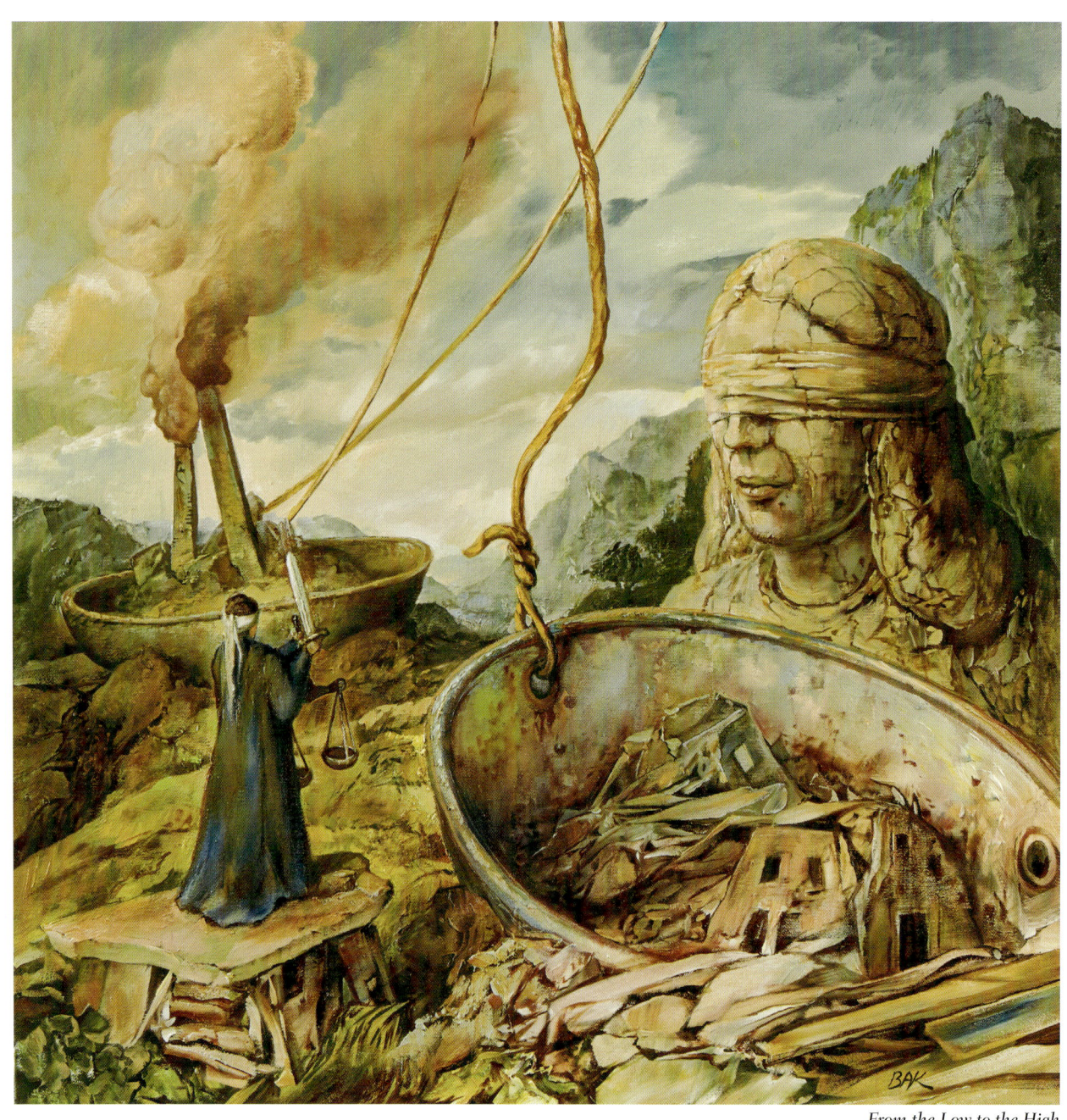

From the Low to the High
Oil on canvas
24 x 24"
BK1952

ICONS OF *JUST IS:*

Suffering Injustice and the Witness of Samuel Bak

By GARY A. PHILLIPS, WABASH COLLEGE

"Is there any meaning in life when men exist who beat people until the bones break in their bodies?"[1] This unsettling question, posed by Henri, a young partisan in Jean Paul Sartre's play *Men Without Shadows,* presents a picture of the horrific world of torture and suffering in occupied France. Apprehended by Nazi collaborators, Henri and four other resistance fighters are interrogated and tortured relentlessly by their Vichy captors in an effort to get them to betray one another. Over the course of three acts, the audience witnesses nonstop psychological and physical violence enacted on and off stage. By play's end, it becomes clear that extracting information is not the real purpose of the beatings; it is, instead, the sheer sadistic pleasure of inflicting pain and suffering upon another human being. To speak out or remain silent in the face of another's suffering is the dilemma of human freedom that Sartre's play represents.

The burden of Henri's question and the world of suffering presented in the play became a focus of Theodor Adorno's critique of certain forms of art that detach from the reality of broken bones or even the right to exist. Of concern are forms of committed art, like Sartre's play, that in their effort to express the meaning of suffering invariably conceal the faces of the tortured and torturer. Contesting Sartre's claim that only prose literature is capable of unmasking this suffering world in order to change it, Adorno insists that poetry, painting, and music do so far more effectively because, in pointing to the horror indirectly, they give expression to the inexpressible; by interrupting efforts to render suffering meaningful, these art forms manage to jolt and revolt in ways that keep us connected directly to the victims who suffer.[2]

A gifted composer, philosopher, and refugee from Nazi persecution, Adorno reflects on the relationship of suffering and art as a wider lens for diagnosing the failure of Enlightenment values and ideals for achieving human freedom, dignity, and justice.[3] This failure is expressed most horrendously in Auschwitz,[4] an emblem of the Nazi-administered world of unspeakable suffering and violence.[5] Critical of all philosophical and theological efforts to attribute meaning to suffering—to "squeez[e] any kind of sense, however bleached, out of the victims' fate"[6]—Adorno insists that art after Auschwitz can render suffering concrete in ways that resist the sort of abstraction that works to distance one person from the material reality of another's pain. Suffering remains "mute and inconsequential" when the lived experience of injustice is abstracted and forced to bear, as in Sartre's case, political meaning.[7] Art that abstracts and aestheticizes broken bones, including art that views itself as ethically committed, commodifies and abases that suffering and, even more disturbingly, has a hand in sustaining the culture responsible for it. Instead, according to Adorno, all art after Auschwitz must be "burdened by the weight of the empirical"[8] and "think in contradictions"[9] if it is to respond truthfully and ethically to individual and community suffering.[10]

But how can art speak truthfully and ethically to suffering when, as Adorno also famously declares, "to write lyric poetry after Auschwitz is barbaric?"[11] His oft-quoted statement is heard by many as a call to silence poetry—indeed art altogether—in the face of the extreme injustice of the Holocaust world.[12] However, when read within the context of his broader critique of the disenchanted and damaged modern world, his accusing statement about poetry should be read not as a prohibition against representations of barbarity but rather as a paradoxical call for art to actively "think against itself" in its creative representations of brutality.[13] In response to atrocity, art's responsibility is but to grapple with the concrete realities of suffering and torture while steadfastly refusing every effort to squeeze sense out of the victim's fate.[14] For Adorno, the weight of the empirical is the demand of justice: "no art which tried to evade [the victims] could stand upright before justice."[15] "The abundance of real suffering tolerates no forgetting," he insists. "[I]t is now virtually in art alone that suffering can still find its own voice, consolation, without immediately being betrayed by it. The most important artists of the age have realized this."[16]

Bak and Bearing Witness

Holocaust survivor Samuel Bak is clearly one of those important artists of our age, in whose artwork suffering finds its voice and injustice is exposed. At age 84, Bak has for more than seven decades painted testimonies to the devastation and loss of Jewish self, family, and culture. A child prodigy, and the only living survivor/artist to have exhibited both in the ghetto and Yad Vashem, Bak has devoted his artistic energies to the task of never forgetting the suffering. His artwork bears witness to persons and communities whose names and faces have been forgotten, especially the million murdered children. His preoccupation with particular bodies and worlds—often presented in fragmented and disfigured, impermanent and provisionally reconstructed forms—has focused aesthetic, moral, and now juridical attention on the materiality of suffering and loss.[17] The beauty of his paintings stands in jarring tension to the barbarity of their subject matter, the effect that of disrupting and demanding attention to real bodies achieved by grounding both art and viewer in this suffering world.

We recall Bak's efforts to disrupt and demand attention demonstrated, for example, in his nearly 100 paintings of the young boy captured in the iconic Warsaw Ghetto Boy photograph. "It is no dream world," Bak describes, "but rather reality experienced and expressed through metaphor."[18] The "poignancy of [the boy's] uniqueness" and "the specific that revolts" ground his effort to paint a memorial to each of the million children lost, an impossible effort to recover "a past that can never be fully remembered or forgotten."[19] The burden of the empirical is a constant weight holding brush to canvas and calling Bak to not forget each individual face and body, like the nameless Jewish child, swallowed up in the abyss.[20] The gravity of injustice keeps Bak connected to the suffering.

Bak's distinctive visual syntax, vocabulary, and style give voice to the incomprehensibility of particular, real lives deprived of justice. Suffering's "mute and inconsequential" character becomes, on Bak's canvases, visual testimony that, through representational strategies, compositional details, and striking colors and textures, express the inexpressible absences in his life: his murdered childhood friend Samek; his martyred father Jonas; his grandparents Shifra, Rachel, Khone, and Hayim massacred in the Ponary woods; and his excised

Vilna Jewish community and culture.[21] Always with particular persons, places, and events as anchors, his canvases offer tenuous constructions of present absences and absent presences that address his loss of family, community, and world. Repetition and gaps, paradox and particularity shape the rhythm and timbre of Bak's voice as it performs a witness to these losses. The creation of a fertile imagination that renders contradiction and paradox with a palette of beauty and brutality, Bak's canvases bear witness to loss and steadfastly refuse to forget the injustice of suffering.[22]

Franz Rosenzweig once wrote that art paradoxically "aggravates the suffering of life and at the same time helps people to bear it," teaching "us to overcome without forgetting." Far from erasing trauma or obscuring injury, art overcomes by "structuring suffering, not by denying it. The artist knows himself as he to whom it is given to say what he suffers ... He tries neither to keep the suffering silent nor to scream it out: he represents it. In his representation he reconciles the contradiction, that he himself is there and the suffering also is there; he reconciles it, without doing the least debasement of it."[23] Samuel Bak acknowledges his own effort to overcome without forgetting when he comments that his paintings protect "the sensitive scar of an ancient wound while still remaining true to the knowledge of the wound itself."[24] Bak is there in his artwork, and so too the suffering.

Just Is *and Justice*

In his recent *Just Is* series, Bak concentrates his creative witnessing and aggravating energy on iconic Lady Justice and the lex talionis, the biblical principle of restitution expressed most commonly as "an eye for an eye." His title—a word play on *justice*—offers an important clue about the metaphorical imagination at work in Bak's representations of a damaged world in which the principles and protections of justice no longer prevail. In his familiar artistic style, Bak draws upon culturally recognizable icons of justice to interrogate and refashion them as alternative iconic images of *just is*. We recognize similar creative efforts with other iconic images: the photographed Warsaw Ghetto Boy; the pensive angel in Albrecht Dürer's engraving *Melencolia I*; and God and Adam's near touch in Michelangelo's fresco, *The Creation of Adam*. By contrasting the iconic form with an alternate image, Bak exploits the negation at the heart of metaphor—the comparison of two things that are both alike and not alike—to foment alternative perspective and action, to unsettle settled comprehension and conscience, and to incite ethical reflection on the part of his viewer. By transforming the standard icons of secular and sacred justice, Bak plays upon the visual and verbal tensions between *Justice* and *Just Is* to provoke wrestling with the status of founding religious and juridical symbols and principles, and their purchase upon life—or rather *deathlife,* to employ Lawrence Langer's discomforting term[25]—after atrocity. How do we envision justice for six million Jews murdered and those who survived the killers? What weight do the Nuremberg Trials, the Convention on the Prevention and Punishment of the Crime of Genocide, or the Universal Declaration of Human Rights bear upon the scales of justice? What moral force can the repeated promises of the biblical lex talionis exert to restore balance, or *shalom* as the Rabbinic tradition envisioned it, to a world where children are tossed into furnaces alive or slaughtered by terrorists at concerts or in classrooms? In the post-Holocaust world, both traditional human and divinely sanctioned justice have collapsed under the weight of unspeakable suffering, leaving the very notions of justice, balance, and restitution devoid of meaning and the consolation of "bracing pieties."[26] In our age of ongoing atrocity, after Rwanda and Darfur, Srebrenica and Breslan, Paris and Orlando, Manchester, and Las Vegas, Bak poses Henri's question in visual terms: Is there any meaningful icon of justice or principle of restitution in life when men exist who beat people until the bones break in their bodies? Bak's *Just Is* images raise these and other vexing questions, but as his style, Bak leaves the work of responding to his viewers.

Iconic Lady Justice and the Lex Talionis

"The arc of the moral universe is long but it bends toward justice." Martin Luther King, Jr.'s iconic words, borrowed from the early 19th century American Transcendentalist preacher Theodore Parker, express unqualified confidence in the spiritual trajectory of life.[27] In the physics of the moral universe, justice exerts a gravitational pull that anchors and buttresses human experience in the face of suffering in-

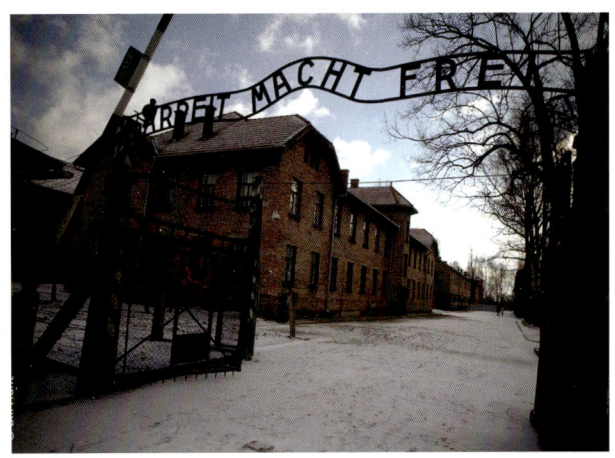
Auschwitz 1 Gate

justice. The celestial imagery evokes the tradition of the Hebrew Bible prophets with its assurances of God's universal justice (*mishpat*) and righteousness (*tzedekah*) that will be extended to all of creation. God's promised justice is orthogonal to a desiccated world wracked with violence inflicted upon the weak and the oppressed. This assurance gives the Prophet Amos confidence to imagine that God's life-giving "justice rolls down like waters, and righteousness like an ever-flowing stream" (Amos 5:24, NRSV). King's moral universe is further bolstered by a Western legal tradition, with its Christian theological roots, grounded in the rule of law and constitutional principles that guarantee justice will be neither delayed nor denied: "No one will we sell, to no one will we refuse or delay, right or justice," the Magna Carta of 1215 promises. In the moral universe, iconic justice confidently stands by and for the principle that those who suffer injustice and are incapable of standing up for themselves will be protected.

In his *Just Is* series Bak paints an alternative universe—*the atrocity universe*—in which the promise of divine justice and assurance of the rule of law, and the culturally familiar icons that have come to symbolize both, are reprised through the lens of his Holocaust experience. In stark contrast to King's moral universe, Bak presents a monstrous cosmos in which the sanctity of individual and communal life is violated, and suffering now structures human relationships, time, and space. The arc of the atrocity universe bends not toward justice but injustice—the gates of Auschwitz, the fields of Cambodia, the hamlets of Kosovo, the mountains of Rwanda, and the jungles of the Congo. The gravity of past and repeated atrocities presses Bak to interrogate the status of justice's standing and the viability of any universal ethical demand for public and private restoration in the face of life after Auschwitz. Questioning the foundations of grand justice, Bak presents us instead with *Just Is*, altered in stature and effect.[28]

Grand Lady Justice and biblical lex talionis here refracted through Bak's experience of suffering injustice belong to a longstanding historical, artistic, and legal tradition. In Western iconography, justice is traditionally figured as a young, vital woman crowned with plant sprigs, draped in flowing robes, and, since the sixteenth century, typically blindfolded.[29] In her left hand she grips a balance scale and in her right a double-edged sword. The substantial ambiguity introduced by the blindfold serves Bak's imaginative ends well. In principle, blindfolded eyes signify impartiality and fairness. In practice they can inhibit efforts to determine if the scales are properly balanced or how the sword is being wielded. As biblical Esau's stolen blessing attests, justice can easily be thwarted by the lack of sight (Gen. 27:1–38).

Iconic Lady Justice's origin is ancient and uncertain.[30] Balance scales and sword link her to Near Eastern and Greco-Roman sister goddesses of justice and morality. The Egyptian goddess Ma'at, the daughter of the sun god Ra, carried a sword but not a scale of justice. Themis, the Greek goddess of divine order, law, and custom and her daughter, Dike, goddess of human justice who maintains social and political order, are both blindfolded and carry scales and sword. The Roman goddess Justitia, who regularly stands vigil atop modern Western courthouse cupolas and guards courtroom entrances, is also depicted with balance scales and sword although she is not always blindfolded.[31] In the medieval period the Christian theological consolidation with pagan justice lead to the classical goddesses of justice joining the quartet of Christian cardinal virtues alongside Prudence, Temperance, and Fortitude to become one of the formidable seven theological virtues partnered with Faith, Hope, and Charity.[32] Before its association with justice in the early modern period, the blindfold connoted stupidity or even the lack of righteousness. But by the late fifteenth century, blindness had become a virtue. Blind justice is meted out objectively, without fear or favor, regardless of identity, money, power, or weakness. Still, the tension between sight and blindness stubbornly infuses her figure. Recurring images of judges with hands or arms severed or undergoing gruesome punishment remind us that in human hands justice is easily perverted and that the veritable icons of justice themselves suffer.[33] Parodies of a peeking Lady Justice with sagging blindfold and eyes partially visible through the masking material signal the uncertainty and precariousness of justice, indeed of all icons. Bak's compositions exploit these complications.

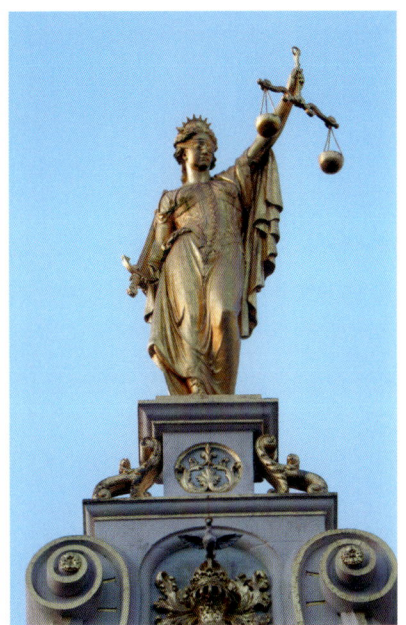

Statue of Lady Justice, Palace of Justice, Bruges, Belgium

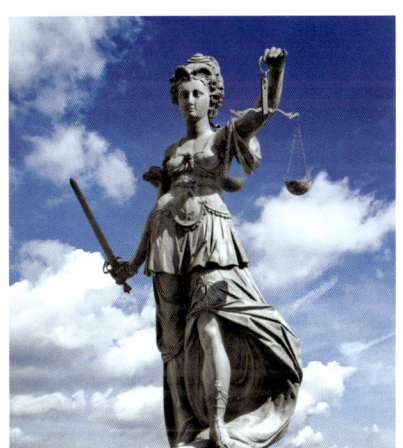

Statue of Lady Justice (Justicia), Frankfurt, Germany

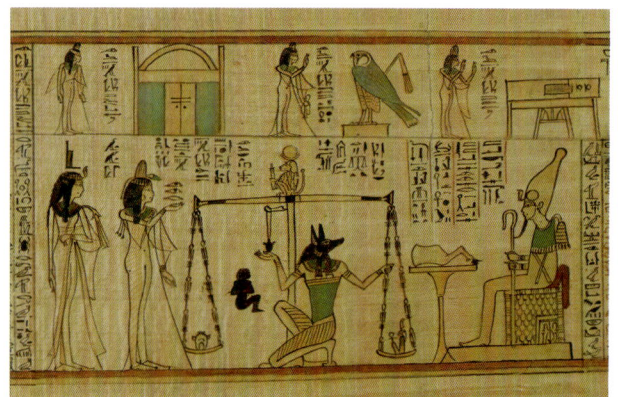

Petitioner's heart-soul (KA), being weighed on the scales of Justice (Goddess Ma'at) by Anubis (scale setter) against the feather of truth (Shu), ca. 1050 B.C., papyrus and paint, collection of The Metropolitan Museum of Art, Rogers Fund, 1930, 30.3.31

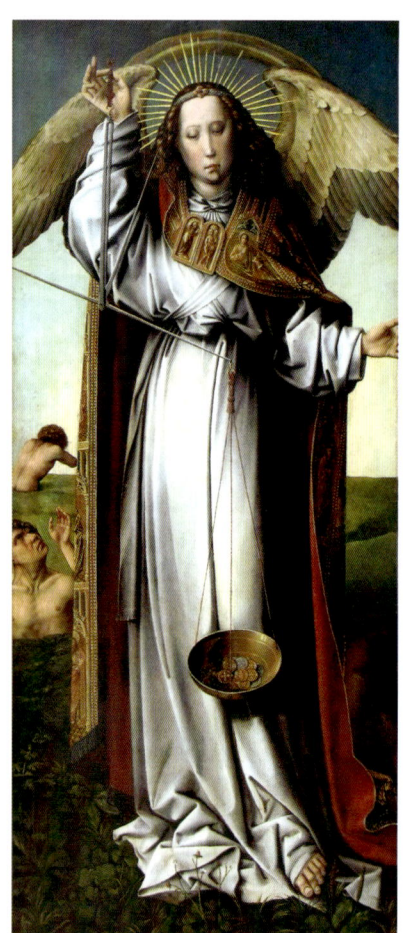

Colijn de Coter (c. 1440–1445–c. 1522–1532), St. Michael Weighing Souls During the Last Judgement

The scales Lady Justice holds have an equally uncertain genealogy. The earliest use of scales of justice is to be found in the ancient Egyptian mythological depiction of the judgment of the dead in the *Book of the Dead*.[34] Anubis judges the fate of the dead, their heart or soul in one pan and an ostrich feather belonging to the goddess Ma'at in the other. In popular medieval Christian iconography, St. Michael weighs believers' souls at the Last Judgment. However, if the scales be tipped or in equipoise, what does either portend? The meaning and consequences vary depending upon culture and context. In ancient Egypt, hearts heavier or lighter than the feather of Ma'at meant immediate demise at the hands of Ammit, the Devourer of souls. For biblical Israel, rigged scales were an abhorrence: "A false balance is an abomination to the LORD, but a just weight is His delight," the writer of Proverbs warns (Prov. 11:1 [NRSV]).[35] The Prophet Hosea reserved a special condemnation for the merchant who oppresses the poor with false balances (Hos. 12:7). However, justice defined according to the principles of equivalence and substitutability—privileged concepts in Enlightenment instrumental rationality—can also paradoxically be made to increase suffering and injustice. Hitler's order to exterminate the men, imprison the women, and remove the children of the Czech village of Lidice and raze it in reprisal for the assassination of Reinhard Heydrich was an act of violent equivalence: 340 souls for one.[36]

The lex talionis has equally deep roots in antique Near Eastern society.[37] Although its precise origin is also lost to us, the ubiquitous presence of the lex talionis, like Lady Justice herself, suggests a near-universal ethical concern for public and private restitution across different cultural systems with its role in these systems varying.[38] The talion is cited in the Code of Hammurabi, Middle Assyrian Laws, as well as in Greek, Roman, and Jewish scriptural and rabbinic formulations in the Talmud and responsa literature. In the biblical literature, the talion is found in multiple places and forms in the books of Exodus and Deuteronomy, Leviticus and the Gospel of Matthew[39] where different combinations of eyes, teeth, hands, feet, lives, burns, wounds, and stripes are paired, weighed, measured, and balanced.[40]

Common to the variations, which in some form likely circulated as a compendium of laws incorporated into the Torah and Christian gospel in diverse ways and at different times, are the paired eyes and teeth, which are discrete enough, literally, to be removed and placed on a scale.[41] Of all the body parts, however, it is the figurative eye that captures the biblical—and so too Bak's—metaphorical and moral imagination.

A pecuniary sense of the talion replaced a corporal one after the 5th century BCE, although the corporal sense of talion returned in medieval Christian Europe and served as legal justification for corporal punishment until the end of the 18th century. In the Rabbinic legal tradition, attested by Maimonides, the plain meaning of the Hebrew alliterative phase *ayin tachat ayin,* "an eye for of an eye," is unquestionably pecuniary and not corporal; a person who causes injury is responsible for making compensatory restitution to the injured party, thus making whole what was broken, restoring peace to situations of conflict and disorder.[42] The weighing of one eye against another, the effort to achieve financial equipoise, affirms the fundamental moral and social responsibility to rebalance the scales, correct injustice, and make life whole (*shalom*) again.[43]

After Eleanor's arrest, Shakespeare's King Henry comforts himself that the system of justice will rectify the wrong and "Poise the cause in justice's equal scales, Whose beams stands sure, whose rightful cause prevails."[44] In the presumed moral universe restitution and restoration do return imbalanced scales to equipoise. But after Auschwitz how can the burden of the weight of six million be measured? What does balance, wholeness, and moral responsibility mean for survivors who live in an atrocity universe anchored in an economy of suffering injustice? What stature and status do the icons of Lady Justice and the lex talionis have once reconfigured for this atrocity universe? Bak shows us in vivid and disturbing detail.

Icons of Just Is

Bak's Lady *Just Is* appears to us in varying conditions, poses, and garbs juxtaposed to once familiar biblical symbols of covenant, law, and justice. Noachic rainbows and Mosaic tablets of the law, talionic eyes and Hebrew letters combine with female figures and

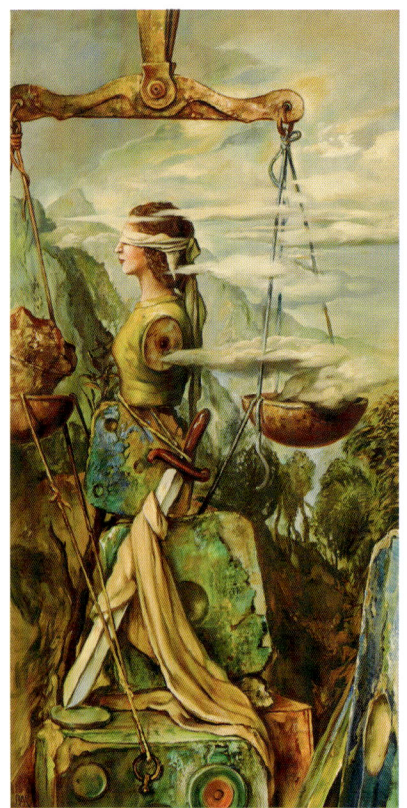
High Up

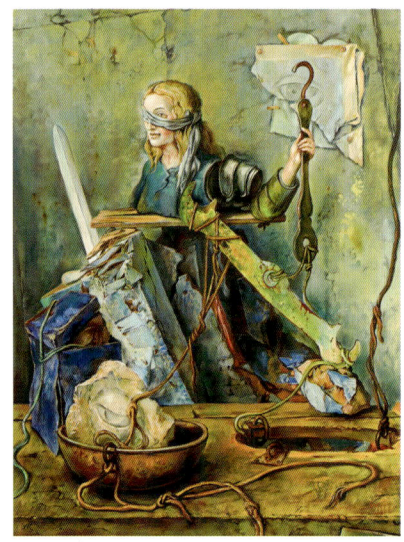
By Hook

balance scales, blindfolds and swords in ways intended to disrupt the perceptual, conceptual, and moral fields of vision at home in the moral universe. Bak's damaged and modified female bodies, defunct and imbalanced scales, and ubiquitous, unblinking stony eyes peer out at us from his canvases—onto a landscape of devastation that is anything but whole, and upon justice that is now virtually unrecognizable.

We first encounter a disarmingly statuesque Lady *Just Is High Up* (BK1963) in the clouds perched on a stack of dice, wagering perhaps that despite a missing arm she, too, can maintain her equilibrium as the intact balance scales do their equipoise. Her stature as assurer of justice is ironically on display for us, while her blindfold prevents this Lady *Just Is* from appreciating the preposterousness of her situation. The pips that dot the faces of the dice beneath her, like so many eyes peering out from the canvas, suggest that the pursuit of justice for those who suffer is little more than an elaborate game of chance, a role of the dice, that often as not turns up the snake eyes that Bak presents here, the worst possible outcome for any gambler.

In *By Hook* (BK1939) Lady *Just Is* appears in pieces, her body a greatly diminished version of her former iconic self. Neither high up in the heavens nor in her customary spot atop the public courthouse dome, her fragmented upper torso, now brought low, precariously balances on a wooden slat atop a stone heap. With arm severed at the elbow, she still manages by hook or by crook to maintain herself and the balance handle upright, quite the balancing act. The configuration gives an ironic twist to a variant of King's maxim—"The moral arc of the universe bends at the elbow of justice."

The talionic eyes around the canvas invite Bak's viewers to connect the dots not only between iconic Lady Justice and the lex talionis, but also between them and the damaged world, where suffering is inflicted upon others for the sheer pleasure of it. A slipped blindfold exposes an eye focused intently beyond the canvas frame. Is Lady *Just Is* aware of her predicament? Does she know if she is still able to stand upright and perform her juridical duties detached from the ruin around her? Is she up to the balancing task? We might ask the same of Bak's art. Can his art represent injustice in ways that maintain connection to the material suffering he expresses in such vibrant colors and paradoxical configurations? What is the balance that Bak's paintings must maintain between the beautiful and the barbaric?

A lone balance pan holds a second eye, its mate completely dropped from sight through the tabletop. What massive force ripped the hole and shattered the balance apparatus? Yet a third eye peeks out from a half-lidded box perhaps wondering the same thing. Are we eyewitnesses to a scene of failed justice or, alternatively, is suffering, yet persistent, Lady *Just Is* presented here a casualty of the catastrophe yet managing somehow to stand her new post? Bak preserves the ambiguity and does not let us forget that answering this question is our responsibility.

In her left hand Lady *Just Is* elevates a hook/question mark extending from the now defunct balance scales. The question mark, a favored image in many Bak paintings, tops the balance handle, which is framed by another eye drawn on a canvas tacked to a wall. Peeking out from behind this talionic eye we see the curved tops of two blank and blindfolded tablets of the law, a trope Bak employs elsewhere in this series (*By Law*, BK1930; *Ever Ready*, BK1942). Is a shrouded Mosaic tablet a way to protect covenantal law from looking out upon a scene of Jewish devastation? If the blindfold were lowered, would we see a Western juridical and Christian theological tradition that appropriates Jewish principles of justice with its talionic law, all the while demonizing Jews and worse? Christian supercessionism and racialized anti-Semitism provided the Nazis with all the justification needed to erase Judaism and all things Jewish, even evidence of the murders. Who and what, by implication, is missing from this picture, no longer in sight, if not the Jews who were made to suffer uselessly? Here, as elsewhere, Bak's unblinking talionic eyes stare back at us *In Search Of* (BK1965) answers to disturbing questions about *Just Is*, what we see, and, importantly, what we choose not to see.

The concern for evidence of injustice leads us to speculate whether the reality that Bak's graphic images present would be ruled *Inadmissible* (BK1931; page 16) in a court of law. A full-bodied Lady *Just Is* stands off in the distance foregrounded by a scene of a near-total devastation. Two belching chimneys, bound up in the wreckage of civilized life bundled and belayed by rope, suspend above a massive debris field that partially obscures our view of her. In *Study for*

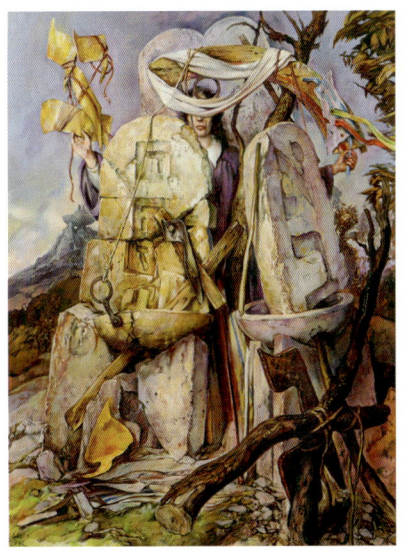

By Law

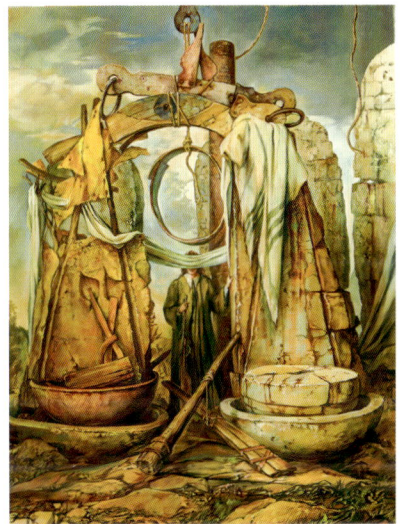

Ever Ready

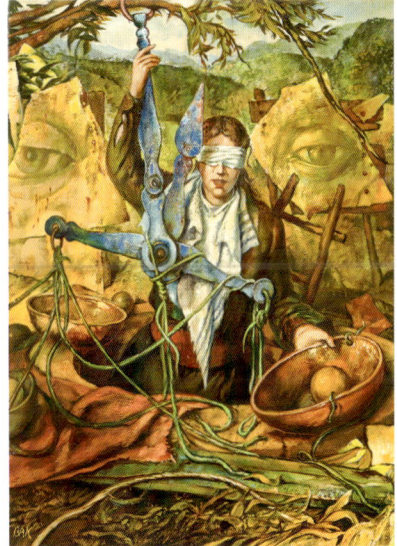

In Search Of

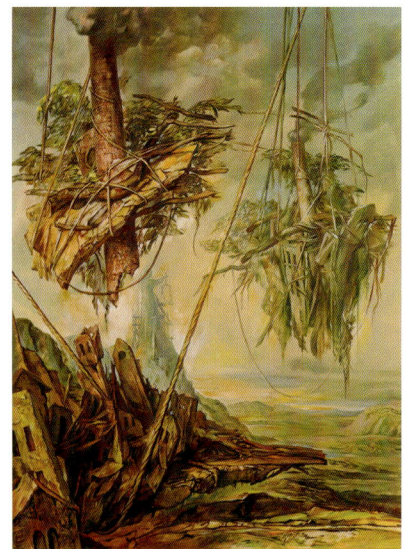

Inadmissible

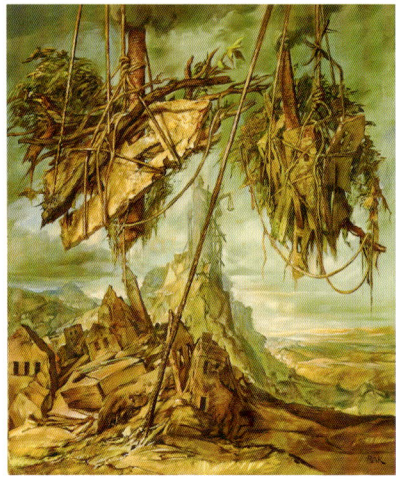

Study for Inadmissible A

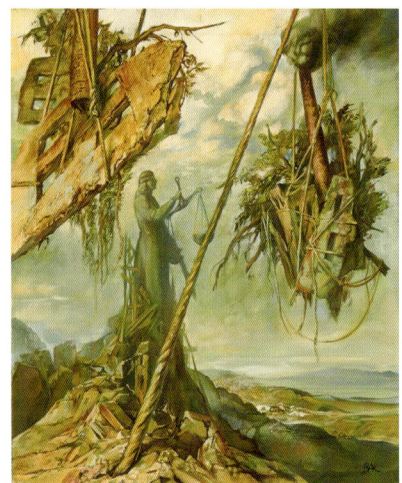

Study for Inadmissible B

Inadmissible A (BK1959) and *Study for Inadmissible B* (BK1961), Bak experiments with perspective on the crime scene by forefronting the evidence and moving Lady *Just Is* progressively away from the damage. It is an important forensic exercise to gain perspective on a crime scene. The suspended wreckage evokes the all-too-common Nazi hangings of concentration camp prisoners, especially children, intended to deliver the message that human suffering and Auschwitz justice are fungible in an atrocity universe where the most vulnerable go unprotected. We must radically suspend our critical and moral faculties to grasp the scale of a Nazi-reasoned cruelty that justified the lynching of children.

Active chimneys hanging in equipoise mimic and mock the scales of justice and the talionic principle of measure, equivalence, and restitution; in the atrocity universe death, not life, is the unbearable unit of measure in this barbarous balancing act that even Amos's prophetic scales prove incapable of calibrating. Are holy texts and their promises of future justice sufficiently weighty to balance out this damage, as in *Scroll of the Living Sea* (BK1949). Can God's promise of justice offset the suffering of six million dead? Even though the Psalmist confidently proclaims, "The LORD loves righteousness and justice; the earth is full of his unfailing love" (Ps. 33:5 [NIV]), how does one balance unfailing love with an earth full of such unfailing cruelty? Bak's empty, broken, and violated balance scales bear witness to the impossibility.

But Bak's balance pans are not uniformly empty. Various configurations hold Lady *Just Is*, talionic eyes, rocks, scrolls, pears, tablets of the law, living and dead trees, swords, as well as the wreckage of Jewish life, a combination that communicate possibility as well as loss. We wonder at the imagination at work and the sense of equivalence Bak poses: What does it mean to weigh the evidence of the death of one child, one ghetto, one shtetl, one death camp, one atrocity against another? Bak's canvases, which we note carry numbers as well as name designations, focus our attention on calculative, quantifiable ways of thinking about atrocity that could tempt us to compare and equate one suffering with another. Only in the Nazi-administered world, which operated comfortably with equivalences between life and death—tattooed numbers for names, emaciated bodies for units of labor, skin and hair for lampshades and mattresses, and medical experiments on children for scientific research—could the measurement of suffering be so rationalized. The sheer incomprehensibility of such tasks and any metrics we might conjure to make sense completely overwhelms the senses. With the disaster concretely before our eyes Bak presses us to ask in what courtroom at The Hague would such horrific evidence be admissible, let alone comprehensible. What jurisprudence would presume to have categories of evidence or damages that could apply? How are the principles of retribution, restitution, and restoration that undergird the biblical lex talionis thinkable in view of the violence committed on this scale?[45] The weight of suffering Bak presents here defies every measure of meaning and morality, the math too severe to account for the empirical reality.

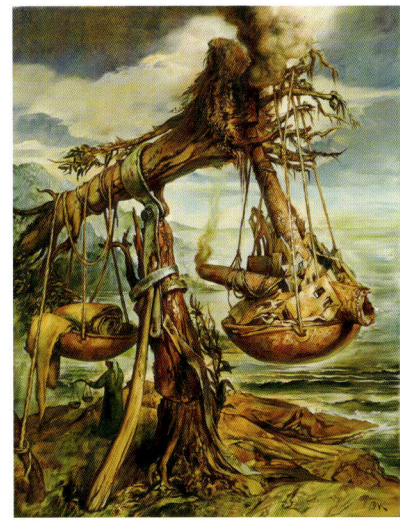
Scroll of the Living Sea

Before leaving this for another scene *Under Investigation* (BK1960), we turn our attention back to *Inadmissible* (BK1931). Lady *Just Is* stands vigil on a remote promontory, a lonely symbol of justice once proudly and prominently displayed atop courthouse domes brought low by forces of destruction. Why does Lady *Just Is* turn away from the catastrophe? She appears shrouded in scaffolding, surrounded and comforted, we could imagine, by traditional principles, ideals, and juridical structures. Does Bak hint at a possible makeover under way? Is Lady *Just Is*

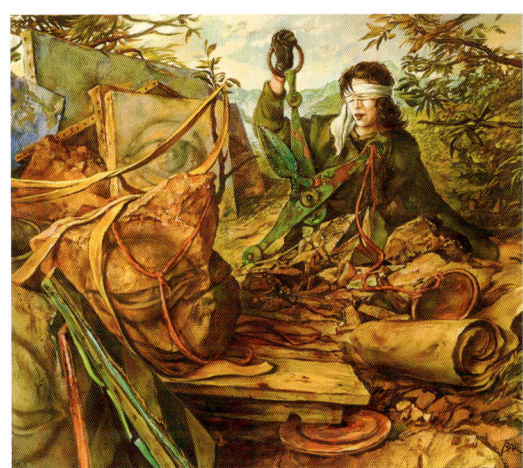
Under Investigation

being restored to her former iconic status as if the devastation is now to be put behind her? Can she turn her attention to restoring the lost gravitas, stature, and standing the moral universe afforded her? Alternatively, and Bak's paintings invite alternative readings, we might see her more favorably "under construction," suggesting we seek a different way for *Just Is* to ensure that those who suffer are protected and not forgotten. The still-belching chimneys alert us that the horror of genocide did not end with Auschwitz and that art's responsibility to represent and bear witness to that horror, as Adorno affirms, must never relax. We are left to decide if, like so many perpetrators and bystanders, artists and viewers implicated in the suffering injustice, we will resort to consoling constructions at home in the moral universe to justify averting our eyes and our thinking from scenes of real life and death hanging in precarious balance.

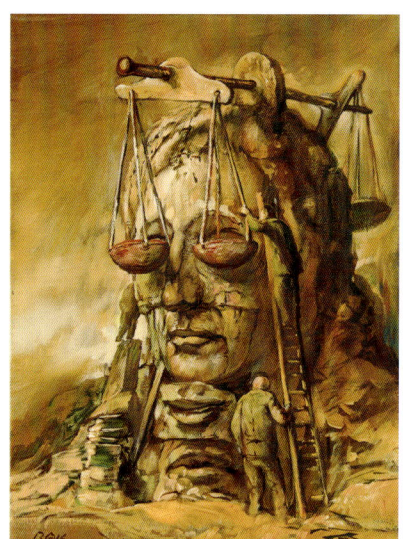

Saving the Face

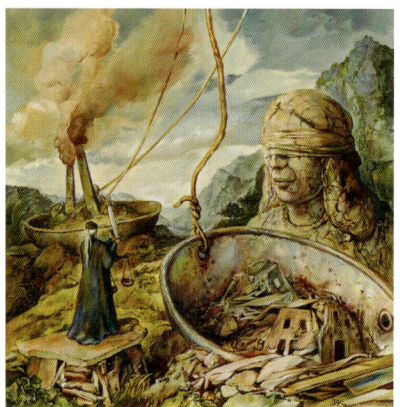

From the Low to the High

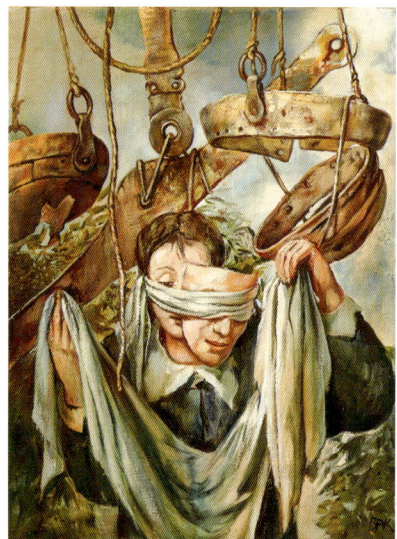

Unmasking

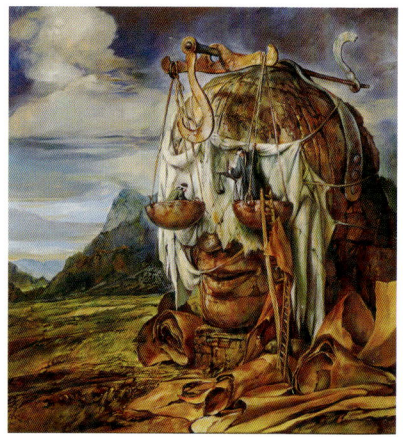

See No Evil

The temptation to turn away and *See No Evil* (BK1935) is amplified when reality fails to cohere with our deepest convictions about the ways things ought to be, like when a survivor's past memory diverges with present experience. A massive bust of Lady *Just Is* is the focus of an intense restoration effort by two diminutive and blindfolded Lady *Just Ises* who work from suspended pan scaffolding and attempt to rehang the fallen blindfold. In the face of the Holocaust reality this is a memorial to not seeing—rather than to not forgetting—the monumental evil around her. The barest hint of a smile conveys the relief that comes when the connection to suffering is interrupted, and we attempt to wrench some consoling meaning out of the suffering. When *Saving the Face* (BK1981) of justice has a higher priority than not forgetting those who suffer injustice, it is no surprise that the very means of ensuring the protection of others distances Lady *Just Is* from the reality before her. What will it take for the scales to fall from her eyes and for her to see again, maybe for the first time? Does it require a heavenly action, as in the Christian New Testament story of the Apostle Paul (Act 9:18) whose seeming scales fell from his eyes when at Jesus' command Ananias laid his hands on him? Or might vision require a human action by Bak's workman who climbs a ladder to remove the scales with human hands not divinely empowered? Do we wait for godly commands to confront the reality or risk taking on that responsibility ourselves?

Such responsibility is expressed in the wider picture of *Just Is* as Bak shows us in *From the Low to the High* (BK1952), where a memorialization of the disaster she and we may prefer not to see surround a blindfolded Lady *Just Is*. The gigantic balance scales and enormity of the wreckage deftly convey a sense of the scale of loss. Billowing smoke from the still-active crematoria chimneys reminds us that, unlike the busts of *Just Is* down low, the rising and dissipating ashes on high make any memorialization of the faces of the million murdered children an impossibility. Compositions that show the impossibility of memorialization give form to Adorno's conviction that "[t]he abundance of real suffering tolerates no forgetting."[46] The negation at the heart of Bak's visual contradiction and paradox discloses the Holocaust world in ways that Sartre failed to appreciate.

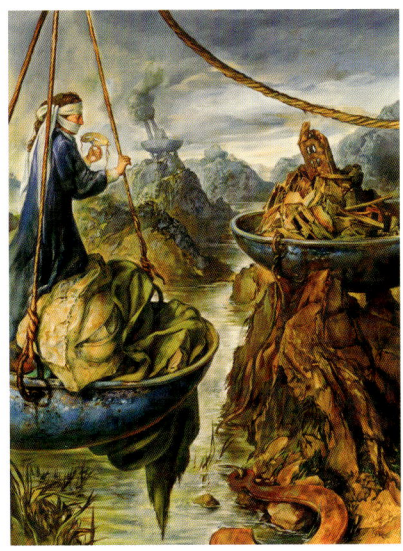

Taking Off

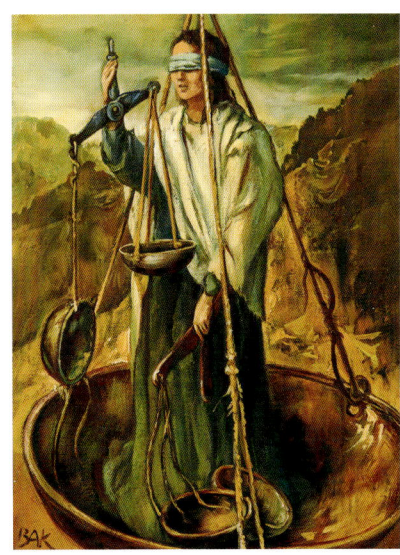

Emblem

From canvas to canvas, encounter with the disquieting realities of Bak's Holocaust landscape tests the limits of our legal and moral comprehension. Because everything about Auschwitz is inconceivable, responsibility not to forget the suffering demands an *Unmasking* (BK1978) of any pretense to impartiality and objectivity that would serve to distance us from the suffering reality. In *Taking Off* (BK1936), Bak repositions Lady *Just Is* from low or protected promontory to inside a balance pan, hoisted high above the devastation alongside her stony-eyed companion. This elevated spot is her new, improvised, courthouse perch. If this is an *Emblem* (BK1982) of her importance now, it carries a certain irony since classical Lady Justice is the one who is meant to hold up the balance scales not be held in them, an inversion Bak exploits elsewhere in the series, as in *See No Evil* (BK1935) and *Settlement* (BK1937). Previously blindfolded, Lady *Just Is* was able to avoid seeing; now unmasked she has little choice but to look and for us to see the distorting effects the blindfold has had on her, as in *Eye with Eye* (BK1984).

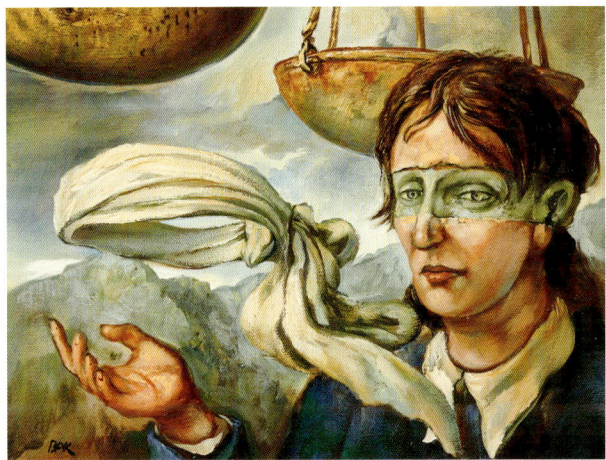

Eye with Eye

With mask in hand, Lady *Just Is* peers out over a flooded chasm below, suggesting that after the cataclysm the masquerade of justice and the pretense of impartially is now over. The detached, matching balance pan holds the remnants of a once vital community that iconic Lady Justice and the lex talionis were in principle charged with, but

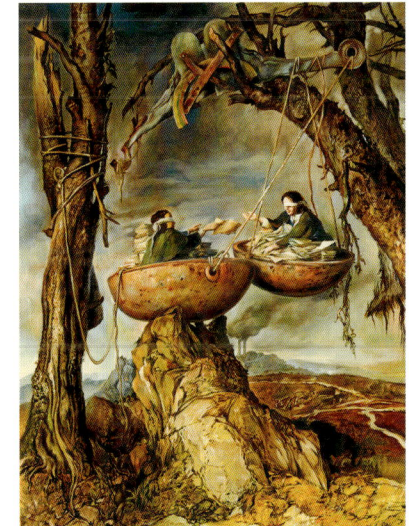

Settlement

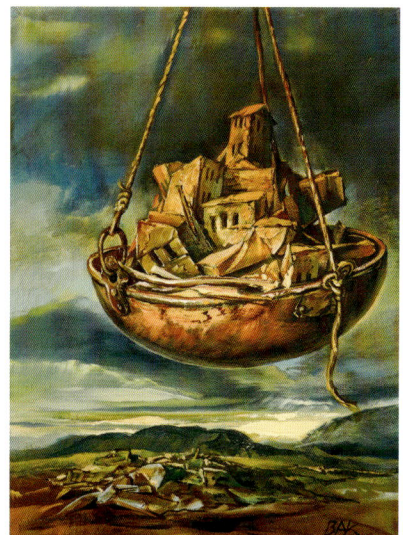

One of Two A

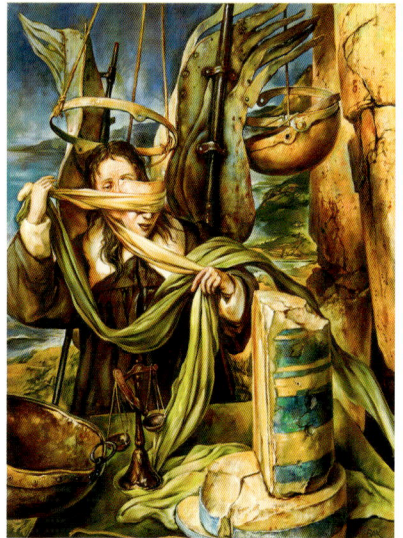

Close By

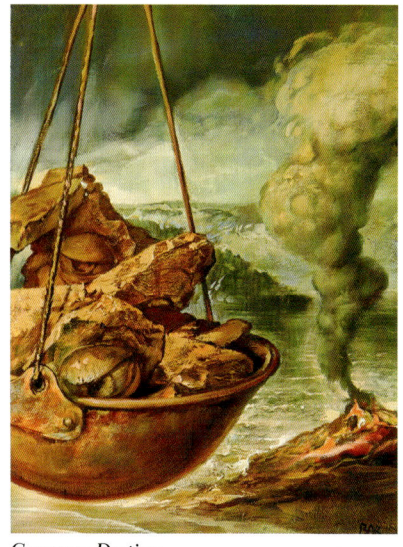

Common Destiny

proved ultimately ineffective in, protecting. In *One of Two A* (BK1983) a matching pan overflowing with the devastation is elevated for all to see. Bak paints a graphic reminder that purported icons, principles, and tools of justice are only effective when they are actually used to protect; social structures can readily turn a blind eye to, and even become actively complicit in, the worst injustices, such as the vaunted German legal system and the volkisch German Christian movement amply demonstrated in their advocacy of Nazi genocidal goals. Theological traditions, enlightenment narratives, and legal systems have their specific cultural and historical roots. How do we gain sufficient critical perspective on ours to see the material reality of injustice that is so *Close By* (BK1940) and in front of our very faces? Although elevation can distance us from the reality, we are reminded it also affords a place from which to see not only a shared past but our *Common Destiny* (BK1985).

One of Bak's creative contributions here and in other series is the *Taking Off* (BK1936; page 19) of theological masks traditionally placed on biblical stories to protect texts and readers from the material reality of suffering. In the earlier *Elegy III* (BK545), a crucified Ghetto Boy is juxtaposed to a propped up and fading rainbow, flood detritus, and despondent angel challenging viewers to give coherence to covenantal promises of life and expression of real suffering and death.[47] In a takeoff on the biblical flood story, Bak bears witness to two world-altering deluges, one ancient and the other modern. Receding waters expose two ships grounded on far distant peaks, one with its stacks still actively streaming smoke that has all but filled the sky. Two near-extinction events—the one Noachic, the other Nazi-inspired—coincide on Bak's canvas in a disturbing association. The Noachic ark was a material sign of God's covenantal commitment to preserve a righteous, blameless man and his family, and a promise to fill the earth with life (Gen. 6:9, 17), whereas the Nazi transport was a sign of Hitler's demonic commitment to end Jewish life and erase all signs of Jewish presence from the face of the earth, even destroying creation in the process. Bak's metaphorical juxtaposition of the two invites us to consider the ways both Genesis narrative and genocidal ideology, inflamed by two millennia of Christian contempt for Jews, can mask real suffering and loss.

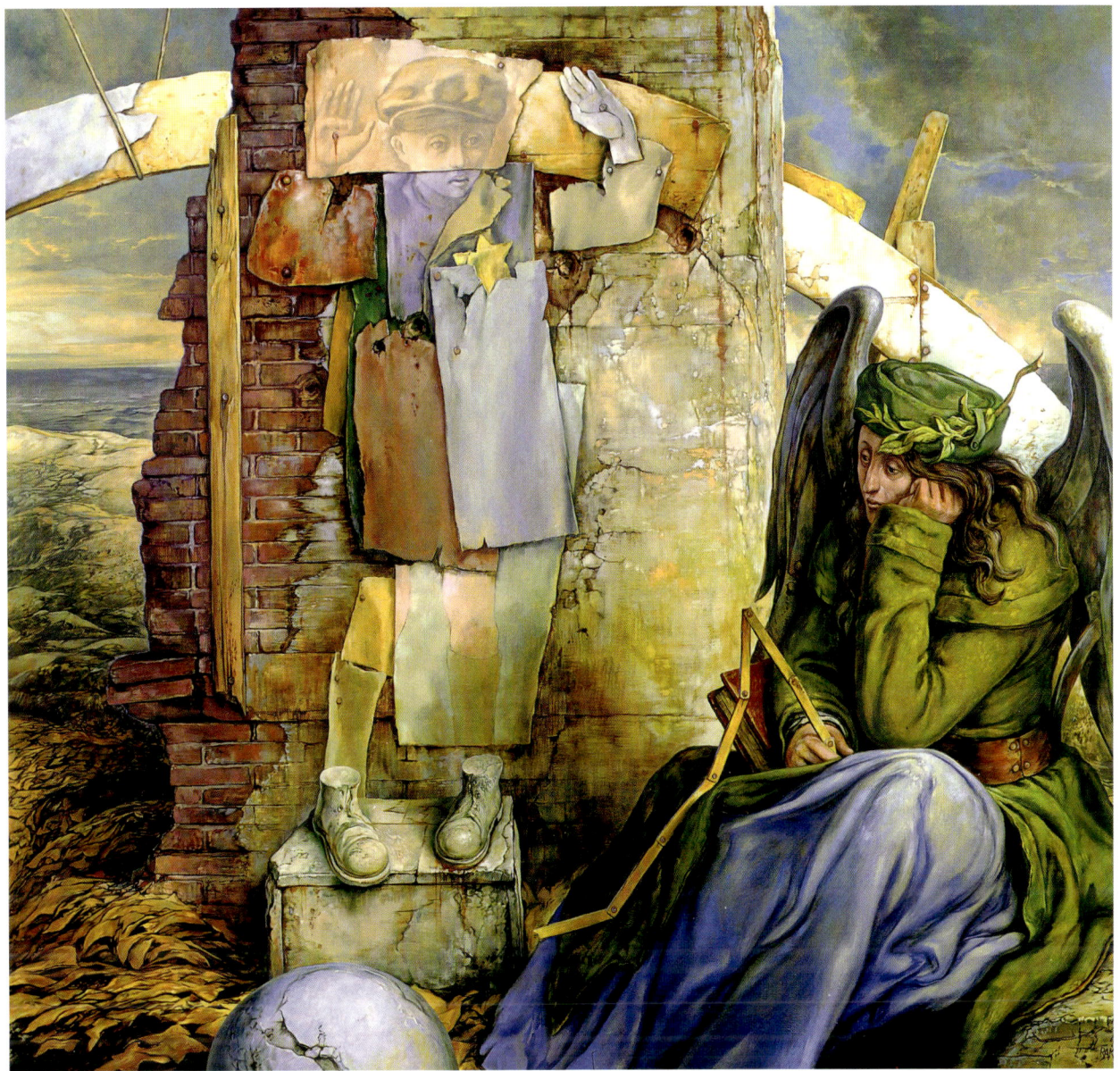

Elegy III, 1997
Oil on canvas
47.5 x 51.5"
BK545

At the conclusion of the biblical flood story God places a familiar rainbow in the sky as a heavenly sign of His commitment to creation and as a reminder never again to annihilate the living with flood waters (Gen. 9:13–16). The Genesis text paints a picture of a self-conscious deity who stammers "I will remember ... I will remember" the suffering and obliteration. Why is God portrayed as intent on assuring he will not forget unless God's forgetting is a real issue? The narrative may be recalling the experiences of Jewish covenantal communities repeatedly traumatized by deportation and exile and here unmasks consoling

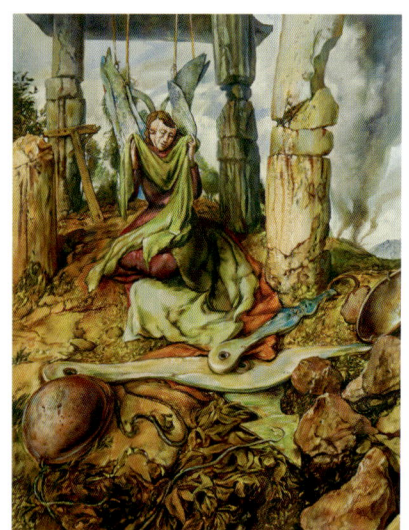

Angel of Middle Ground

efforts to paint a rosy theological picture of a covenant partner who glosses over the forgetting of suffering injustice with heavenly promises, signs, and wonders. Like the Bible, Bak's *Just Is* images remember past sufferings that through incongruous connections challenge our self-consciousness about forgetting and neglect, about the masks we use to cover up, the props we use to hide our memory failures, and our complicity in the suffering of others.[48]

Lady *Just Is* sees the consequence of the deluge around her, but what confidence do we have that she, like God, will continue to remember? What heavenly sign will she rely upon? In contrast to a number of other post-deluge representations, Bak here paints no rainbow, installs no colorful sign in the heavens that would signal unqualified confidence in either deity or future. Like the *Angel of Middle Ground* (BK1947), Bak's and our eyes are focused upon the damaged world as the sign that evokes memory. The wafting ashes linked to grounded ships and destruction draws our attention to contradictory accounts of biblical salvation, to the material remains of Jewish life after atrocity, here on the ground, where suffering is encountered. Memories are both sharpened and threatened by concretion and particularity that compel us to look down not up, to the ground and not the heavens, at human devastation not starry wonder.

The juxtaposition of biblical and Nazi destruction narratives draws our attention to another painful absence that haunts Bak: where are the missing children in both biblical narrative ark and pictured pan? Have they too been forgotten in both story and painting? In the foreground, Bak's balance hook once again resurfaces, detritus left behind as a questioning reminder that forgotten victims of atrocity demand never to be forgotten and that those who suffer are not aided by consoling explanations that differentiate between divinely versus humanly inspired violence. What is our responsibility to unmask the ideological and religious causes of, and complicity in, atrocity toward the innocent and the ways they conceal suffering, to remember our failures to not forget, to think against treasured assumptions and comforting fictions with the help of texts and works of art in touch with suffering, and to recognize, as the ship's still-working chimney insists, that ongoing suffering tolerates no forgetting?

In *Nap* (BK1929), Lady *Just Is*, alone for the moment, seeks relief from this unrelenting reality and its implications for religious and juridical traditions. If we are honest, so, too, do we, Bak's viewers. Lady *Just Is* is exhausted by the overwhelming nature of a Jewish excision that, as *High Winds* (BK1944) visualizes in a frozen moment in time, has left a devastated Jewish world completely untethered to the traditions of justice that had presumably secured it, a destruction Lady *Just Is* has paradoxically had some role in creating. Having abandoned her post to catch a little shut-eye, she stretches out beneath a severed tree incongruously held upright by wooden staves in a gravity-defying scene that stretches the limits of realism and credulity. Elsewhere Bak shows how impossibly *Balanced* (BK1954) justice is where feather absurdly outweighs tree, the very threat to life and future that prompted the Egyptian Goddess Ma'at into action.

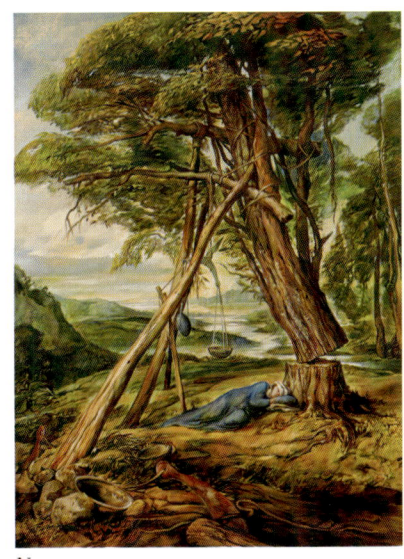

Nap

Lady *Just Is* seems unaware of the danger looming directly overhead as perhaps we, too, are of the continuing threat of ongoing genocides. The contrast in size between her diminutive figure and surroundings underscores *Just Is's* insufficiency in the face of catastrophe. Empty balance scales hang limp from a detached tree limb. Apparently the tools of vigilant justice need a breather too. Is this an indication that Lady *Just Is* has abandoned responsibility to protect the innocent and restore life, and if so for what reasons? Perhaps it's a matter of practicality because the very principles of undersized justice make it no longer viable in the atrocity universe. After the wholesale erasure of Jewish life and culture, this icon of *Just Is* presses us to consider whether the burden of response to suffering is a precarious balancing act owing as much to irrational as rational factors. After all, would it not be a relief to justify the paroxysms of violence against Jews over the centuries as mythical irrationality that has run its course rather than as deliberate, enlightened reason on the part of a Nazified Christian European culture intent on punishing and then erasing Jew-

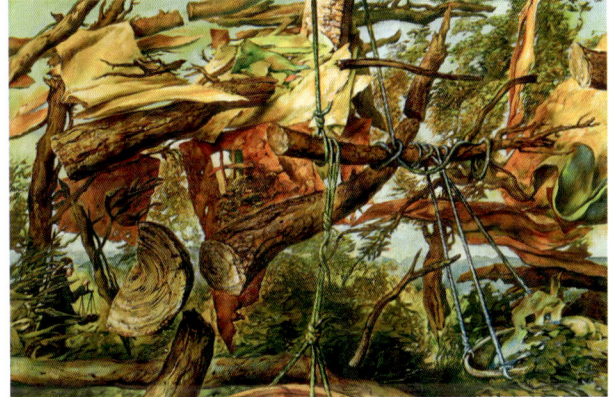

High Winds

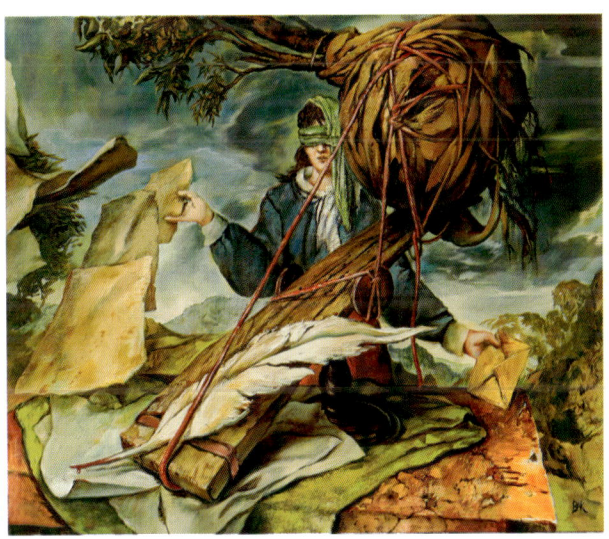

Balanced

ish life? Would chimerical anti-Semitism[49] or instrumental rationality offer the more satisfying theory of the destruction? Which explanation allows her and us to sleep better?

The concept of sleeping justice runs deeply counter to the juridical expectations of an ever-vigilant Lady *Just Is,* ever-protective and ever-alert to danger. However, as Bak repeatedly intimates, the innocent may no longer count on justice as protector or its icons as assuring. We recall once again that the biblical corpus preserves scars of its many ancient wounds, experiences of past disasters and disappointments with its own sleeping and forgetful divine protector. The Psalmist directly charges God, who supposedly neither slumbers nor rests, with sleeping though the oppression and affliction of his people (Ps. 44:23–5): "Rouse yourself! Why do you sleep, O Lord? Awake, do not cast us off forever! Why do you hide your face? Why do you forget our affliction and oppression? For we sink down to the dust; our bodies cling to the ground. Rise up, come to our help" (Ps. 44:23–26 NRS). The Jews have not forgotten God, which leads the Psalmist to lament sarcastically the absence of God's saving help that is surely known only in the land of forgetfulness (Ps. 88:12). Where were the covenantal and constitutional protectors when defenseless Jewish children needed them most? They are "forsaken among the dead, like the slain that lie in the grave, like those whom you remember no more, for they are cut off from your hand" (Ps. 88:5 NRSV). With Jewish life cut off and *Just Is* not prone to paying attention, can we expect any promise of protection, any Torah, any Magna Carta—and the icons that used to stand for them—to stand up against present dangers? It is left to artists like Bak to challenge us not to forget and to give voice, consolation, to the suffering. Bak's paintings remind us that memory work is both exhausting and threatening, but that the lack of consciousness and conscience (which go hand-in-hand) only extends the forgetting and the violence. The burdens of the empirical and of memory are linked, and they rest not only upon the artist but also we who engage Bak's art.

If anything, Bak's foray into representations of *Just Is* shows us that Lady *Just Is's* standing—or non-standing—implicates the foundations of Jewish covenantal life and thought.[50] Bak pursues her standing in *By Law* (BK1930; page 15) with its dense constellation of religious symbols and signs. Clustered about Lady *Just Is* are the familiar symbols of the Noachic and Mosaic salvation narratives—but also the Torah, Talmud, and kabbalistic texts—in marked conditions of disarray and disrepair. The fragmentary construction both protects and exposes her. She elevates in her right hand the Hebrew letter *tsade*—in Yiddish *tzadik* stands for "righteous person"—and in her left a rainbow-colored Noachic arch beneath which hang suspended incomplete and fractured tablets of the law. The fragile and broken arms of the *tsade,* reminiscent of broken Lady *Just Is* herself, are roped together, a

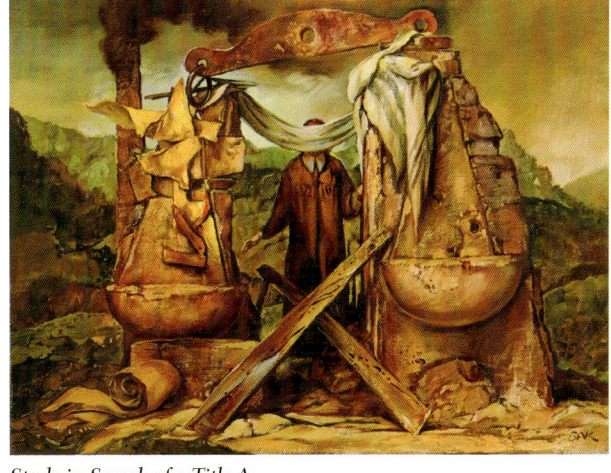

Study in Search of a Title A

visual midrash on the makeshift nature of the righteous after the catastrophe. While Proverbs confidently assures that "When the tempest passes, the wicked are no more, but the righteous *(tzadik)* are established forever," (10:25 NRSV) the remnants Bak pictures raise doubts. Elsewhere in *Even-Handed* (BK1928) and *Study In Search of a Title A* (BK1972) Bak places the stone-carved *tsade* in a balance pan pointing to the burden of the righteous in a world where life-affirming commandments have petrified. In *Factor of Time* (BK1957) the tsade leans up against a broken Mosaic tablet carved with double *yods,* the unpronounceable name of God, serving both as a reminder and an accusation that covenantal justice and forgetfulness go hand in hand. The fallen number "6," signifying the commandment prohibiting murder, and the number "3," the commandment prohibiting the taking of God's name in vain, serve as timely reminders that atrocities in the name of a deity are all too common. The hands of the clock indicate that time is ticking away as we await the next genocide.

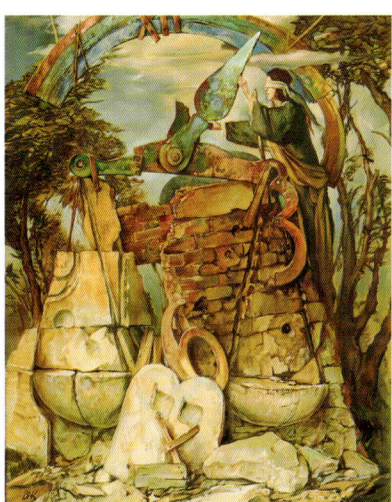

Factor of Time

As an act of Jewish midrash Bak invites us to connect Lady *Just Is* to the *tzadik,* described in the Zohar as the "Righteous one who suffers," to the vibrant Lurianic kabbalistic tradition with its vast cosmogony intended to explain the reality of exile and evil in the world where God has been shattered, evoking the Ghetto Boy of *Gathering Ground* (BK1214; page 26), into the ten sefirot. Lady *Just Is* may be one of the thirty-six *tzaddikim nistarim* or *Lamed Vav Zaddikim,* the anonymous righteous, that the Talmud confidentially assures lives in the damaged and fallen world among us at all times and who shows compassion and bears the burdens of those who suffer. As *tzaddikah,*

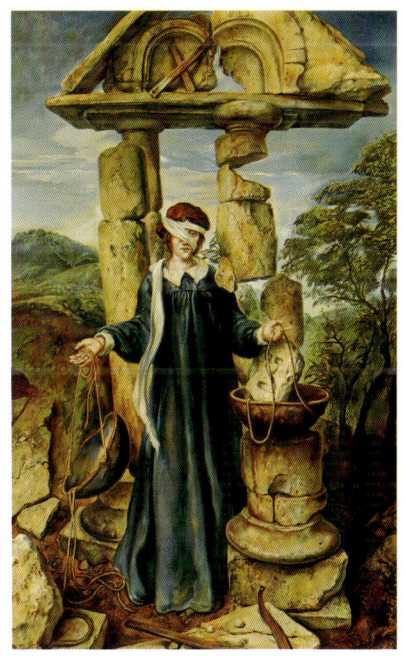

Even-Handed

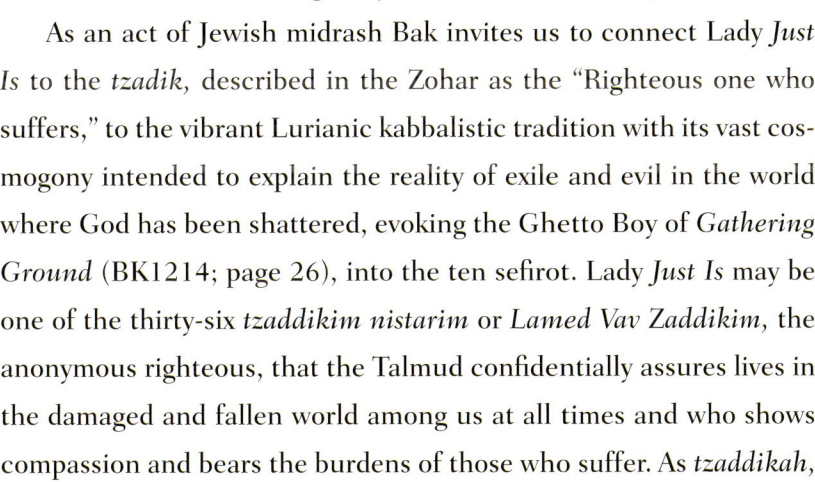

25

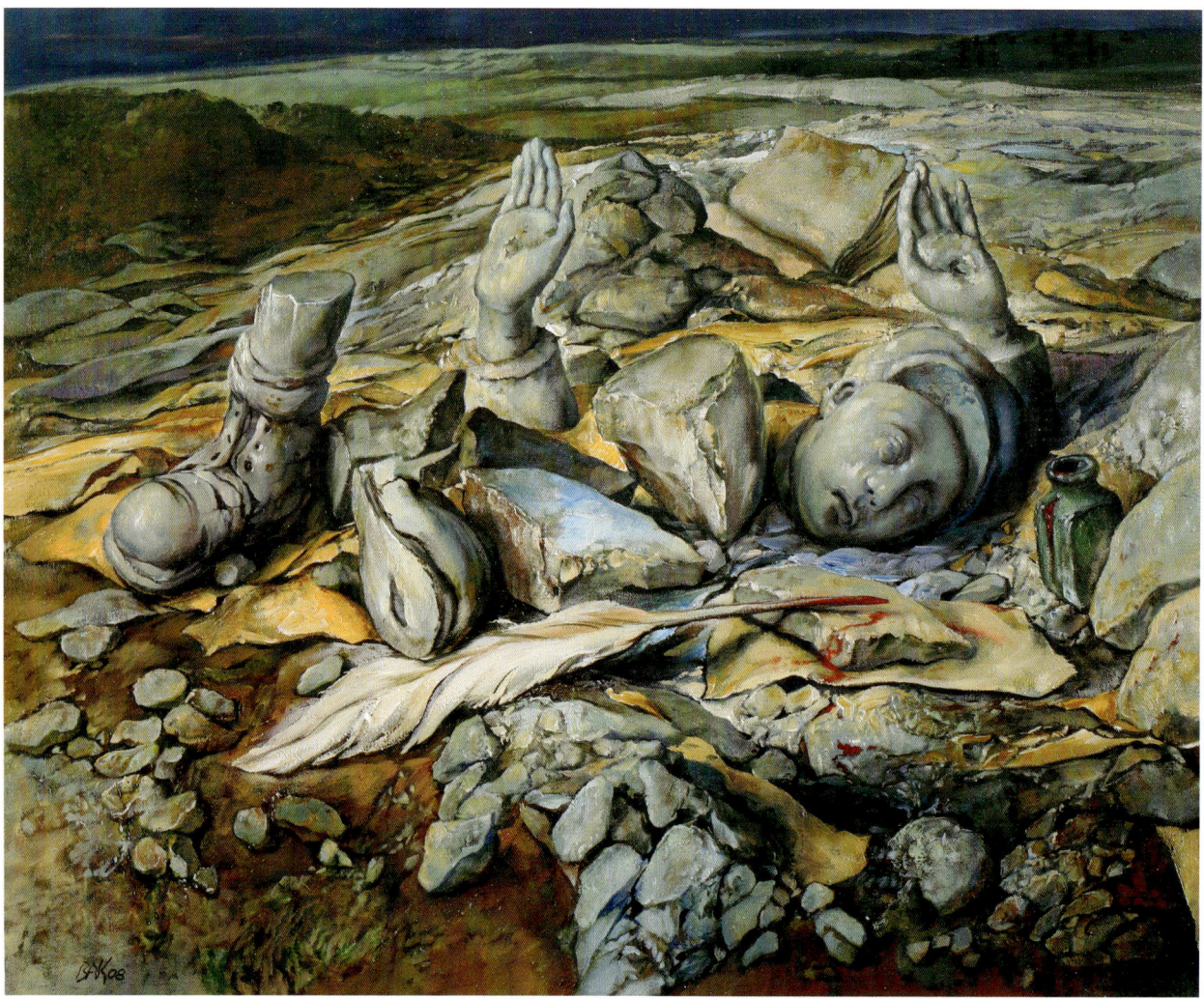

Gathering Ground, 2008
Oil on canvas
30 x 24"
BK1214

she may be a hopeful but mixed reminder that evil is real and does not have the last word unless we allow it, and that restoration of the world, *tikkun olam,* is possible through the re-gathering of the sefirot, the shards, the pieces, and the restitution of shalom reconfigured for a damaged world. Bak's fabrications are brutally honest, hopeful, and realistic creative acts.

Lady *Just Is's* wooden sword looks permanently sheathed in the balance pan supporting one of two Mosaic tablets. The letter *vav,* the sixth letter/commandment signifying the biblical prohibition against murder, is riveted through the sword handle, a jolting and revolting connection of biblical law and mass murder, a trope Bak also explores in other series. Behind Lady *Just Is* our eye catches sight of another set of pristine tablets blindfolded by a cloth-draped broken rainbow, the intersection of two covenantal symbols of promise that Bak's atrocity universe now vacates.

Perched on a distant mountain peak, tucked beneath the *tsade*, the silhouette of a ship once again recalls the biblical flood narrative and the salvation of Noah, that *tsaddik* who was blameless in his generation (Gen. 6:9), and who survived the deluge with his family intact. In an unsettling opposition, we can imagine the S.S. *St. Louis,* that modern Jewish ark that failed abysmally to deliver to safety its human cargo of 937 blameless Jewish children and adults seeking safe haven from the Nazi calamity. We are reminded that the biblical narrative makes no mention of children brought to safety[51] and that the Genesis narrator included them among wicked humankind, whose minds and hearts were evil all the times (Gen. 5:5). Whereas the kabbalistic tradition struggles to nuance the problem of evil, "[n]either the Bible nor the Nazis make any distinctions, or exceptions, in their zeal to solve the problem of 'evil' and 'pollution.' And there is nothing in Jewish or Christian theology that can make satisfactory sense of it. No lex talionis, no Torah of any kind, can bring [the children] justice."[52] Nothing. The double smokestacks stand as a sobering reminder that there was no sanctuary for many of the S.S. *St. Louis's* forgotten and never found. By the standards of 1939 international law, the denial of refuge may have been legal, but by what moral law and in what moral universe could we ever call the suffering of children defensible? Bak's atrocity universe and *Just Is* icons leave us with the unsettling reminder that when we justify suffering or suffer injustice using symbols and narratives that distance us from the reality, we implicate ourselves in erasing the names from the ship's passenger manifest.

Across other canvases in this engaging series, Bak exploits biblical letters, symbols, and experiences of covenant to refashion his alternative icons of *Just Is.* For example, in *Scripture* (BK1938) Lady *Just Is* holds up the letter *ayin* (literally "eye") written on a page in Hebrew cursive and Phoenician pictograph; and in *Ever Ready* (BK1942; page 15) she is dwarfed by tablets of the law inscribed with the familiar double *yods,* the unpronounceable name of God,[53] that as we encountered in *Factor of Time* (BK1957; page 25) can also be read discomfortingly as double *vavs,* the repeated sixth letter/commandment prohibiting murder. Bak's visual grammar relies

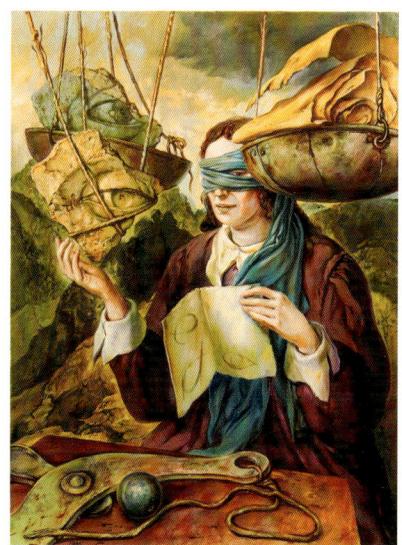

Scripture

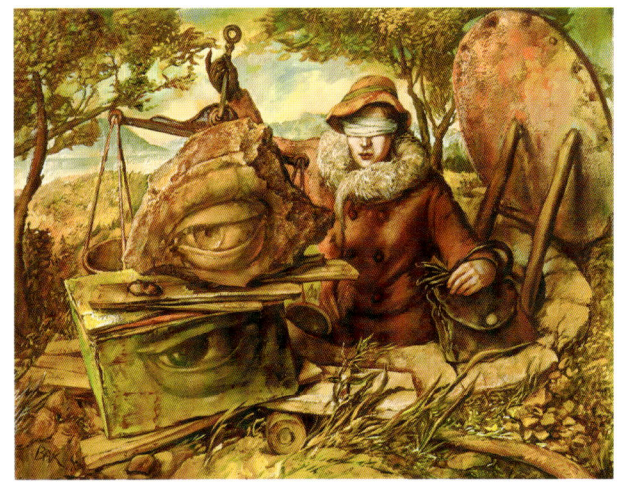

Emergence A

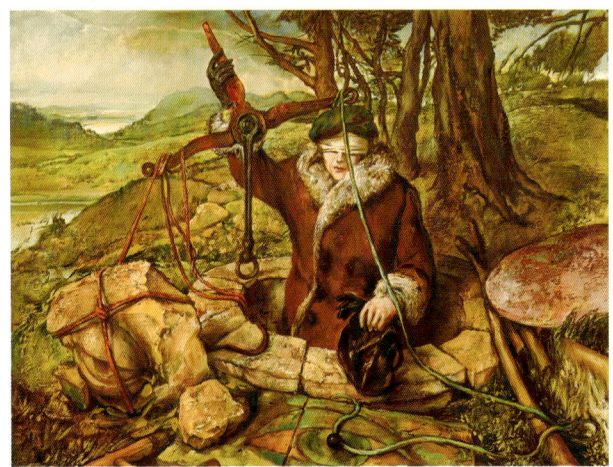

Emergence B

upon a repetitive syntax: numerous canvases with multiple representations of Lady *Just Is,* letters, eyes, tablets, covenants, balance scales, ropes, swords, ships, scrolls, carts, pans, faces, arms, and masks. These iterations, not unlike the numerous appearances of Lady Justice and the lex talionis across various cultures, historical periods, legal systems, and biblical texts, signal something central about the nature of his testimony. It is inviting to see Bak's iterations [54] as a type of visual stutter, a manifestation of what Freud describes as repetition compulsion related to past traumatic experience. [55] Bak's paintings return repeatedly to scenes of devastation and injustice. He repeats familiar tropes and themes. He duplicates the pattern of refashioning icons. Might the iterations of his icons of *Just Is* also be related to the Jewish aniconic effort to negate and destabilize every image so that no one dare acquire iconic status? In this instance it is not God who is the focus of the aniconic prohibition demanded by the Torah but *just is* as demanded by Auschwitz. These iterations are Bak's metaphorical manner of negatively constructing the not forgetting, working through, and witnessing to old wounds where attention has shifted away from the consolation of a saving force to the desolation of a suffering face. [56]

Despite the unremitting devastation and damage, Bak involves us in art's not forgetting work with measured promise and possibility, caution and care. He reiterates iconic Lady Justice as much different, and the talionic eyes as plucked out and unblinking, both reconfigured by and for an atrocity universe where the lofty promises of Enlightenment freedom and biblical justice have not materialized and where genocide is the reality. However, we must resist the temptation to view the icons of *Just Is* as simple expressions of psychological neediness or resignation—it *just is* what it is—but instead consider them as fortifying acts of memory and moral courage. *Emergence A* (BK1967) and *Emergence B* (BK1958) both picture Lady *Just Is* as a modern-dressed woman with glove and bag in hand, instead of sword, stepping up into action, asserting herself and the talionic eye's presence in the atrocity reality, in touch with the brokenness of the world around her and acting assertively on her own will. Far from lofty Roman Justicia located above, this Lady *Just Is* emerging out of the ground readies herself. We are reminded of biblical scenes where women emerge from the narrative to take on transformative roles:

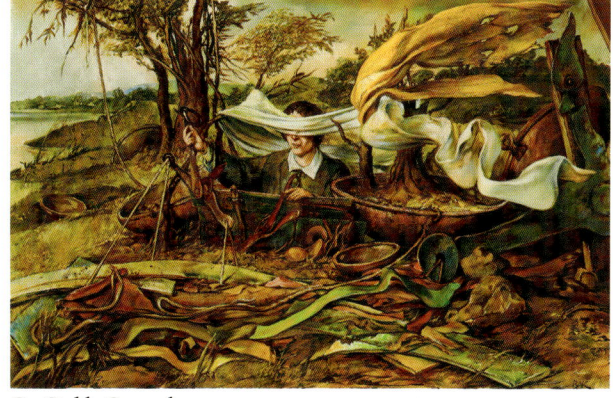
On Stable Ground

biblical matriarchs Rebekah (Gen. 24), Rachel (Gen. 29), Deborah (Judg. 5), Esther (Esth), and the Samaritan Woman (John 4) adopt real-world transformative roles that alter destinies. An encouraging figure, Lady *Just Is* finds herself *On Stable Ground* (BK1945) standing upright in the atrocity universe and before us with heightened moral realism and honesty, no longer wilting under the romanticized delusion of iconic Lady Justice and talionic restitution but *Growing* (BK1977) more capable of standing on her own without benefit of props, blindfolds, masks, swords, theodicies, or consolations. Adorno characterizes art that does not forget suffering as art that "stand[s] upright before justice."[57] Do we follow her lead and stand up before *Just Is*? Bak's artwork holds out hope for this possibility.

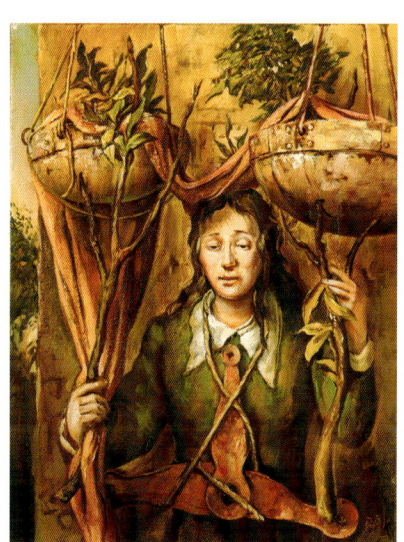
Growing

Bak expands upon this possibility in *Long Lasting* (BK1941) where we are offered a commanding view of the atrocity universe surrounding Lady *Just Is* and a different sense of time and space emerges. Retrieving another favored image, Bak fashions the Holocaust world as a pear pealed apart to expose a cored-out sphere, its central contents exploded before our very eyes. The traditional hoped-for restoration of God's universal justice (*mishpat*) and righteousness (*tzedekah*), appears now all but an empty dream, a permanent disjuncture from the present reality of damaged life. In this arid setting Amos's vision of rolling waters and ever-flowing stream of divine justice seems little more than a pipe dream, some opiate-induced hallucination needed to escape from, not be in touch with, suffering reality.

Positioned before a still-belching crematory chimney, Lady *Just Is* stands blindfold free, able now to grasp the reality surrounding her for what it is. She is also on the cusp of some action. Poised to descend a short flight of steps, she directs herself toward what appears

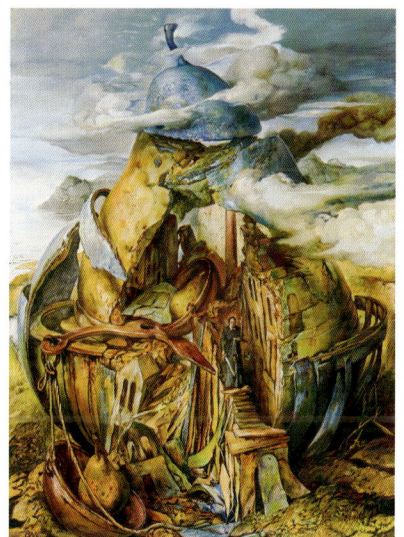
Long Lasting

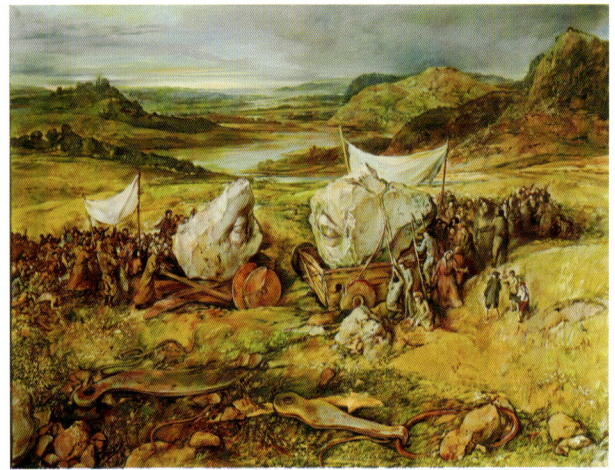

Eye for Eye

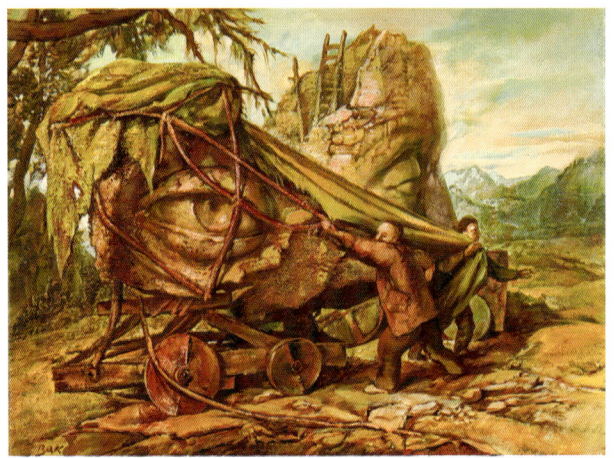

Tit for Tat

to be a repositioned—and maybe repurposed—tablet of the law. Bak paints a modern post-Holocaust Mt. Sinai wrapped not with kiln smoke that went up because God had descended upon the mountain with fire (Exod. 19:18) but with crematory smoke of Jews wafting skyward as a consequence of the Nazi destruction that descended upon them.[58] In a remake of the Exodus narrative's central scene, it is Lady *Just Is,* rather than Moses, who descends the mountain in the direction of a blank tablet marked by bullet holes and reflecting the colors of the damaged world at its base. The blank tablet, like a blank canvas, awaits a third, post-biblical inscription of the Law. Bak paints an alternative mitzvah, a 614th commandment, a new categorical imperative,[59] which gives primacy to the voice of Auschwitz, to a worldly suffering inscribed not by the finger of God, or by Moses' hand, but with the paint brush of a secularized, Holocaust child-survivor who incomprehensibly escaped the fate of a million other children.[60] If before Auschwitz Emmanuel Kant proposed the Enlightenment's categorical imperative of human freedom, now after Auschwitz "Hitler has imposed a new categorical imperative upon humanity in the state of their unfreedom: to arrange their thinking and conduct, so that Auschwitz never repeats itself, so that nothing similar ever happen again."[61] Lady *Just Is* may just be arranging her and our thinking and conduct to engage a new moral law, a new mitzvah, a new Torah, a new Bible, a new universe, a new talion, a new *Just Is.*[62] Presenting Lady *Just Is* standing squarely amid, not above or removed from, the destruction, Bak asks if she, and we, are ready to stand upright before *just is* in this damaged world. As with much of Bak's representation of loss, we oscillate in a dialectical way between uncertainty and hope.

This contradiction intensifies as we consider the alternative principle of *Just Is* in the atrocity university presented in an *Eye for Eye* (BK1932). Here we witness what, on first view, are the consequences when traditional justice falls out of the hands of an impartial Lady *Just*

Is and into those of partisan crowds. She is not visible in this frenzied scene, perhaps absorbed off canvas with her own affairs or blended back into the crowd; we cannot be sure. Set incongruously in a bucolic setting amid rolling hills and lakes, two carts standing nose to nose suggest a scene of confrontation. Clustered behind each cart are gathering crowds pressing forward under the banner of their respective causes—although tellingly both standards are blank. If they intend to promote some particular ideology or cause they lack the words to express it. Are we witnessing two clashing communities on the brink of violence and yet further suffering? Imagine a *Tit for Tat* (BK1975), each side getting set to settle a score, to exact a literal talion by taking the other's eye in payback for some wrong, imagined or real, to balance the scales violently, certainly one interpretation of the ancient tradition of the talion. In their haste to get even they seem unaware that the wheels have come off their transports. When the figurative wheels come off, when the icons no longer effect peace, when domination over the other governs our communal lives together, they can perpetuate a suffering world where the literal loss of an eye, tooth, hand, and foot is sure to escalate to more horrific losses of life and limb, culture and creation.

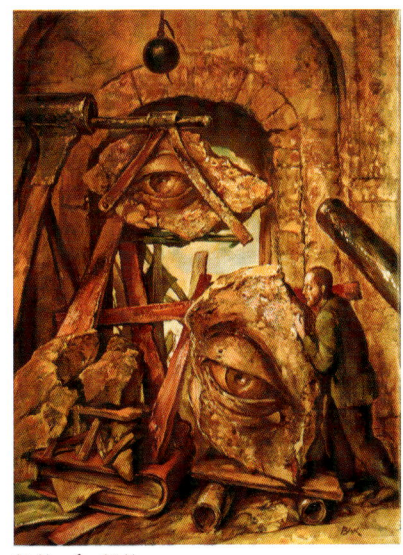

N Eye for N Eye

From a different perspective we imagine instead two opposing parties raising the iconic white flag of shalom, implying that violence toward the other

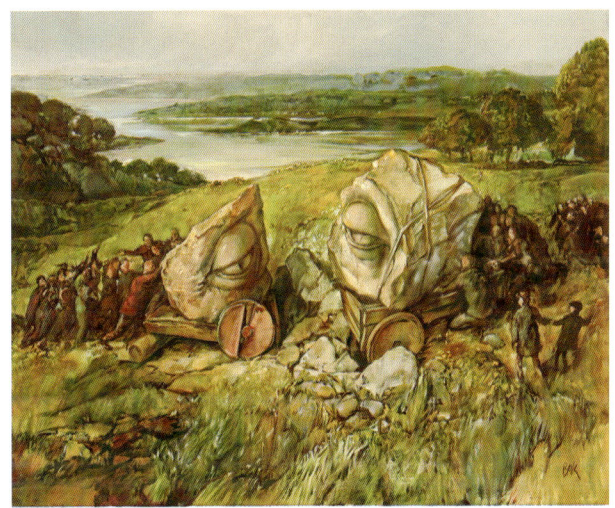

Collective Memory

has given way to being for not against the other—*N Eye for N Eye* (BK1971) where Bak embeds the letter "N" and number "4" into the scene to give support to the individual eyes and to invite his viewer to imagine structures in today's damaged world that could do the same. Do the crowds in *Eye for Eye,* see, perhaps for the first time, the consequences of taking justice, the narratives of freedom and salvation, and their supporting icons into their own hands? Have they pulled back from the brink? It *Just Is* possible that we are witnesses to a scene of collaboration, not confrontation, in which the crowds have combined their *Collective Memory* (BK1968) of suffering and injustice and now see together in a promissory act of community and a parallax moment of common vision. A single eye on its own is in capable of accurately discerning distance; depth perception requires two eyes working together, one with and for the other. It is a promising thought. At the same time, even with two eyes perception is not always assured. It *Just Is* possible that despite our best intentions vision may not be clear enough, thinking in contradictions may not be critical enough, and art may not bear witness effectively enough to not forget the suffering and return us all to a literal plucking out of each other's eye. That possibility also exists. As Bak turns his talionic eyes toward us he asks if we are prepared to accept the reality both of uncertainty and possibility of living after atrocity in a damaged world.

Living After

Henri's question, "Is there any meaning in life when men exist who beat people until the bones break in their bodies?" has a partner question: "Can we live after Auschwitz?"[63] Bak's artwork paints both questions as a testimony to suffering *Just Is*. We live after genocide with continuing unsurety and the ethical demand neither to forget nor to suffer injustice. We live after with those who suffer at the hands of people who have traded rifle butts for hijacked airplanes and bullets for a suicide bomber's vest. We live after with legal traditions and biblical principles that are fractured and implicated in injury to the world. And we live after with art that is both beautiful and barbarous committed to the task of keeping us in touch with the pain of others. With peace in tatters, Bak shows us the pieces, fragments of his and our world, shards like the sefirot, and that is what we have to work with living after Auschwitz. Bak's art addresses us with representations of remnants of justice reconfigured as *Just Is* emerging from and in response to the wreckage that bears witness to a suffering past as well as to a possible alternative future where violence does not structure life. In this way, his icons of *Just Is* offer a tenuous way forward toward living after with art not detached from but in touch with the world, not forgetful of but remembering suffering injustice and its attendant costs.

Above all else, Samuel Bak's artwork leaves us with the predicament and precariousness of ethical choice. Bak prompts vexing questions about the nature and work of justice after atrocity that refuse to yield either to easy dismissals of art or romanticized assumptions about the bent of morality. The refusal to forget or evade suffering,

Adorno reminds us, enables art honestly "to stand upright before justice"[64]; by refusing to forget or evade suffering Bak gives us art that stands upright before *Just Is*. The density and complexity of the realities he renders on canvas challenge us to think against pre-Auschwitz thinking, to embrace the burden of the empirical, and to hear and to see the familiar and the given now in unconventional terms. The metaphorical effect of contrasting Justice with *Just Is* increases our aural, visual, and moral acuity; it offers a creative witness to suffering and trauma, and serves as an ethical call to action. When we now hear the word *Justice* as *Just Is* and see the icons of Lady Justice and the lex talionis in such altered forms, we can choose to resign ourselves to justice no longer in touch with the living and the dead, with *deathlife*. Or, following Bak's artistic and moral invitation, we can choose instead to hear in his voice and see in the beauty and barbarity of his paintings possibilities of alternative icons of *Just Is* that enable us to bear witness to suffering injustice and challenge us to take up the collective work of restoring shalom to this damaged world. With eyes wide open and icons provisionally refashioned for the uncertain work ahead, Bak places the loss and repair of this suffering world, of *tikkun olam,* before our eyes and in our hands leaving us to decide what our next step will be.

---

[1] Cited in Theodor W. Adorno. "Commitment," in *The Essential Frankfurt School Reader,* edited by Andrew Arato and Eike Gebhardt (New York: Continuum, 1985), 312.

[2] According to Sartre, prose alone "discloses the world with the intention of changing it. Only prose uses language to confer meaning on objects in the real world, thereby demonstrating that to speak is indeed to act," Jean Paul Sartre, *What is Literature and Other Essays* (Cambridge: Harvard University Press, 1988), 11. He dismissed painting and other nonverbal art forms because they cannot be heard. Adorno criticizes this view of committed art arguing that it is insufficiently self-critical. Painting, poetry and music are especially able to express the inexpressible. See Adorno's discussion in "Commitment," 302.

[3] Adorno's mixed Jewish and Christian parentage subjected him to educational and professional discrimination, forcing him to flee Germany for the United States in 1933. See Stefan, Müller-Doohm. *Adorno: A Biography* (Malden, MA: Polity Press, 2005), 173-175.

4   Adorno identifies with the Marxist oriented Frankfurt School of Critical Theory and promoted a philosophical and materialist critique of modernity with focus on topics that included instrumental rationality, aesthetics, suffering/injustice, fascism, authoritarianism, anti-Semitism, the administrative world, and the culture industry. His contributions to aesthetic theory and postwar Germany educational reform are significant. For excellent overviews see Martin Jay, *Adorno* (Cambridge: Harvard University Press, 1984), J.M. Bernstein, *Adorno: Disenchantment and Ethics. Modern European Philosophy* (Cambridge: Cambridge University Press, 2001); and Daniel Coluccieller Barber, "Theodor Adorno," In *Religion and European Philosophy: Key Thinkers from Kant to Žižek,* edited by Philip Goodchild and Hollis Phelps (New York: Routledge, 2017), 127–40.

5   Adorno equates suffering or damaged life with injustice. He rarely uses the latter term preferring "suffering" instead because it allows him to avoid conceptual abstraction and reification, a major concern in his critique of modernity. See J.M. Bernstein, "Suffering Injustice: Misrecognition as Moral Injury in Critical Theory," *International Journal of Philosophical Studies* 13 (2005): 304.

6   Theodor W. Adorno, *Negative Dialectics,* translated by E. B. Ashton (New York: Continuum, 1992), 361. For a rich discussion of Adorno's anti-theodical thought see Carl B. Sachs, "The Acknowledgement of Transcendence: Anti-theodicy in Adorno and Levinas," *Philosophy and Social Criticism* 37 (2011): 273–94.

7   Theodor W. Adorno, *Aesthetic Theory,* translated by Robert Hullot-Kentor (Minneapolis: University of Minnesota Press, 1997), 18.

8   Ibid., 19.

9   Adorno, *Negative Dialectics,* 145.

10 On the relationship between Bak and Adorno see an earlier version of this essay written for a special Religion and Genocide issue of *Religions.* Gary A. Phillips, "Icons of Just Is: Justice, Suffering, and the Artwork of Samuel Bak," *Religions* 8/6 (2017):108, accessed June 17, 2017, doi:10.3390/rel8060108.

11 Adorno, "Commitment," 312. Lawrence Langer acknowledges art's central paradox: "art signals its limited success through ultimate failure" (Lawrence L. Langer, *Using and Abusing the Holocaust* (Bloomington: Indiana University Press, 2006), 81. Robert Gibb's speaks of the "Janus face of art" (Robert Gibbs, "Unjustifiable Suffering," in *Suffering Religion,* edited by Robert Gibbs and Elliott R. Wolfson (New York: Routledge, 2002), 31.

12 On Adorno's multiple and changing statements about the barbarity of poetry and the different ways it has been interpreted and misinterpreted see Michael Rothberg, "After Adorno: Culture in the Wake of Catastrophe," *New German Critique* 72 (1997): 45–81; and Klaus Hofmann, "Poetry after Auschwitz—Adorno's Dictum," *German Life and Letters* 58 (2005): 182–94. Adorno eventually "clarifies" the statement: "Perennial suffering has as much right to expression as a tortured man has to scream; hence it may have been wrong to say that after Auschwitz you could no longer write poems." (*Negative Dialectics,* 362). See Lyn Hejinian, *The Language of Inquiry* (Berkeley: University of California Press, 2000), 334, note 3.

13 "Thinking against itself" is Adorno's shorthand for dialectical thinking that applies reason negatively to interrogate and critique itself. Adorno preferred modernist art for precisely this self-critical character. In particular, he valued the atonality of Arnold Schoenberg's musical compositions and the minimalism of Samuel Beckett's plays for their tensions and contradictions. (Adorno, *Negative Dialectics,* 365). On Modernism's self-criticism see James Thompson, *Twentieth-Century Theories of Art* (Ottawa: Carleton University Press, 1990).

14 The ethical challenge in making suffering meaningful is the focus of Emmanuel Levinas's phenomenological analysis of useless suffering, theodicy, and ethical responsibility for the one who suffers for nothing. Emmanuel Levinas, "Useless Suffering," in *The Provocation of Levinas: Rethinking the Other,* edited by Robert Bernasconi and David Wood (New York: Routledge, 1988), 158. Suffering is "useless" because it violates the integrity of the person as a self and escapes the capacity to incorporate it into meaningful

communicative structures. On the connections to Adorno see Andrew Edgar, "The Art of Useless Suffering," *Medicine, Health Care and Philosophy* 10 (2007): 395–405. On the chastened view of ethics from a Levinas perspective atrocity see John Roth, *The Failures of Ethics. Confronting the Holocaust, Genocide and Other Mass Atrocities* (New York: Oxford University Press, 2015), 98–101.

[15] Adorno, "Commitment," 313.

[16] Adorno, "Commitment," 312.

[17] Bak eschews abstraction in favor of concretion. He abandoned his early abstract and semi-abstract painting style for a representational—characterized differently as pictorial realist or near surrealist—approach because he found the former hindered the telling of his personal story and proved insufficient for expressing the immense weight of his own experience. See Samuel Bak, *Painted in Words. A Memoir* (Boston: Pucker Art Publications, 2001); Eliat Gordon Levitan, "The Ghosts of Samuel Bak. Vilna Stories," accessed June 17, 2017. http://www.eilatgordinlevitan.com/vilna/vilna_ pages/vilna_ stories_s_bak.html; Elizabeth Pols, "Beyond Time: The Paintings of Samuel Bak," *Paken Treger. Magazine of the Yiddish Book Center,* Spring, 2010, accessed June 17, 2017, http:// www.yiddishbookcenter.org/language-literature-culture/pakn-treger/beyond-time-paintings- samuel-bak.

[18] Richard Raskin, *A Child at Gunpoint. A Case Study in the Life of a Photo* (Aarhus: Aarhus University Press, 2004), 150.

[19] Danna Nolan Fewell and Gary A. Phillips, *Icon of Loss: The Haunting Child of Samuel Bak* (Boston: Pucker Art Publication, 2009), 5.

[20] Bak resists the banalization and cultural exploitation of the famous Warsaw Ghetto photo and by implication the real child captured by the Nazi photographer (Raskin, *A Child at Gunpoint,* 151; Fewell and Phillips, *Icon of Loss*).

[21] See Bak, *Painted in Words;* Lawrence L. Langer, and Samuel Bak, *Return to Vilna in the Art of Samuel Bak* (Boston: Pucker Art Publications, 2007).

[22] Across the body of his work, Bak represents the tensions and contradictions of absence and presence, suffering and hope in manifold ways. For example, he paints concentration camp musicians playing silently, lonely teddy bears standing sentinel for missing children, birds grounded from flight, living forests wholly excised from the earth, chess pieces frozen to their boards, floating rock formations that defy the laws of gravity, mourning angels whose messages go undelivered, broken and bullet-marked Mosaic tablets that have shed their commandments, impenetrable books and blank canvases that inhibit reading, keys incapable of opening their intended locks; and yet, we also encounter new growth on desiccated tree branches, concentration camp victims reaching pointedly for a deity's outstretched hand, ghetto boys bravely effecting their own rescue, and burial shrouds that serve double duty as freedom sails.

[23] Franz Rosenzweig, *The Star of Redemption,* translated by Barbara E. Galli (Madison: University of Wisconsin Press, 2005), 399. For further discussion see Gibbs, "Unjustifiable Suffering," 6.

[24] Raskin, *A Child at Gunpoint,* 154.

[25] Lawrence Langer, *Using and Abusing the Holocaust* (Bloomington: Indiana University Press, 20060, 295.

[26] Langer points out the danger of "redeeming" and "salvation" vocabulary and the "bracing pieties" that "prods us away from the event toward a consoling future" (*Holocaust Testimonies: The Ruin of Memory,* 2).

[27] Theodore Parker "Of Justice and the Conscience," in *Ten Sermons of Religion* (Boston: Crosby, Nichols and Company, 1853), 84-85, accessed June 17, 2017), https://archive. org/stream/tensermonsofreli00inpark/tensermonsofreli00inpark_djvu.txt 1853. This is a condensing of Parker's longer statement that King revised and employed without attribution many times in sermons, public addresses, and on marches.

[28] Theodor W. Adorno, *Minima Moralia: Reflections from Damaged Life,* Radical Thinkers Classics, translated by E. F. N. Jeffcott (London: Verso, 2005). Adorno plays upon a similar contrast in the title *Minima Moralia* in contrast to Aristotle's classic *Magna Moralia.* Bak minimizes the figure of Lady Justice to reflect the change in justice's much-altered, post-Auschwitz status.

[29] William Ian Miller, *Eye for an Eye* (Cambridge: Cambridge University Press, 2006), 1–6; Judith Resnik and Dennis E. Curtis, "Images of Justice," *The Yale Law Journal* 96 (1987): 1727–28, accessed June 17, 2017, http://digitalcommons.law.yale.edu/fss_papers/917/.

[30] Resnik and Curtis, "Images of Justice," 1729–30; Miller, *Eye for an Eye,* 1–4.

[31] Adorno associates blindfolded justice with modernity's success in maintaining men and women in a state of unfreedom: "The blindfold over the eyes of Justitia means not only that justice brooks no interference but that it does not originate in freedom." Max Horkheimer and Theodor W. Adorno, *Dialectic of Enlightenment. Philosophical Fragments,* edited by Gunzelin Schmid Noerr, translated by Edmund Jephcott, Culture Memory in the Present (Stanford: Stanford University Press, 2002), 12.

[32] Resnik and Curtis, "Images of Justice," 1728.

[33] Ibid., 1728. On the severing of arms Resnik and Curtis ("Images of Justice," 1750) discuss the mural "Les Juges aux mains coupées, Cesar Giglio, circa 1604, Salle du Conseil (Council Chamber), Town Hall of Geneva, Switzerland.

[34] Miller, *Eye for an Eye,* 3–6.

[35] Ibid., 6.

[36] On the critique of modernity's quantitative reduction of reason and life see Adorno, *Negative Dialectics,* 43–45; Horkheimer and Adorno, *Dialectic of Enlightenment.* On the razing of Lidice see http://www.holocaustresearchproject.org/nazioccupation/lidice.html.

[37] Miller, *Eye for an Eye,* 17.

[38] See Dorothy Jean Weaver, "Transforming Nonresistance: From Lex Talionis to 'Do Not Resist the Evil One,' In *The Love of Enemy and Nonretaliation in the New Testament,* edited by Willard M. Swartley (Louisville: Westminster John Knox Press, 1992), 37; David Daube, *New Testament and Rabbinic Judaism* (New York: Wipf and Stock, 1956), 25–26; Tikva Frymer-Kensky, "Tit for Tat," Biblical Archeologist 43 (1980): 230–34; Nahum Sarna, *Exodus,* The JPS Torah Commentary (Philadelphia: Jewish Publication Society, 1991), 125.

[39] Exod. 21:23–25; Lev. 24:19–21; Deut. 19:21; Matt. 5:38. Daube David, "Eye for Eye," In *New Testament Judaism. Collected Works of David Daube,* edited by Calum Carmichael, vol. 2 (Berkeley: University of California Press, 2000), 182 argues that Matthew surely follows prevailing rabbinic use.

[40] Miller, *Eye for an Eye,* 58.

[41] Sarna, *Exodus,* 126; Miller, *Eye for an Eye,* 26.

[42] Moses Maimonides. *Laws of Wounds and Damages,* accessed June 17, 2017, http://www.chabad.org/library/article_cdo/aid/1088908/jewish/Chovel-uMazzik-Chapter-One.htm.; Miller, Eye for an Eye, xii; Daube, "Eye for an Eye, vol. 2, 178–79; David Daube, "Lex Talionis," In *Studies in Biblical Law* (Cambridge: Cambridge University Press, 1947), 102–53.

[43] See Daube's discussion of the complex lex talionis textual history in "Lex Talionis" cited in Miller, *Eye for an Eye,* 16.

[44] *Henry VI,* 2.2.214.

[45] Langer, *Using and Abusing the Holocaust,* 88–90 discusses the singularly unhelpful categories of retributive and restorative justice in relation to atrocity and the complications in comparing justice after apartheid with justice post-Holocaust.

[46] Adorno, "Commitment," 312.

[47] For more on Bak's explicit engagement with biblical themes of Torah, covenant,

and creation see Danna Nolan Fewell and Gary A. Phillips, "From Bak to the Bible: Imagination, Interpretation, and *Tikkun Olam*," *ARTS: The Arts in Religious and Theological Studies* 20 (2009): 21–30.

[48] See Fewell and Phillips, "From Bak to the Bible," 22-23.

[49] Gavin I. Langmuir, *Toward a Definition of Antisemitism* (Berkeley: University of California Press, 1990), 14–15.

[50] For an intertextual reading of a *By Law* see Gary A. Phillips, "An Eye for an I: An Intertextual Reading of Matthew 5:38 and the Artwork of Samuel Bak," in *The Press of the Text: Biblical Studies in Honor of James W. Voelz,* edited by Andrew H. Bartlet, Jeffrey Kloha, and Paul R. Raabe (Eugene: Pickwick Publications, 2017), 179–99.

[51] Fewell and Phillips, ""Genesis, Genocide and the Art of Samuel Bak: "Unseamly" Reading After the Holocaust," 84.

[52] Ibid.

[53] As a strategy to keep attention on the concrete, Adorno (*Negative Dialectics,* 402) uses the Jewish prohibition against images as a kind of "inverse theology" that directs attention away from God and to the damaged life of this world. Bak's visual strategy works in a similar way. See Pritchard, "Bilderverbot Meets Body in Theodor W. Adorno's Inverse Theology," 291–318.

[54] Fewell and Phillips, *Icon of Loss,* 5.

[55] Sigmund Freud, *Beyond the Pleasure Principle,* Standard Edition, translated by James Strachey, Anna Freud, Alix Strachey, and Alan Tyson, vol. 24 (London: Hogarth Press, 1920), 20.

[56] On Adorno's use of negative images as a way of affirming future redemption see Pritchard "Bilderverbot Meets Body in Theodor W. Adorno's Inverse Theology," 311. On Adorno's consideration of the Jewish prohibition of images see Adorno, Aesthetic Theory, 93; Neil Levi, *Modernist Form and the Myth of Jewification* (New York: Fordham University Press, 2014) 140–42. Levi 2014, pp 140-42.

[57] Adorno, "Commitment," 314.

[58] The sadists in the camps told their victims, "Tomorrow you will be wiggling skyward as smoke from this chimney" (Adorno, *Negative Dialectics,* 362).

[59] Geoff Ostrove, "Adorno, Auschwitz, and the New Categorical Imperative," *Perspectives on Global Development and Technology* 12 (2013): 298–309.

[60] Bernstein "Suffering Injustice: Misrecognition as Moral Injury in Critical Theory," 319 describes Adorno's new categorical imperative as asserting the primacy of injustice over justice. While bleak in outlook Adorno, like Bak, maintains hope in this damaged world.

[61] Adorno, Negative Dialectics, 365. Or as Fackenheim states the new moral imperative: not to give Hitler a moral victory becomes the 614th mitzvoth. See Emil Fackenheim, *God's Presence in History: Jewish Affirmation and Philosophical Reflections* (New York: New York University Press, 1970), 80.

[62] Primo Levi describes the stories of incomprehensible suffering related by Auschwitz prisoners as "stories of a new Bible" in *Survival in Auschwitz,* translated by Stuart Woolf (New York: Simon and Schuster, 1996), 65–66.

[63] Theodor W. Adorno, "Metaphysics: Concepts and Problems," In *Can One Live After Auschwitz? A Philosophical Reader,* edited by Rolf Tiedemann, translated by Rodney Livingstone and others (Stanford: Stanford University Press, 2003), 435. Langer cautions that Auschwitz has altered the conditions and conception of survival and therefore the way we should speak of "surviving Auschwitz" in "The Dilemma of Choice in the Deathcamps," In *Holocaust: Religious and Philosophical Implications,* edited by John K. Roth and Michael Berenbaum (New York: Paragon House, 1989), 223.

[64] Adorno, "Commitment," 314.

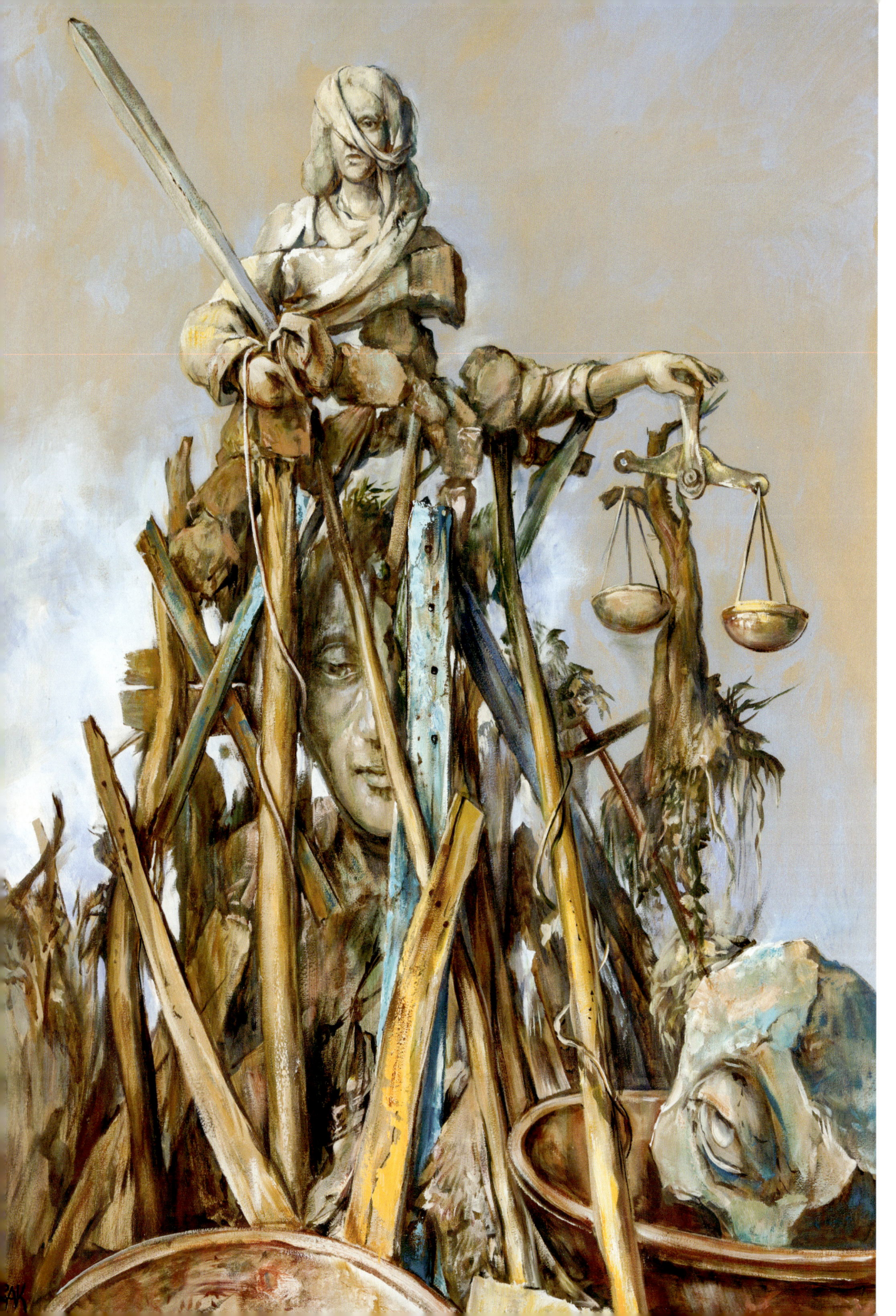

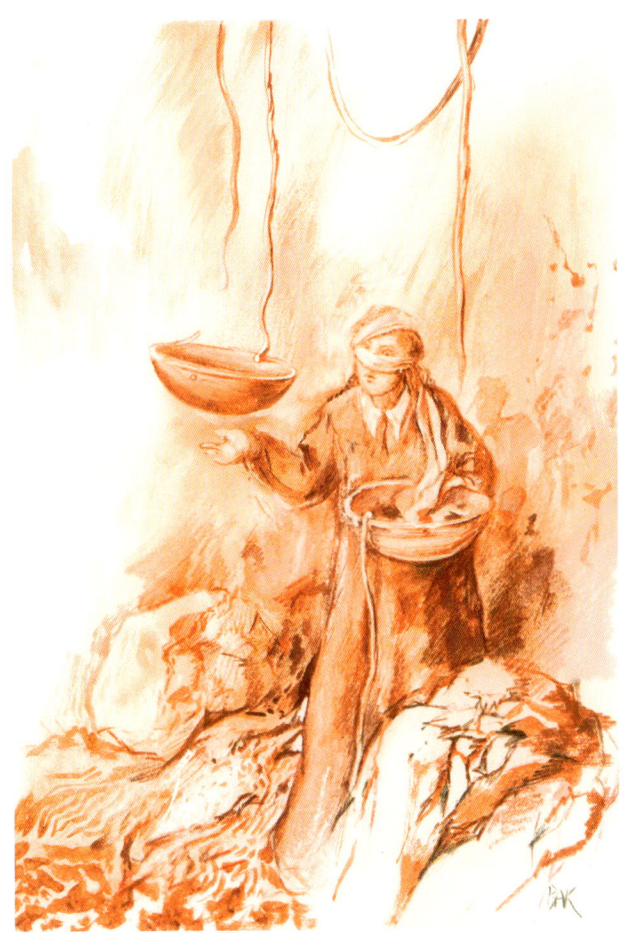

Delicate Issue
Watercolor on paper
14.5 x 10"
BK2015

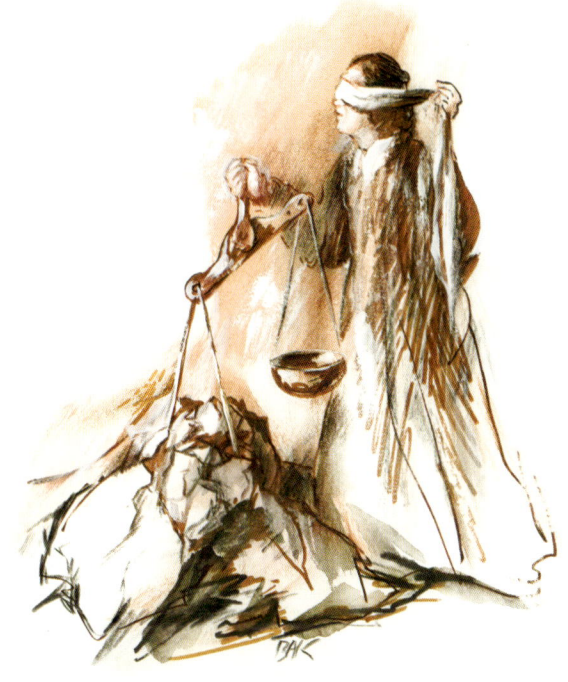

Weighty Argument
Watercolor on paper
14.5 x 10"
BK2014

LEFT:
Facing
Acrylic on canvas
36 x 24"
BK1995

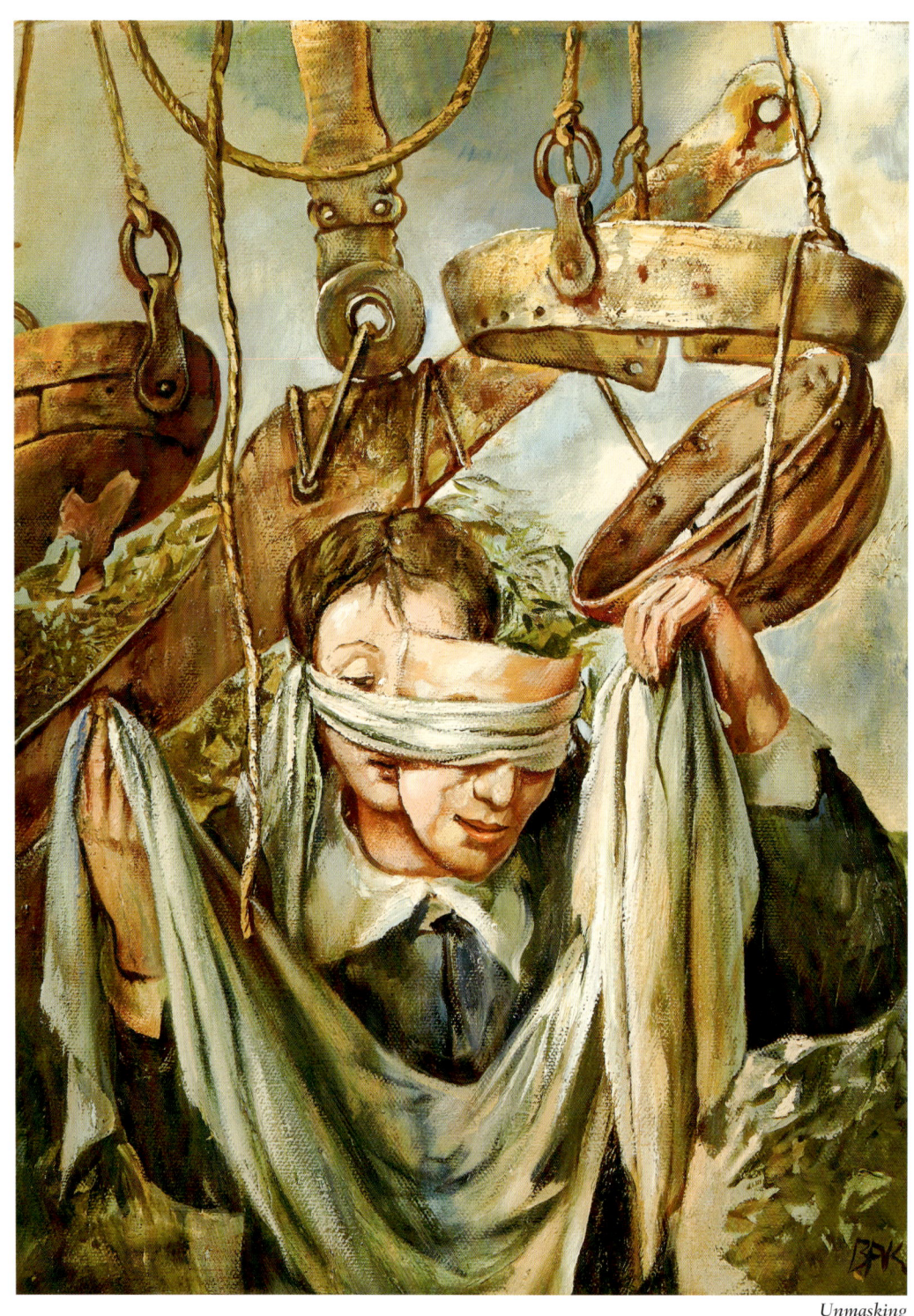

Unmasking
Oil on canvas
14 x 11"
BK1978

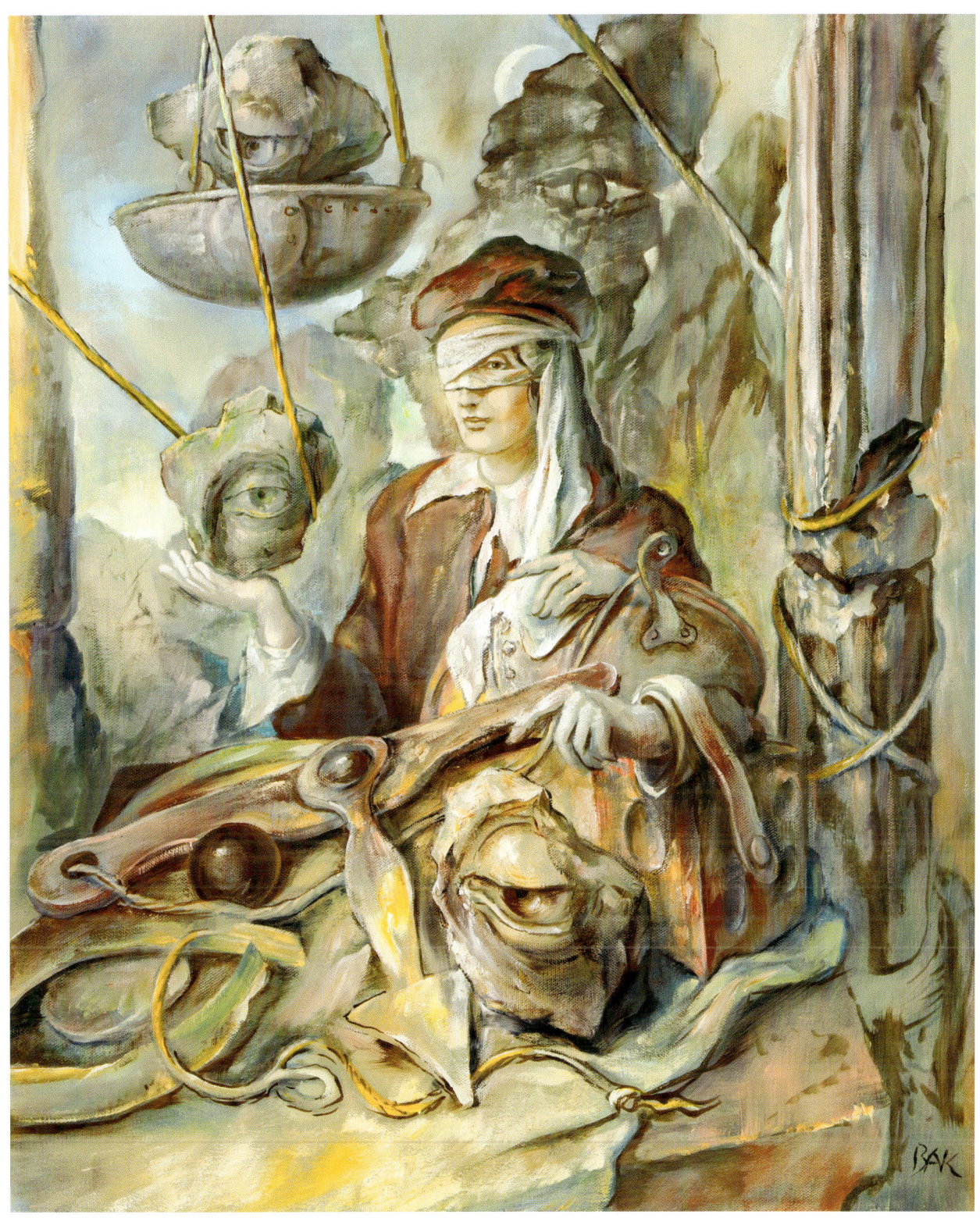

In Search of a Portrait B
Acrylic and oil on canvas
24 x 20"
BK1997

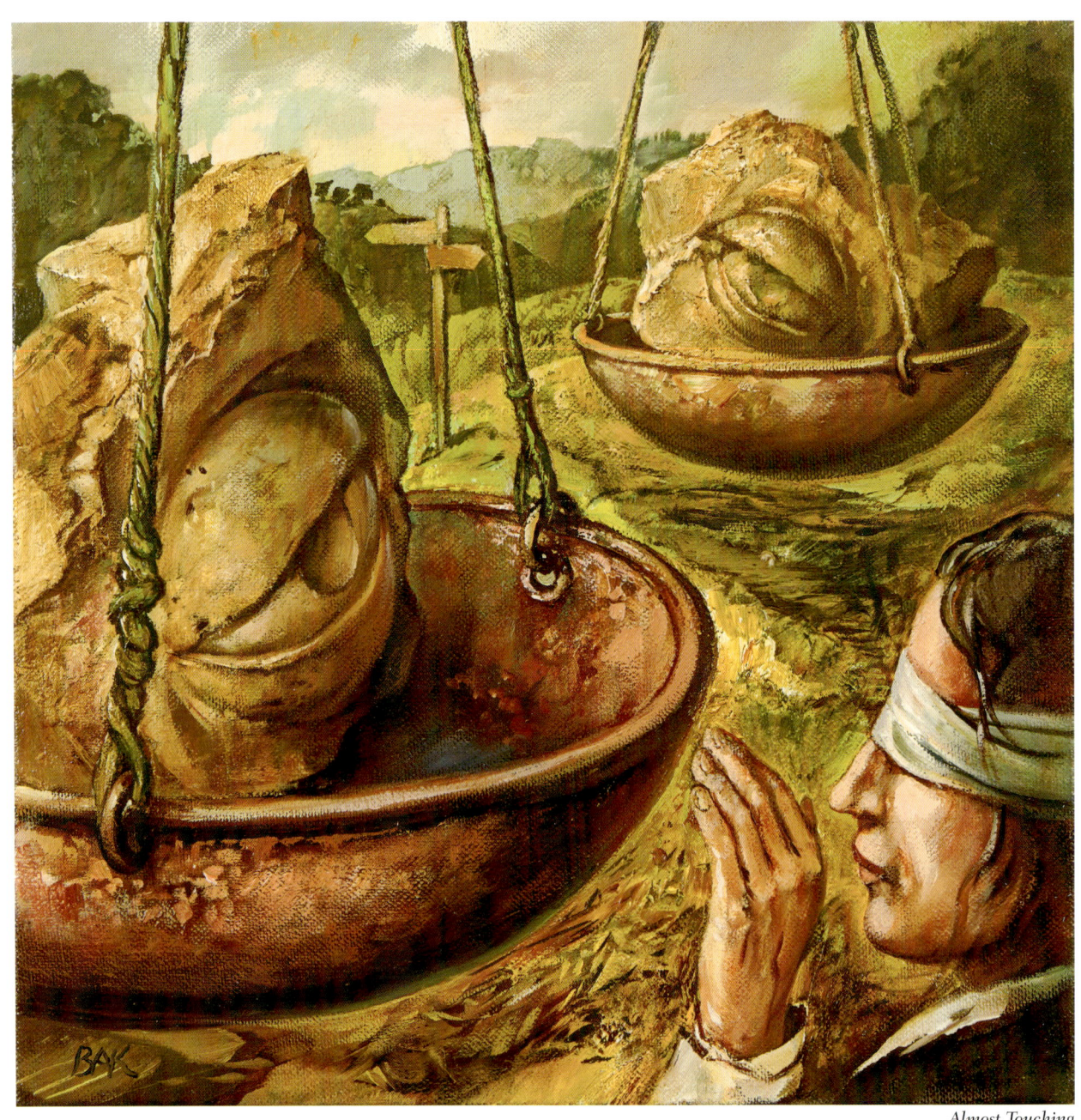

Almost Touching
Oil on canvas
12 x 12"
BK1980

42

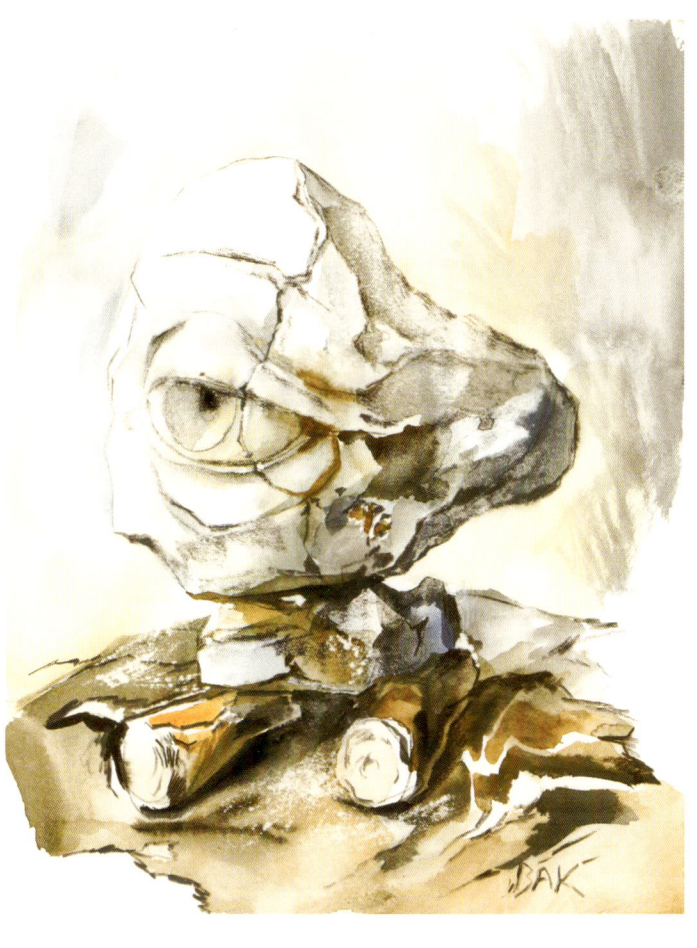

The One and Only
Watercolor on paper
12.75 x 10"
BK2018

Very Involved
Watercolor and egg tempera on paper
8 x 11.75"
BK2022

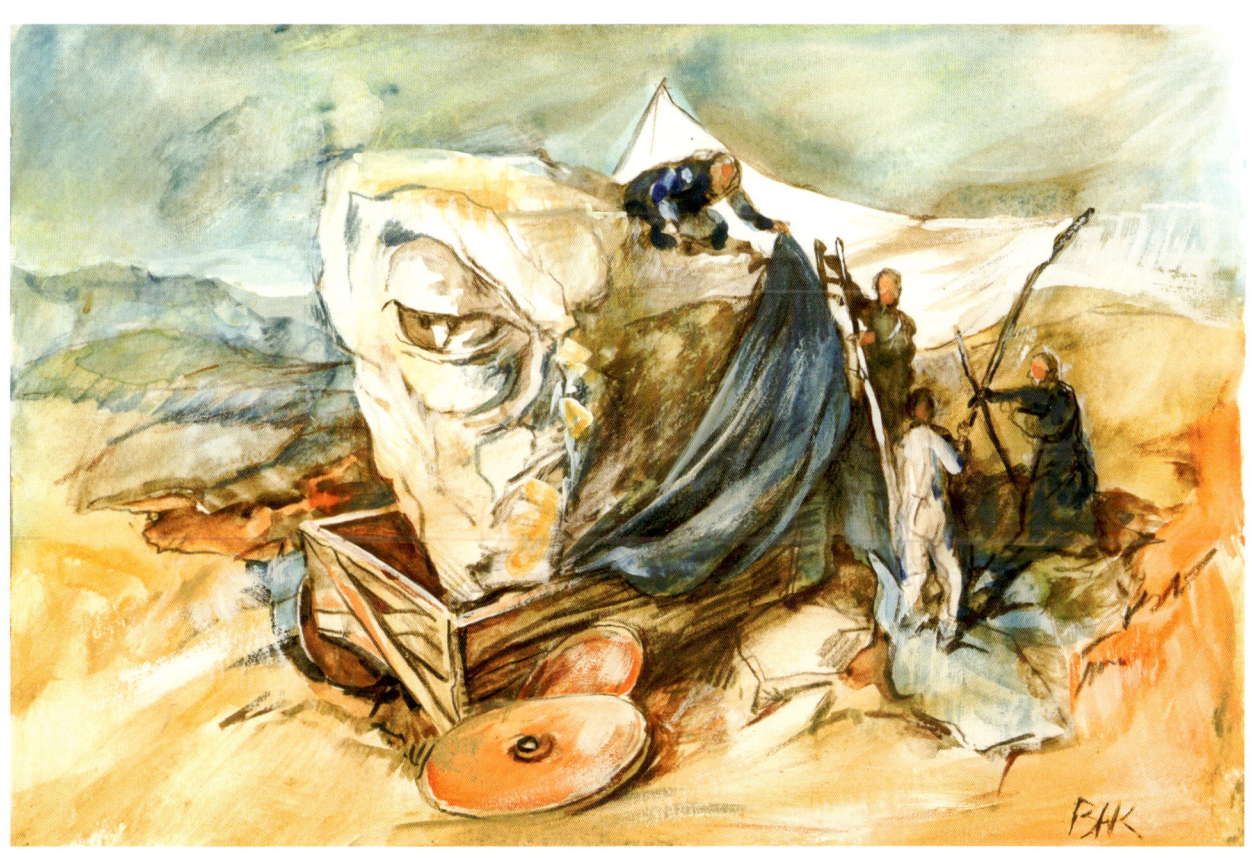

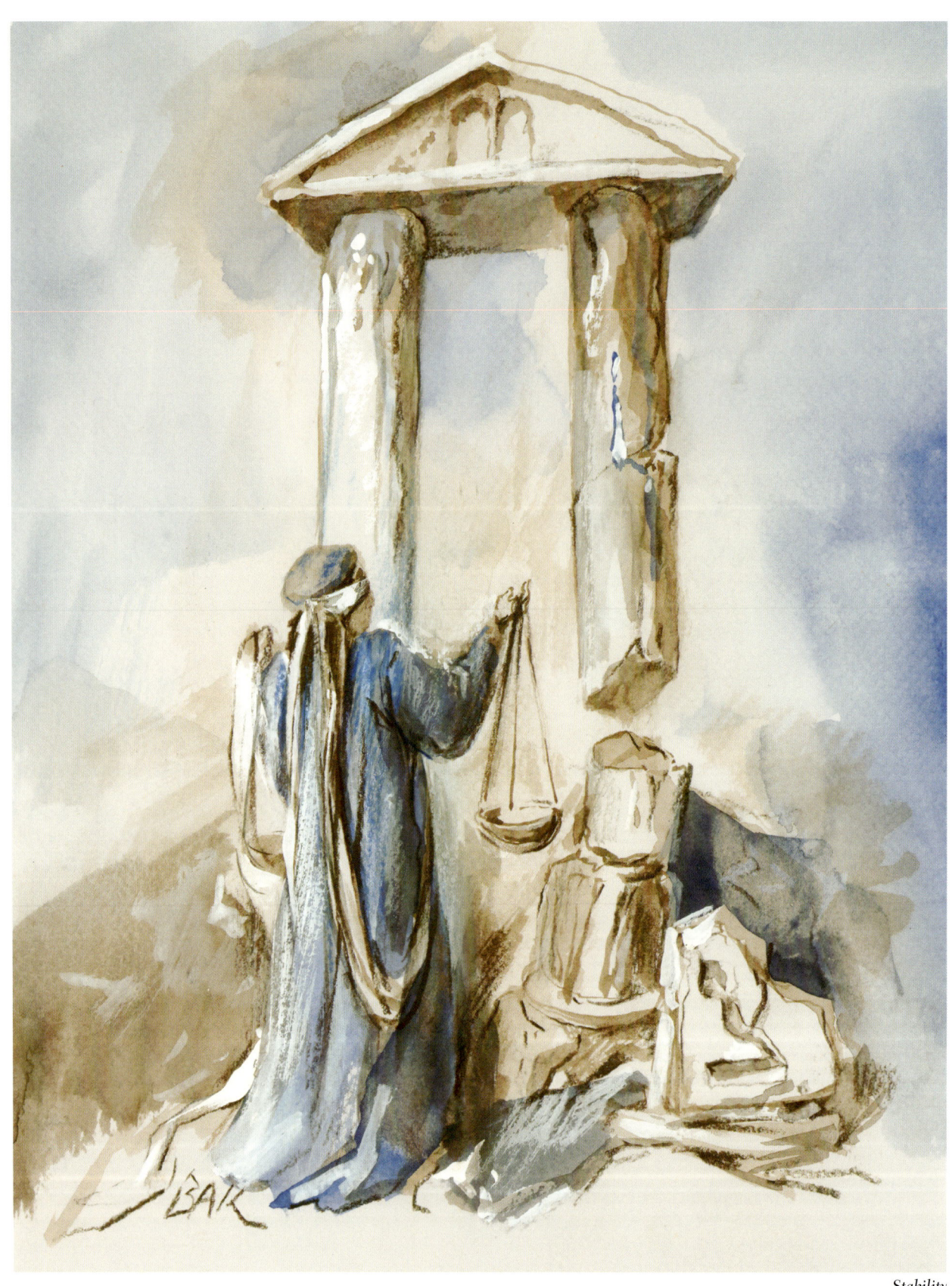

Stability
Watercolor on paper
11 x 8.5"
BK2017

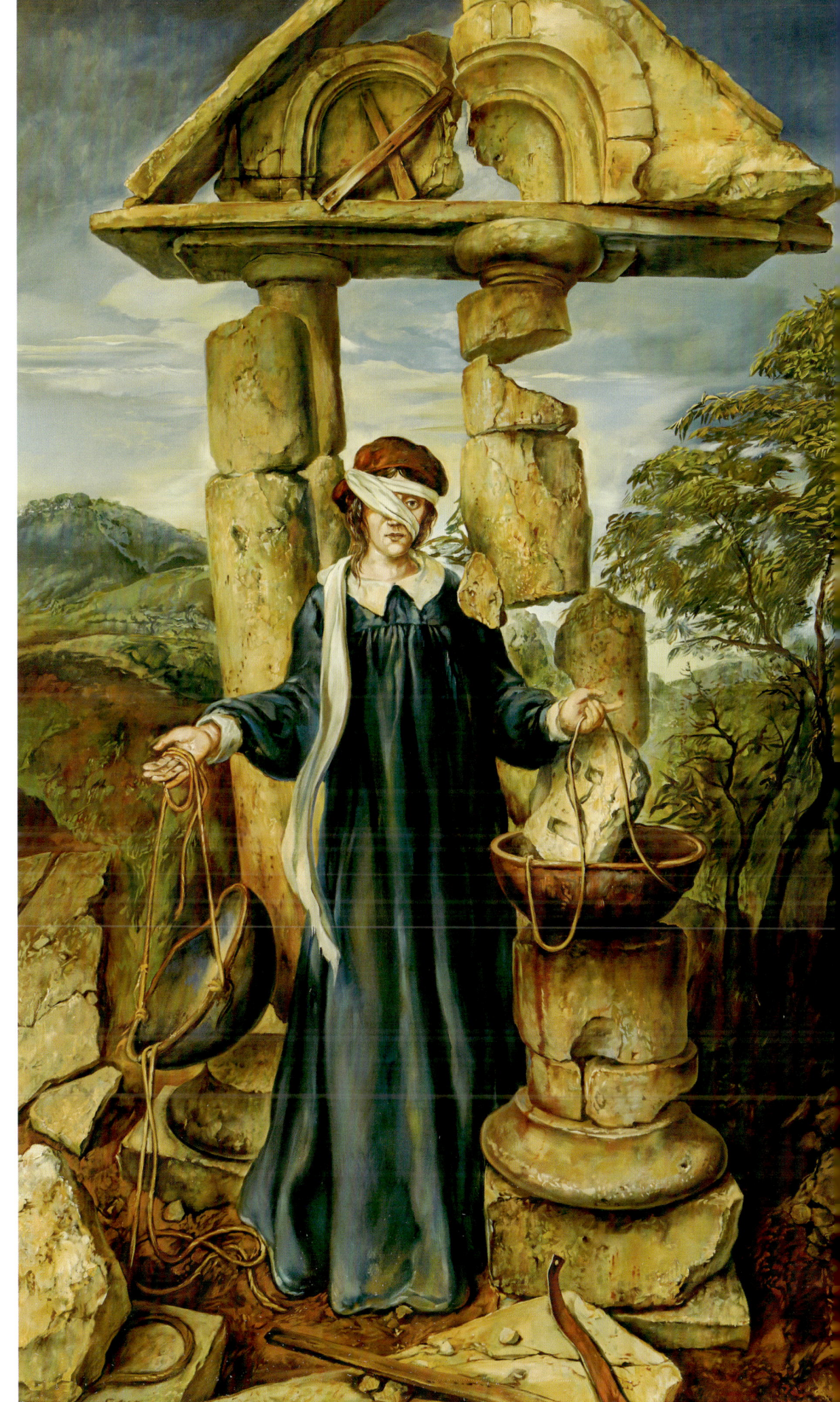

Even-Handed
Oil on canvas
63.75 x 38.25"
BK1928

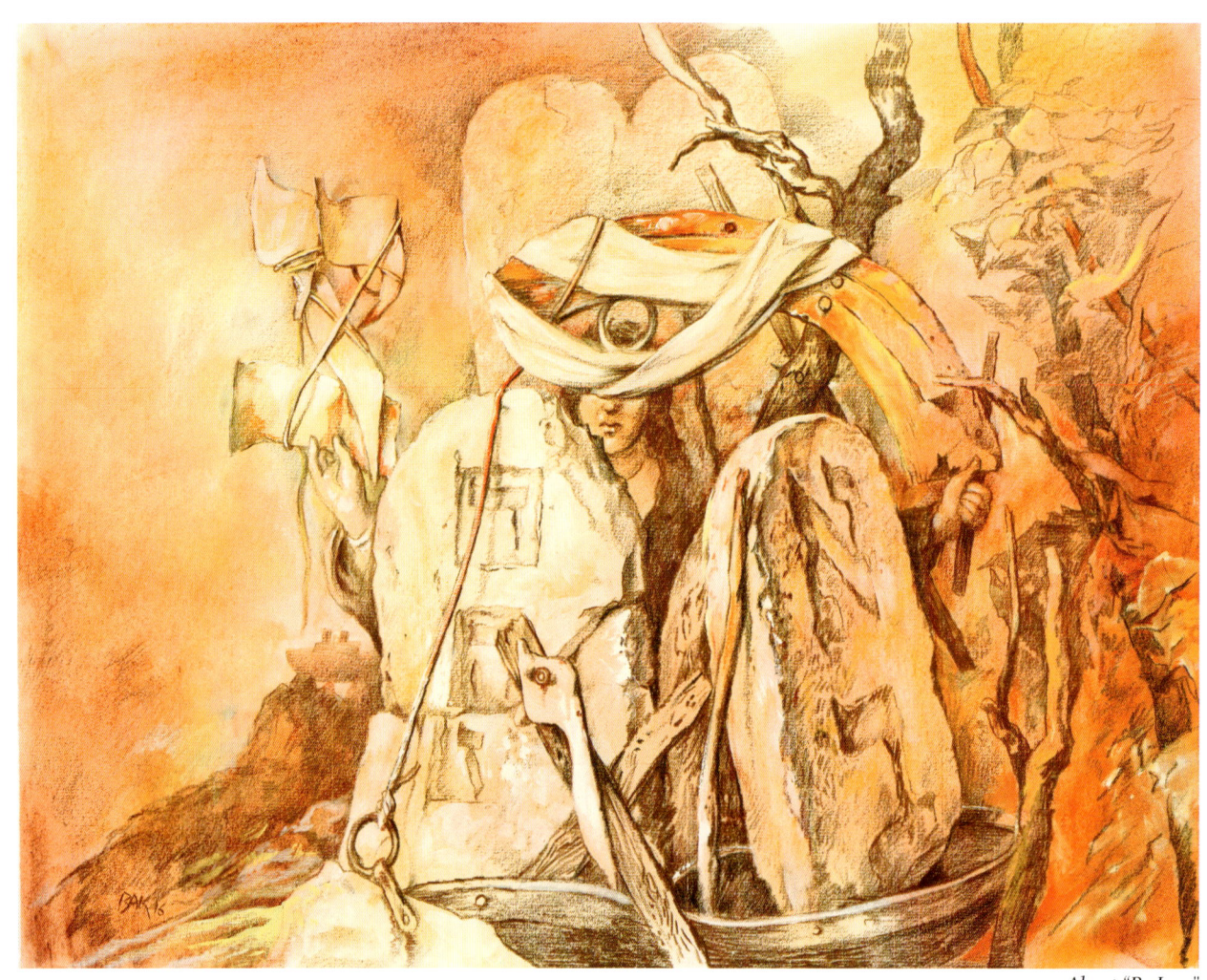

About "By Law"
Crayon and pastel on paper
19 x 24.5"
BK2026

RIGHT:
By Law
Oil on canvas
48 x 36"
BK1930

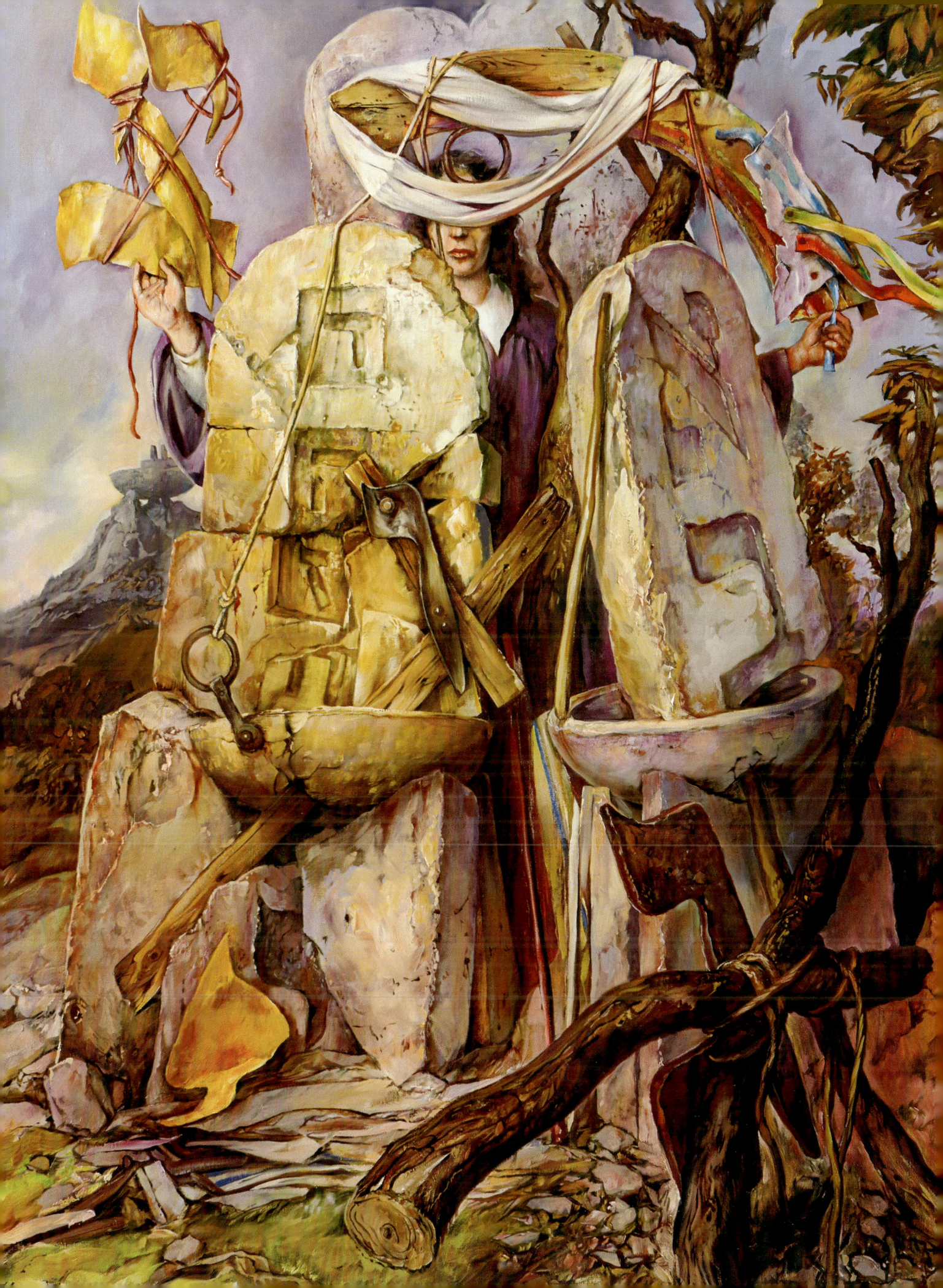

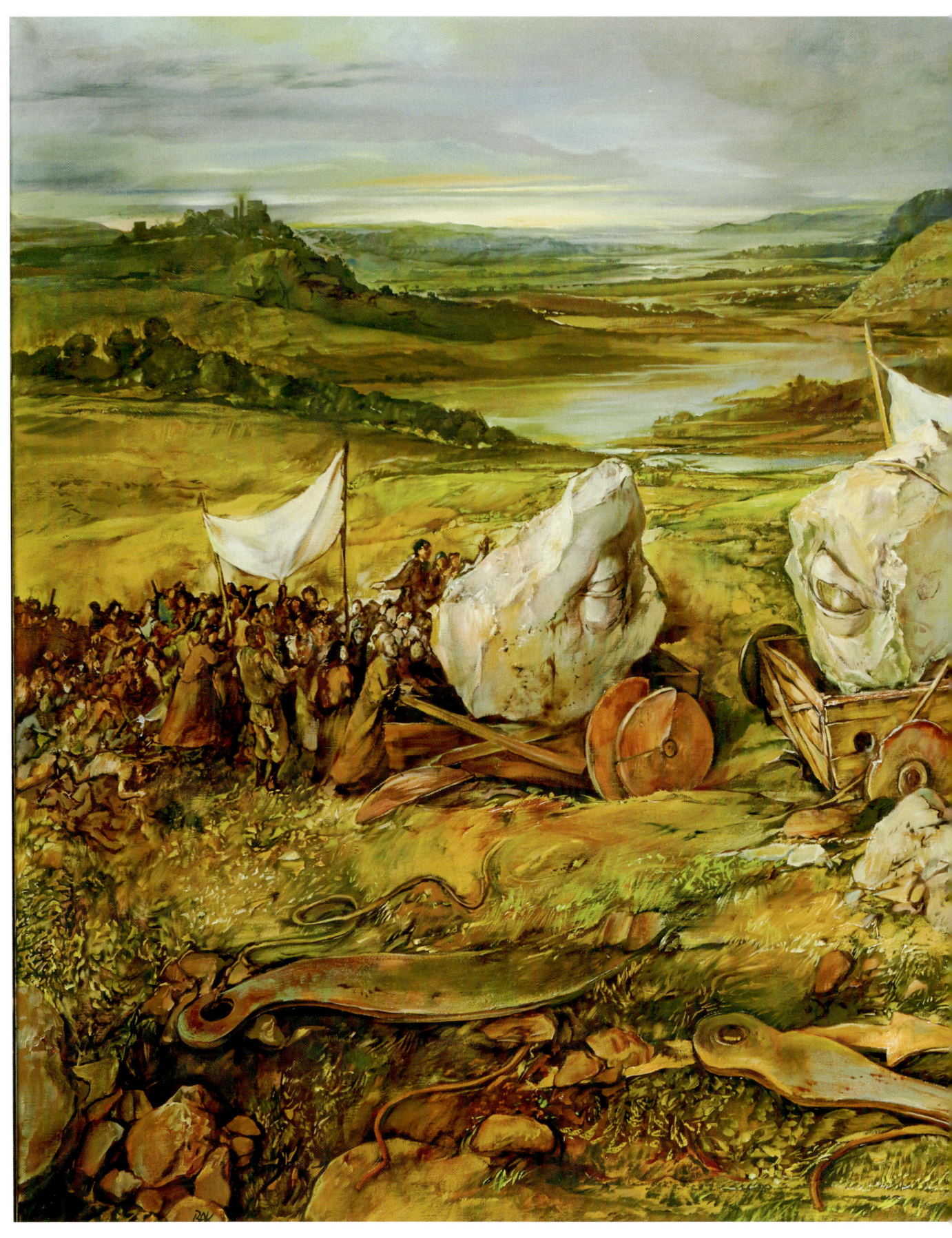

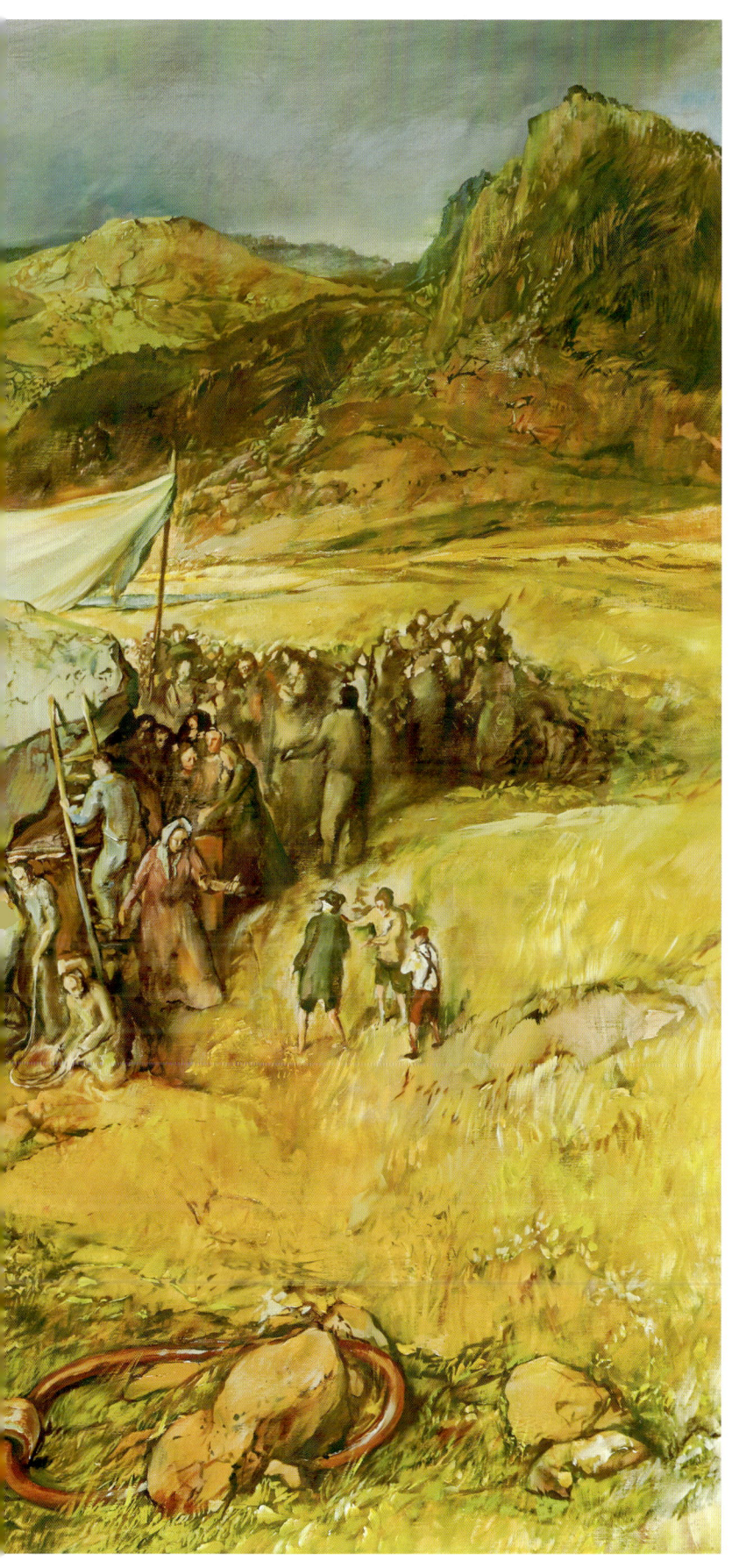

Eye for Eye
Oil on canvas
36 x 48"
BK1932

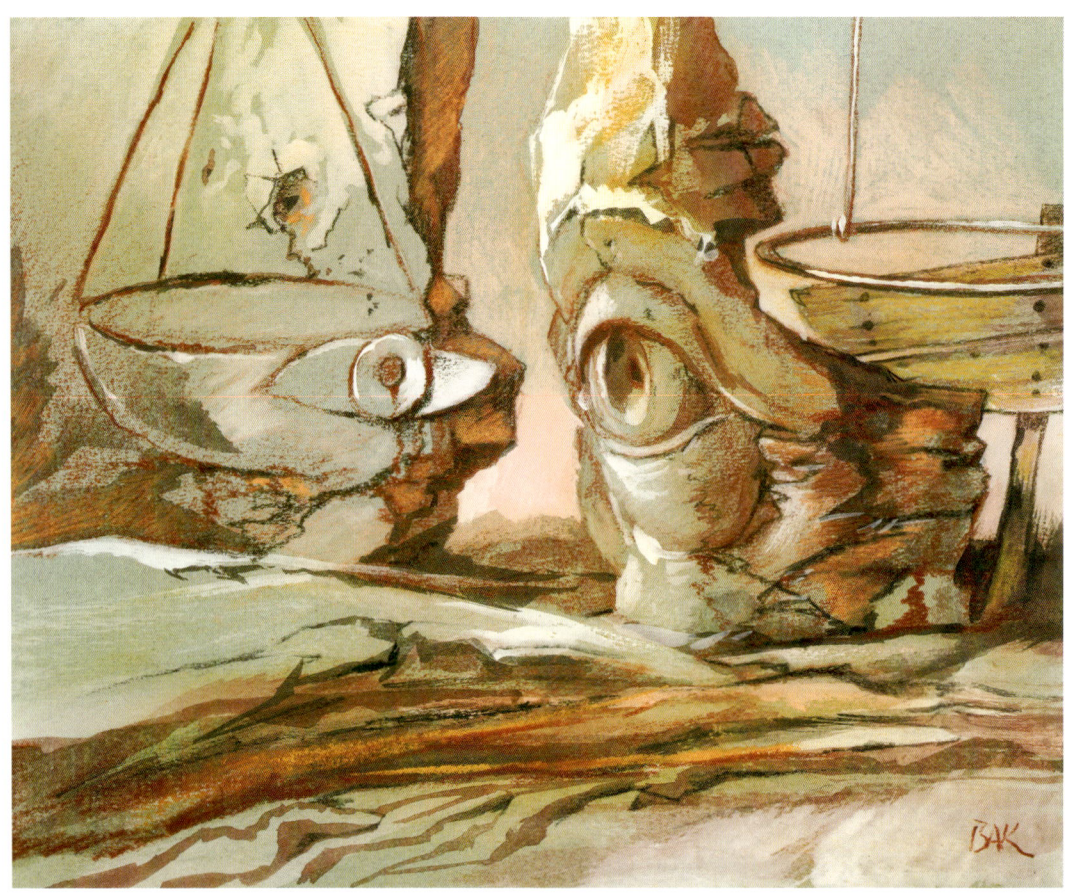

A Different View
Crayon and
tempera on paper
8.5 x 11"
BK2020

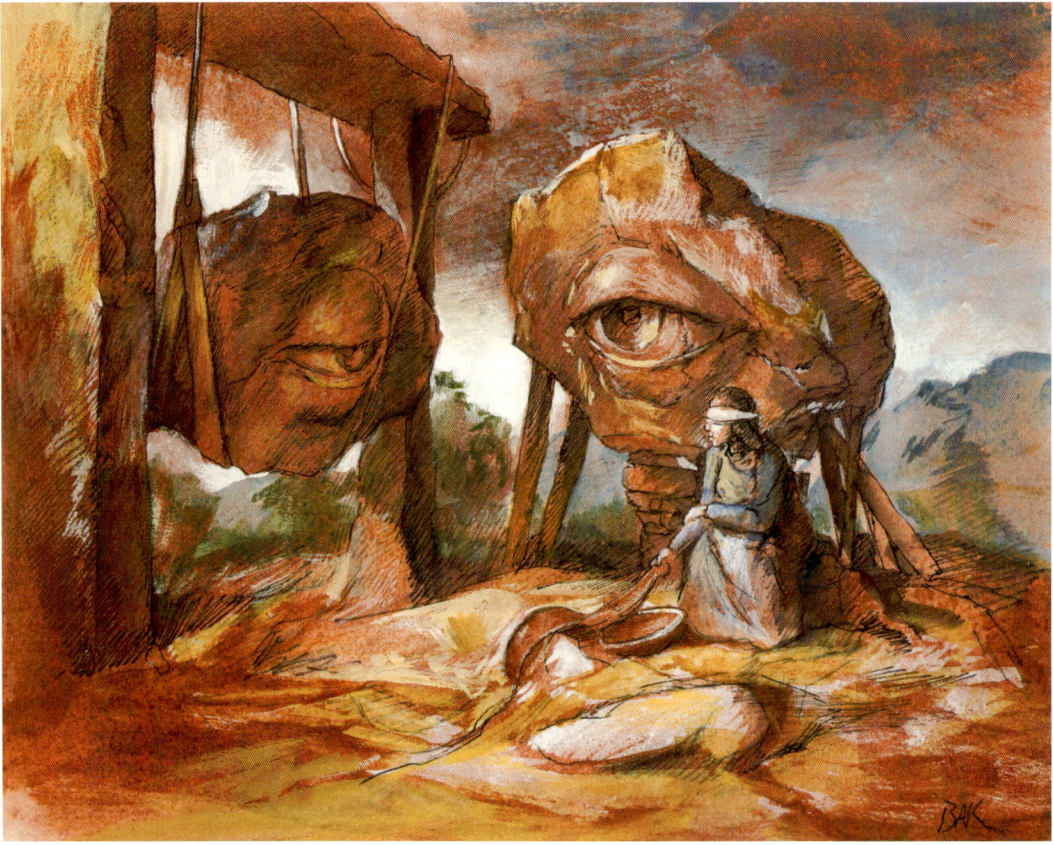

Resting Figure
Mixed media
on paper
8.5 x 11"
BK2021

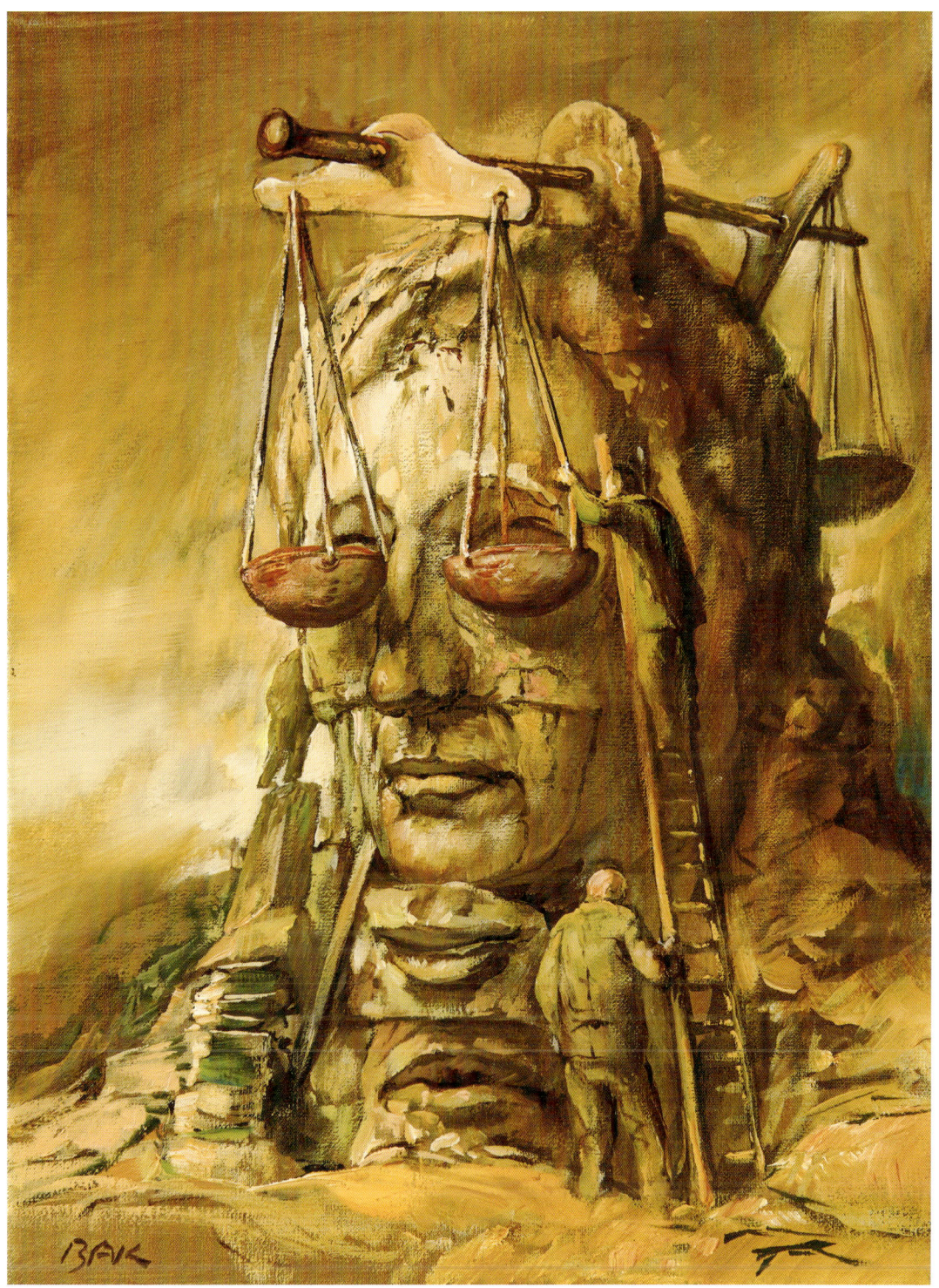

Saving the Face
Oil on canvas
12 x 9"
BK1981

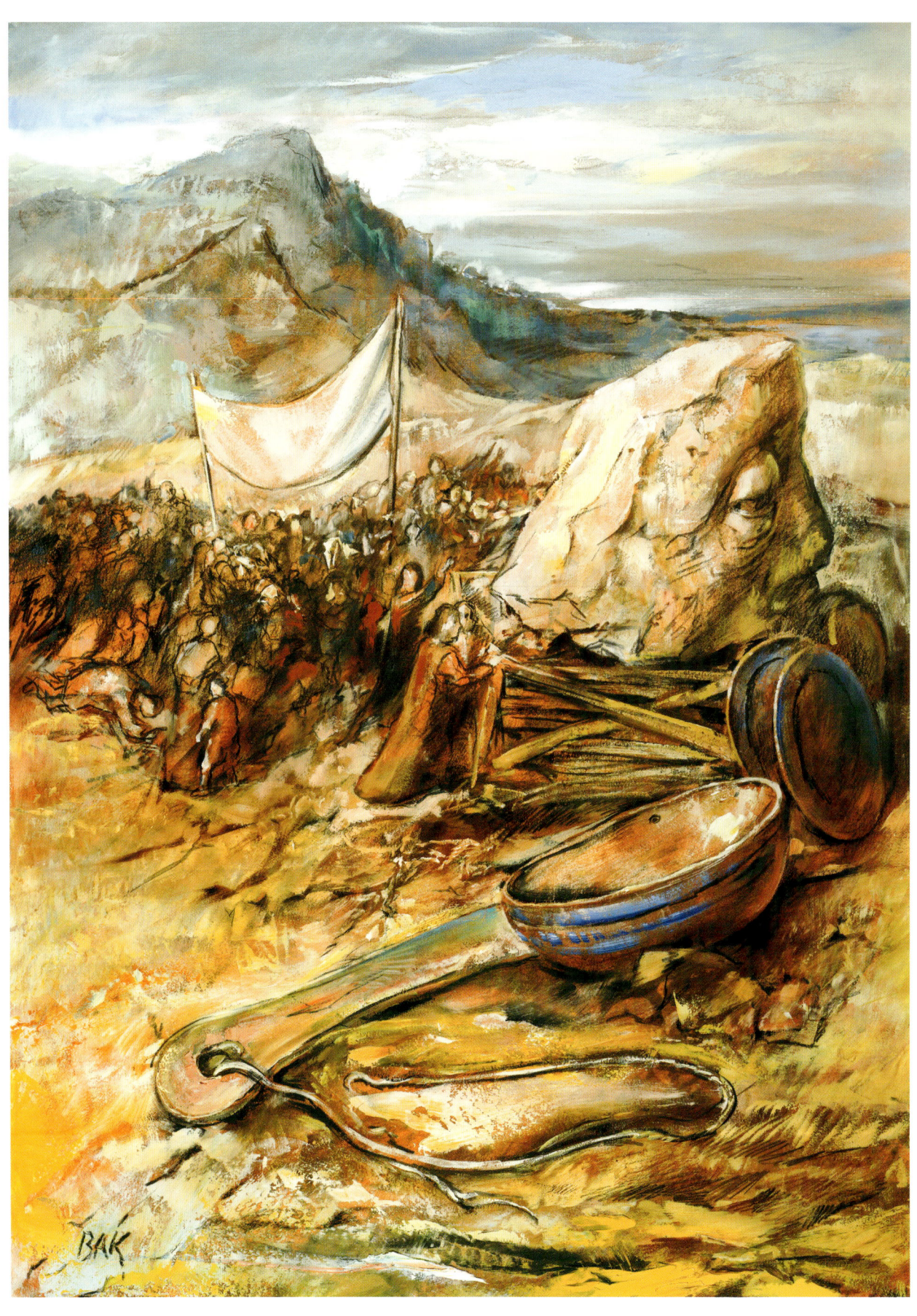

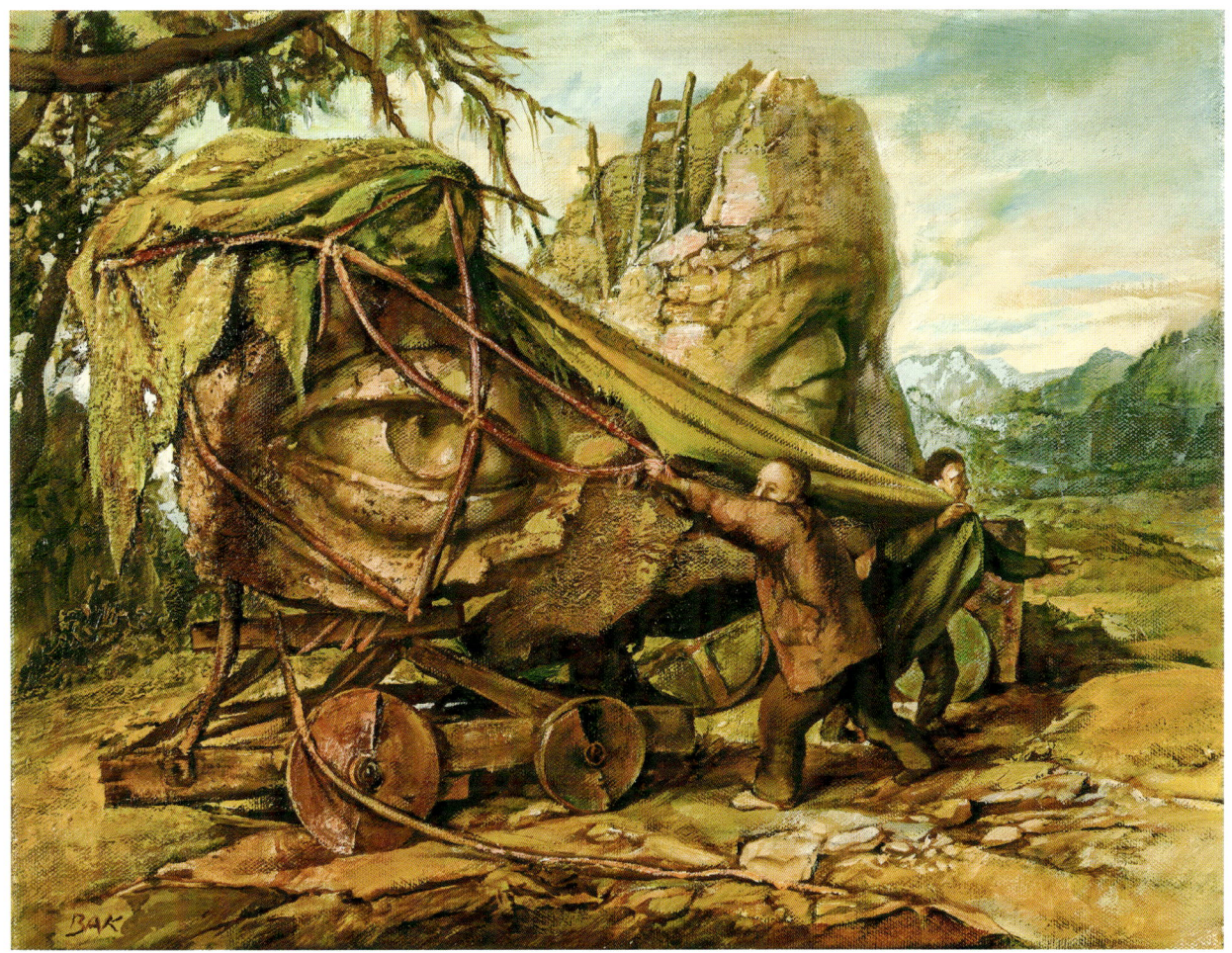

Tit for Tat
Oil on canvas
12 x 16"
BK1975

LEFT:
On the One Side
Charcoal and oil on paper
29.75 x 22"
BK2023

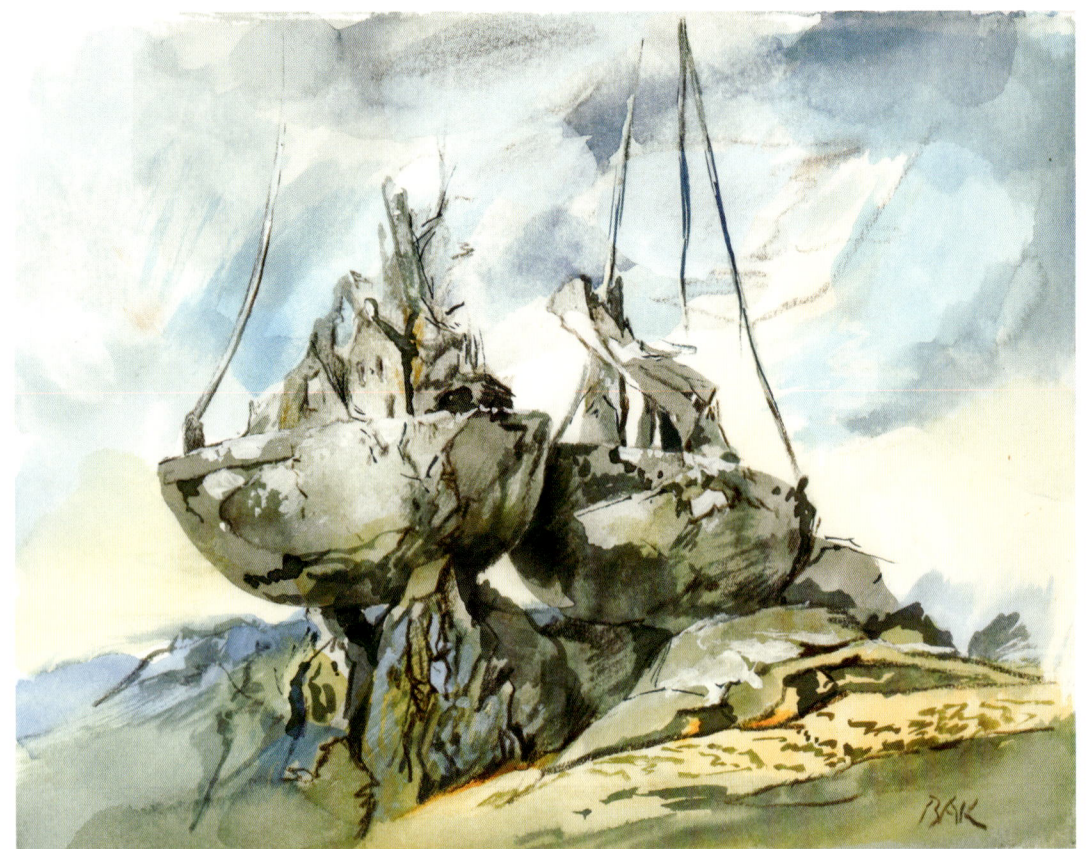

On Both Sides
Watercolor
on paper
8.5 x 11"
BK2002

Postponed
Crayon and
gouache
on paper
10 x 12.75"
BK2011

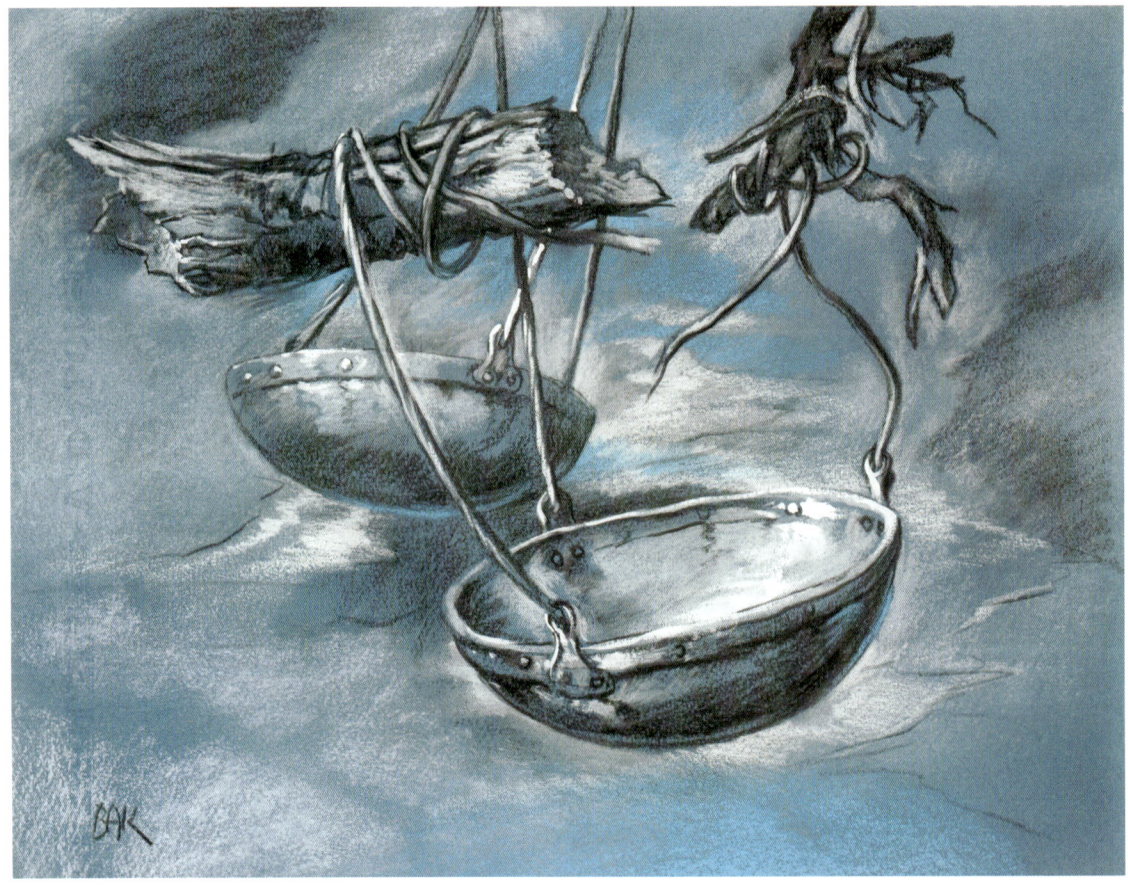

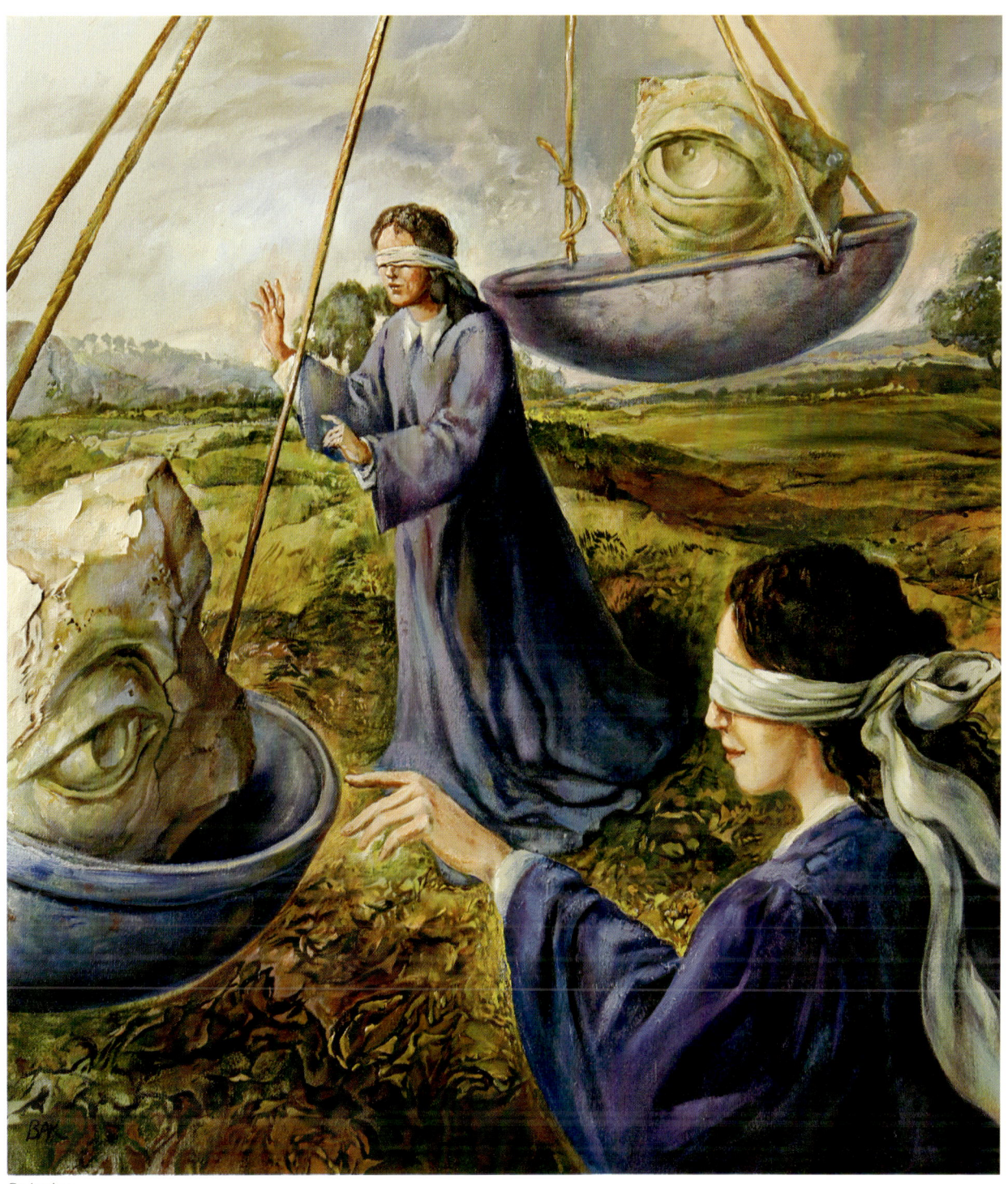

Swinging
Oil on canvas
24 x 24"
BK1953

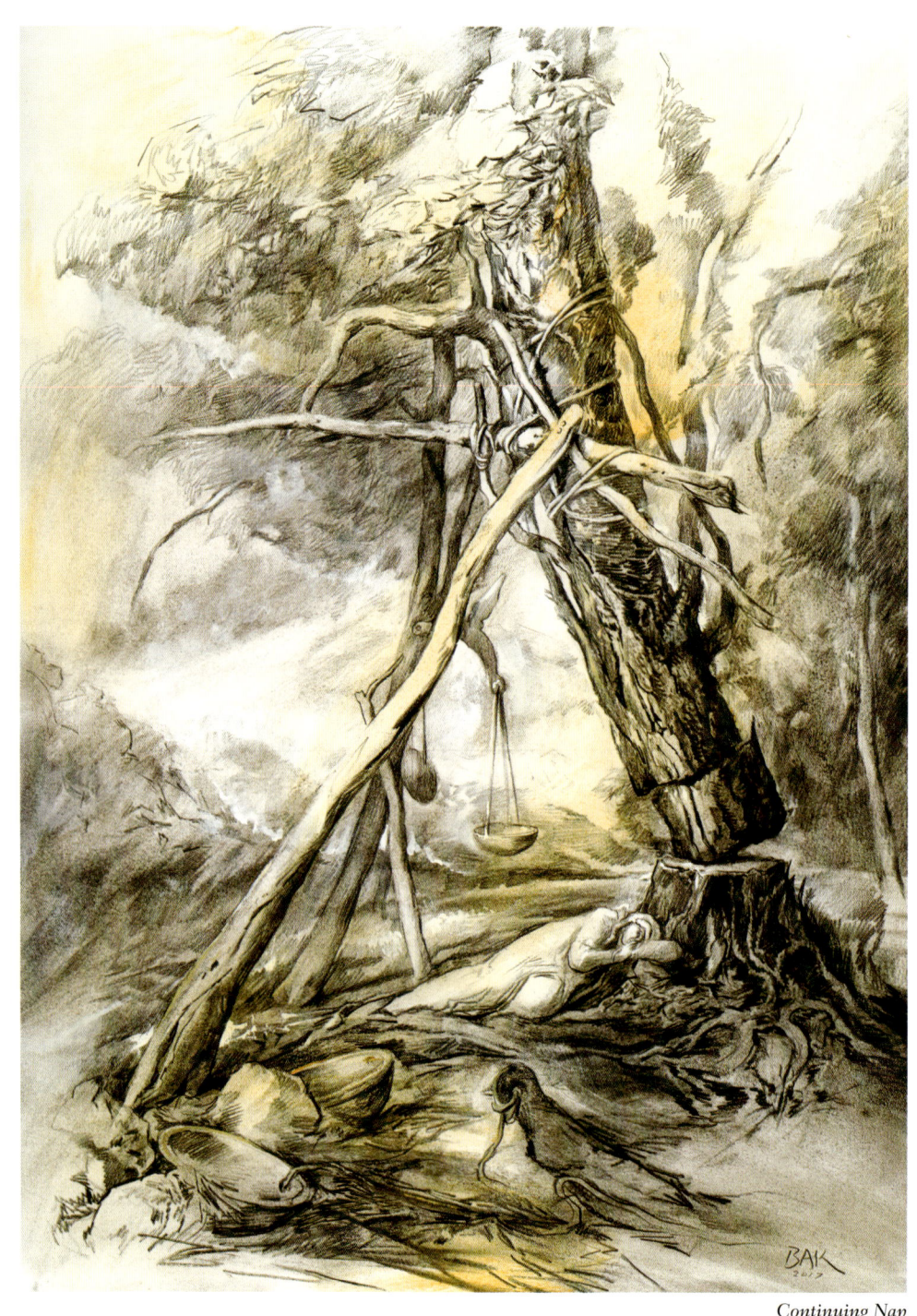

Continuing Nap
Charcoal, crayon, and pastel on paper
29.75 x 22"
BK2024

RIGHT:
Nap
Oil on canvas
48 x 36"
BK1929

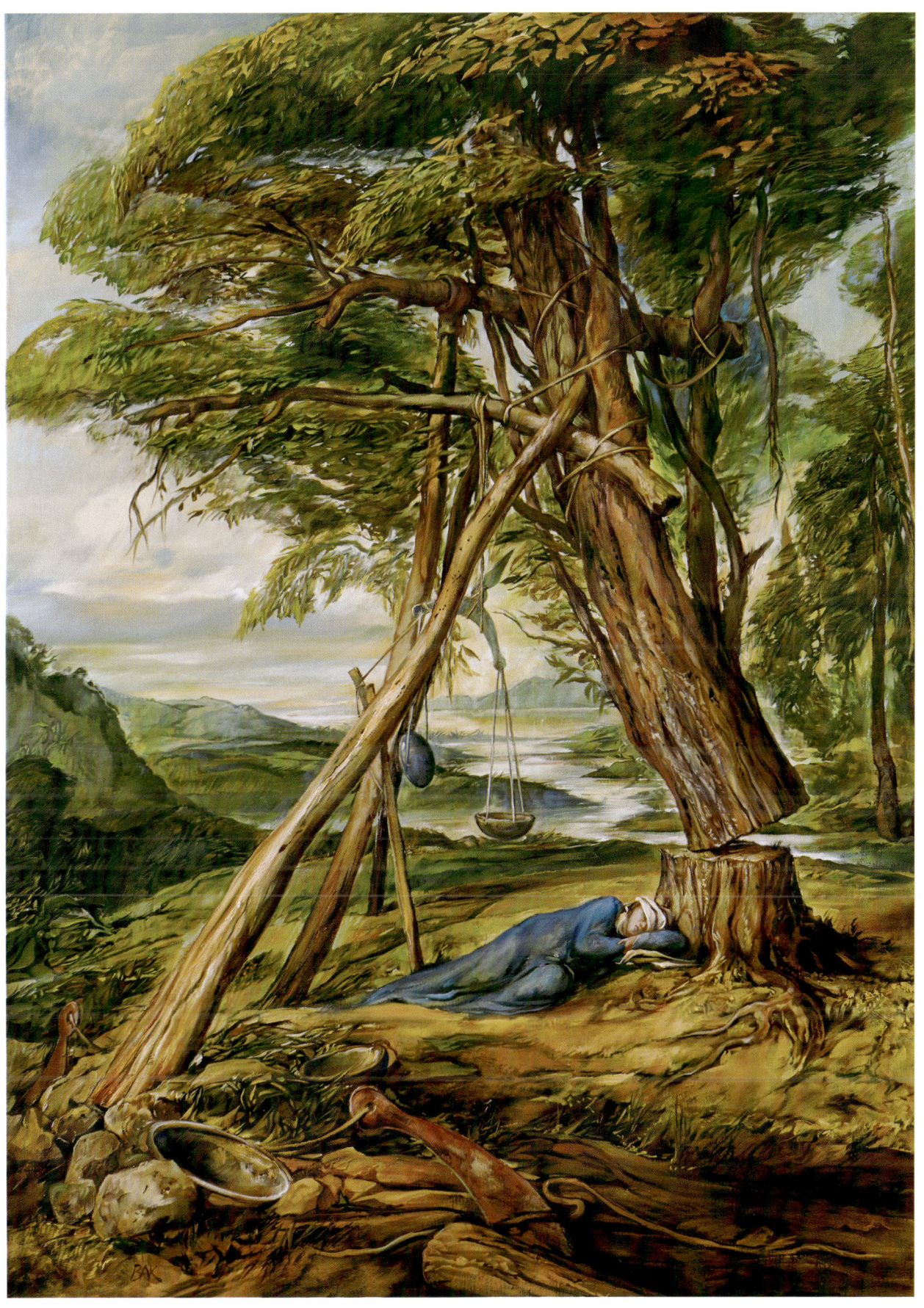

57

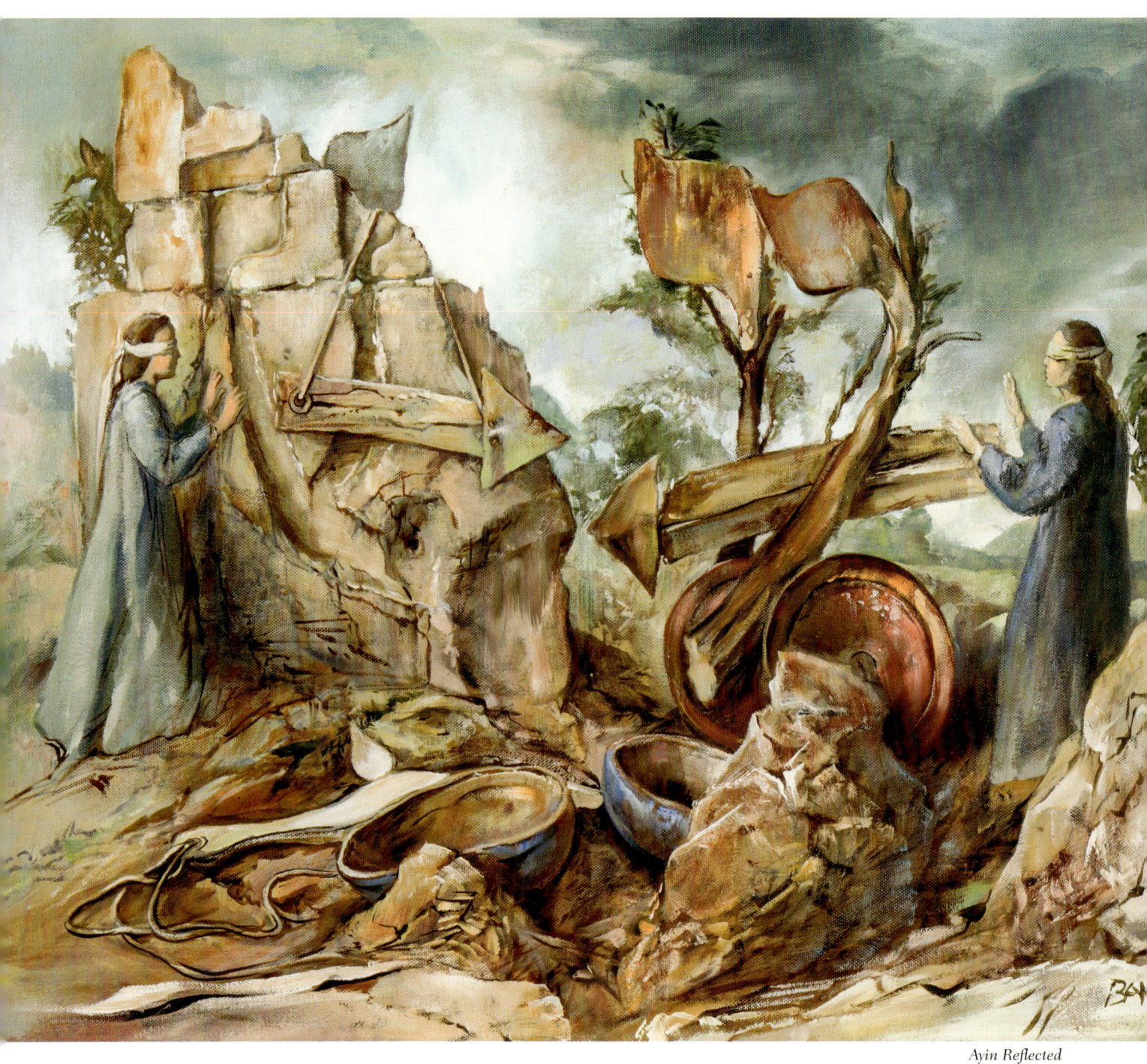

Ayin Reflected
Acrylic and oil on canvas
20 x 24"
BK1998

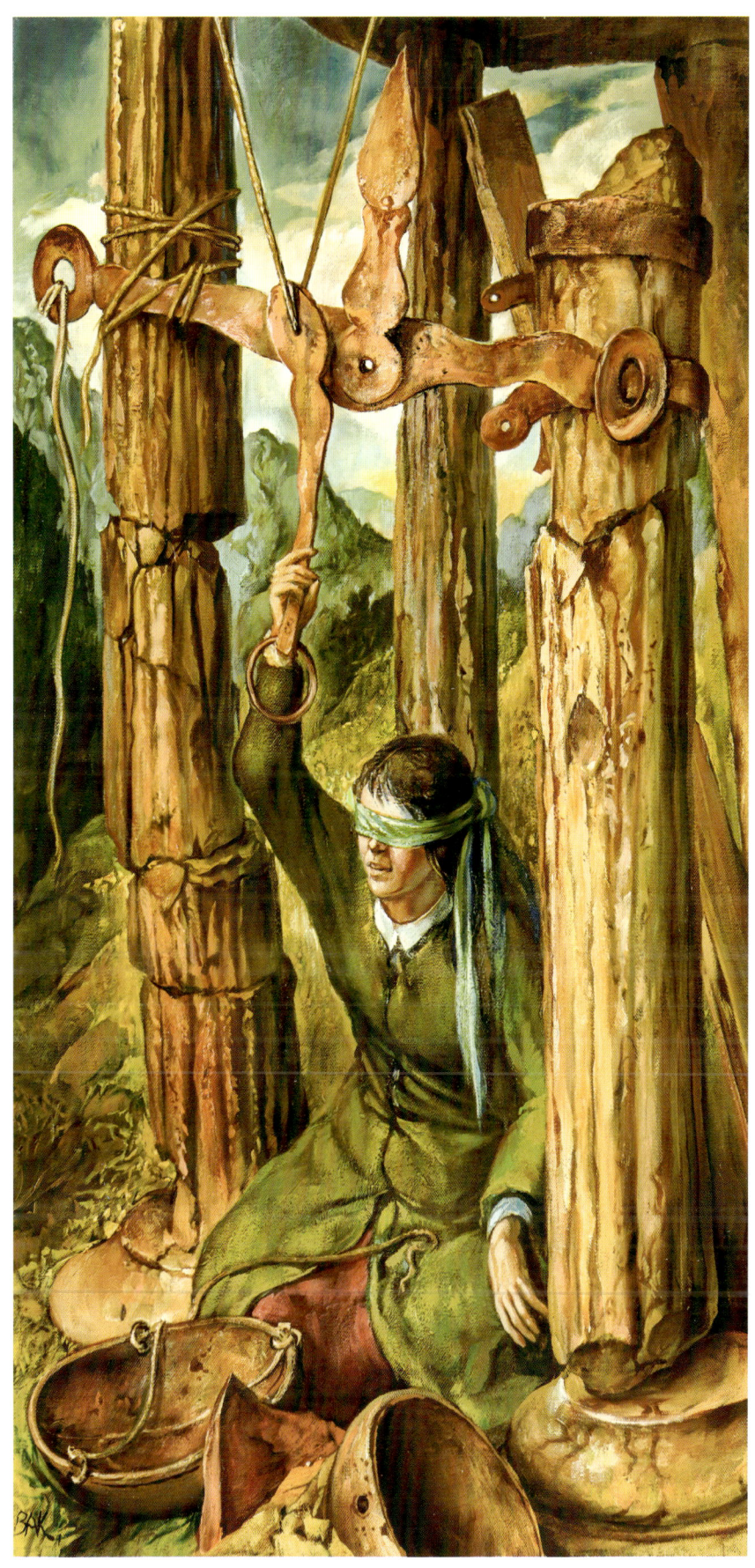

Set in Stone
Oil on canvas
30 x 15"
BK1964

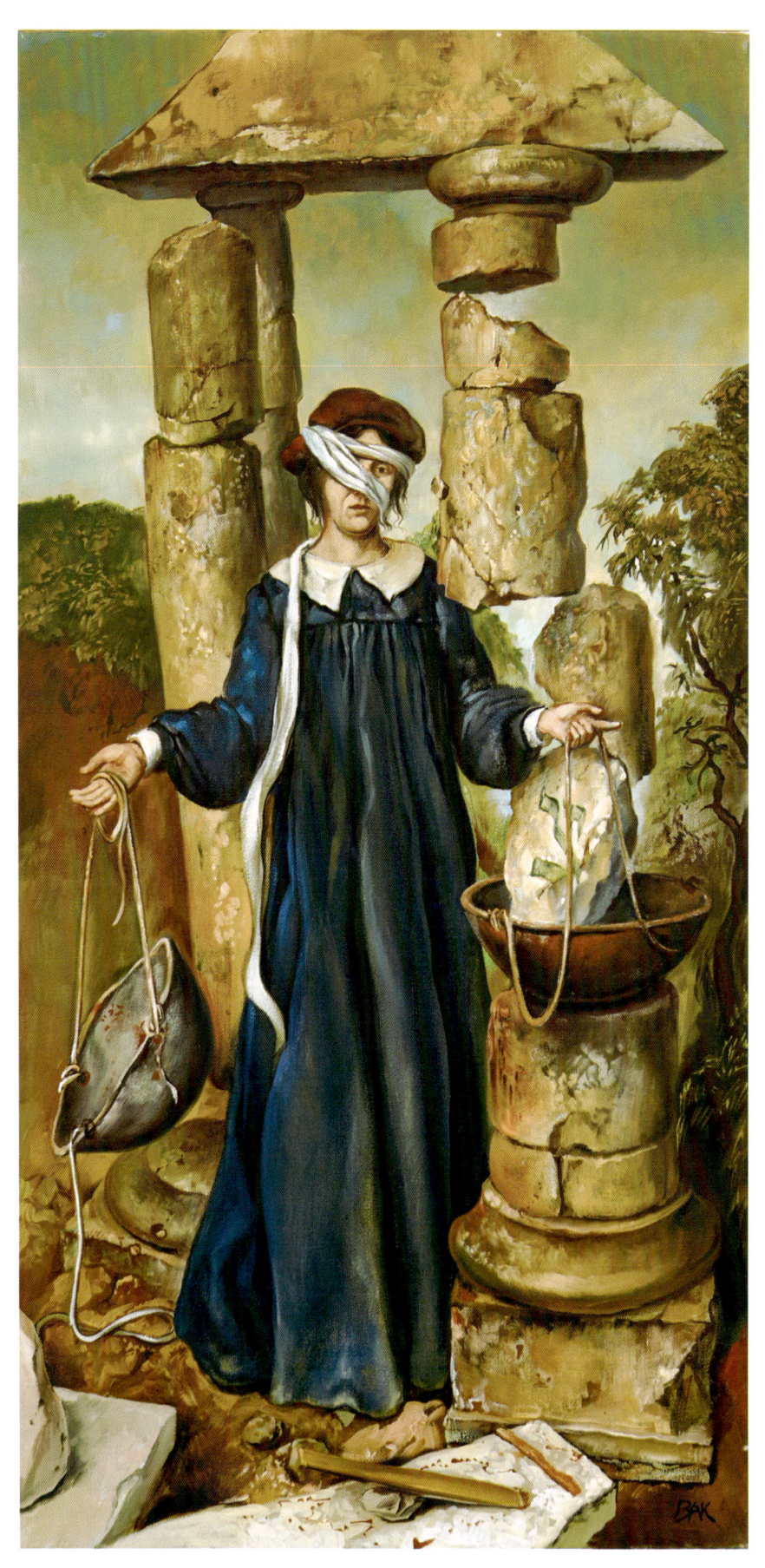

Study for Even Handed
Oil on canvas
30 x 15"
BK1962

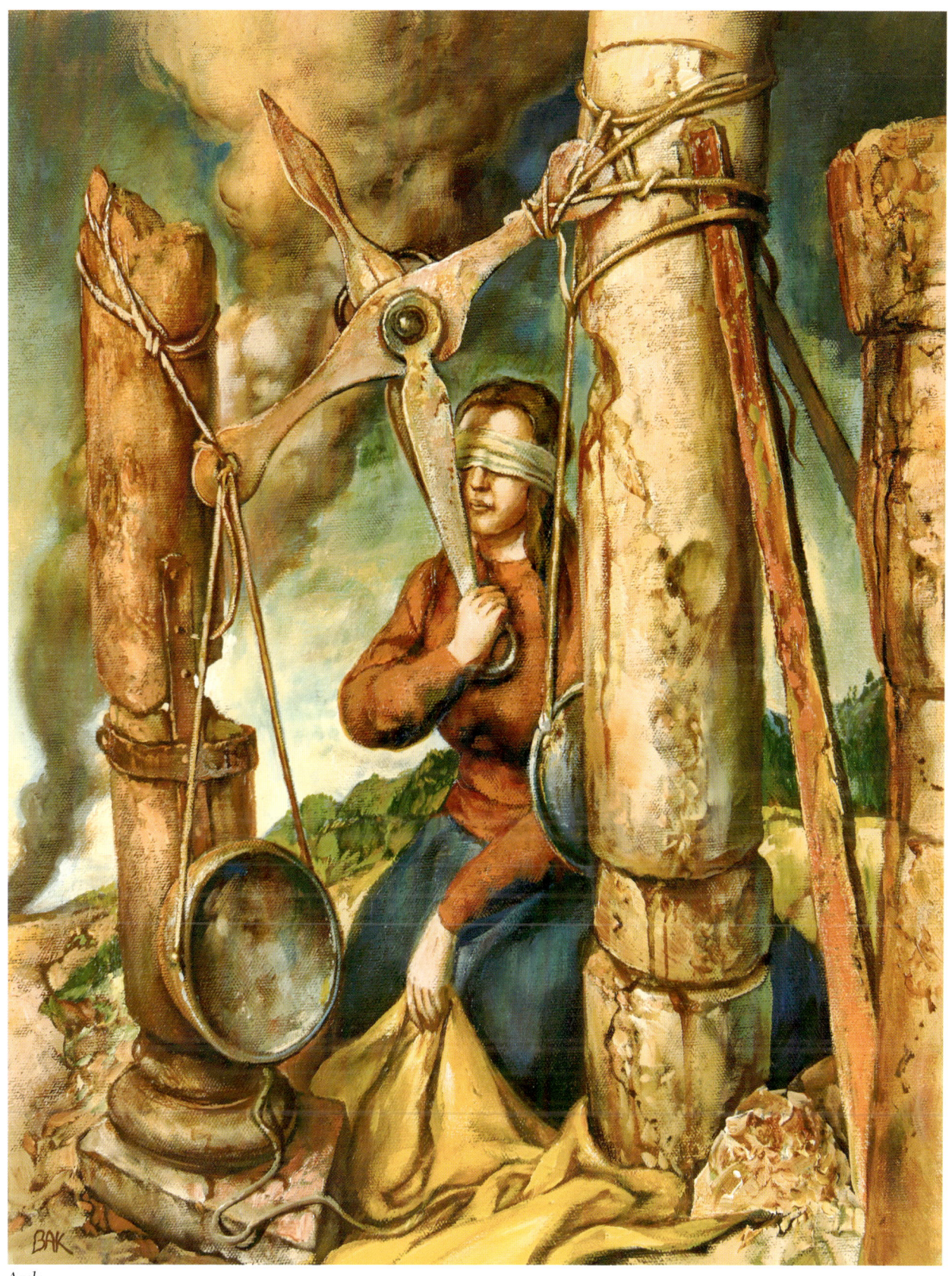

Ageless
Oil on canvas
18 x 14"
BK1966

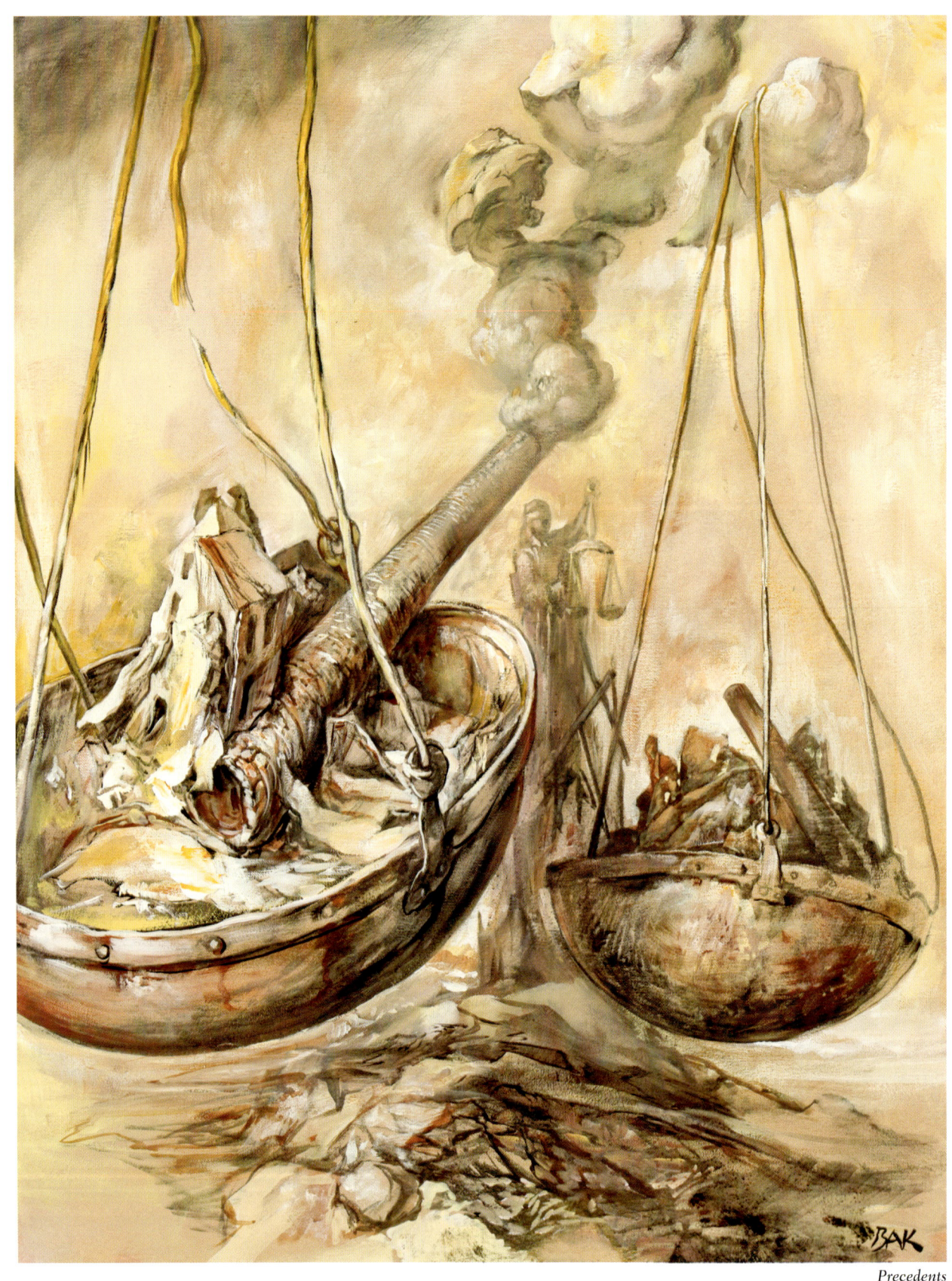

Precedents
Acrylic on canvas
28 x 22"
BK1996

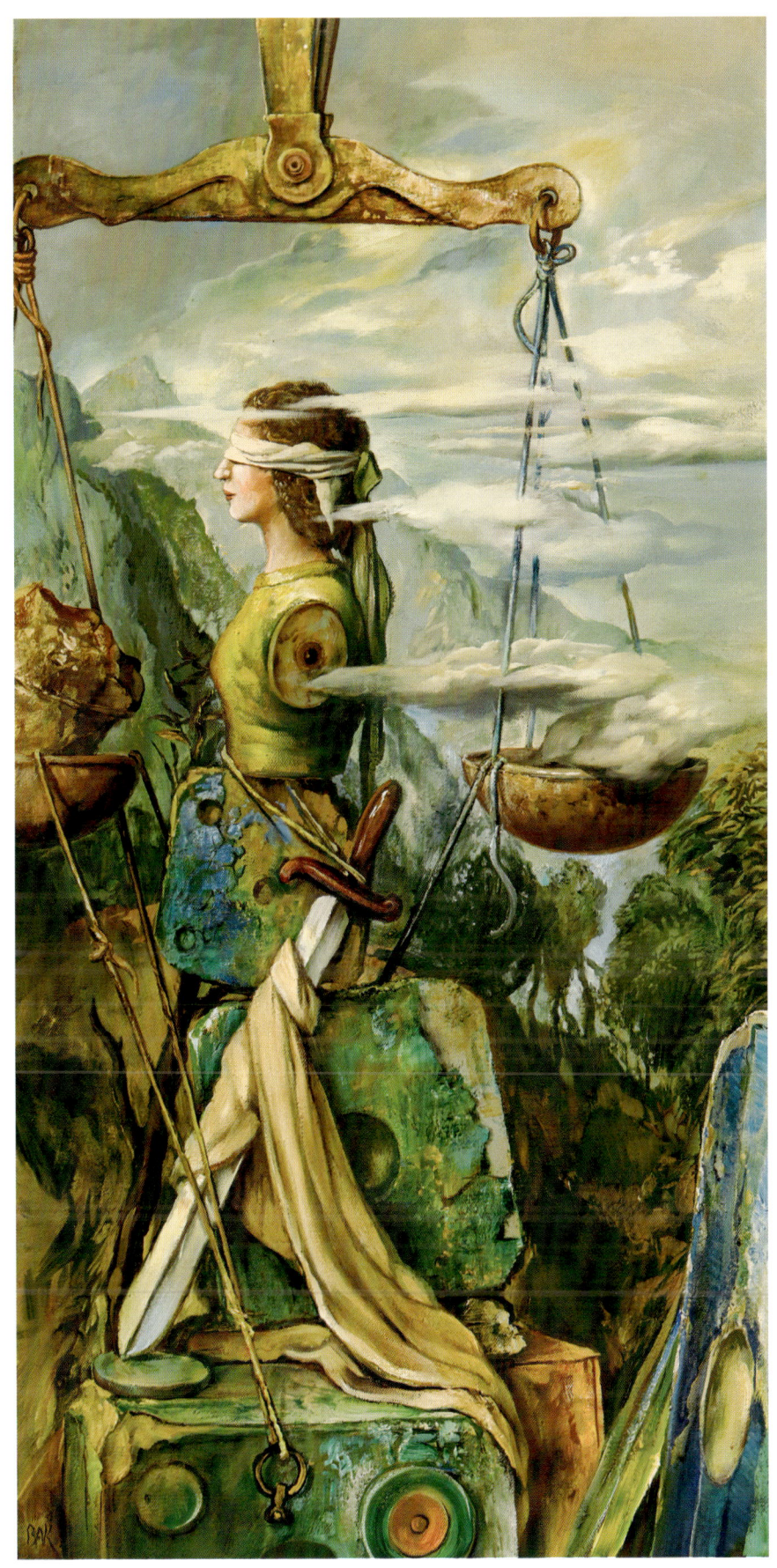

High Up
Oil on canvas
30 x 15"
BK1963

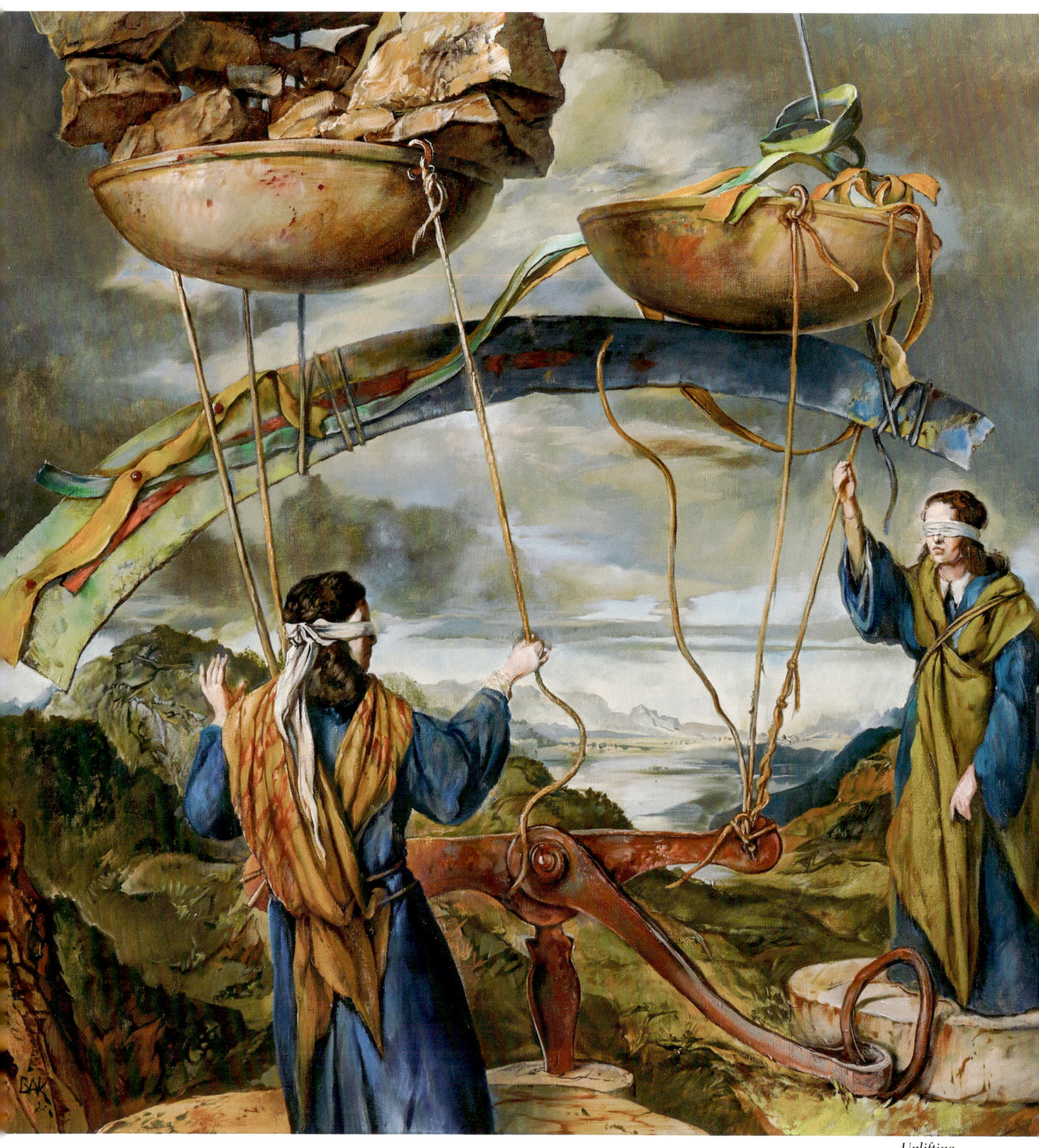

Uplifting
Oil on canvas
36 x 36"
BK1934

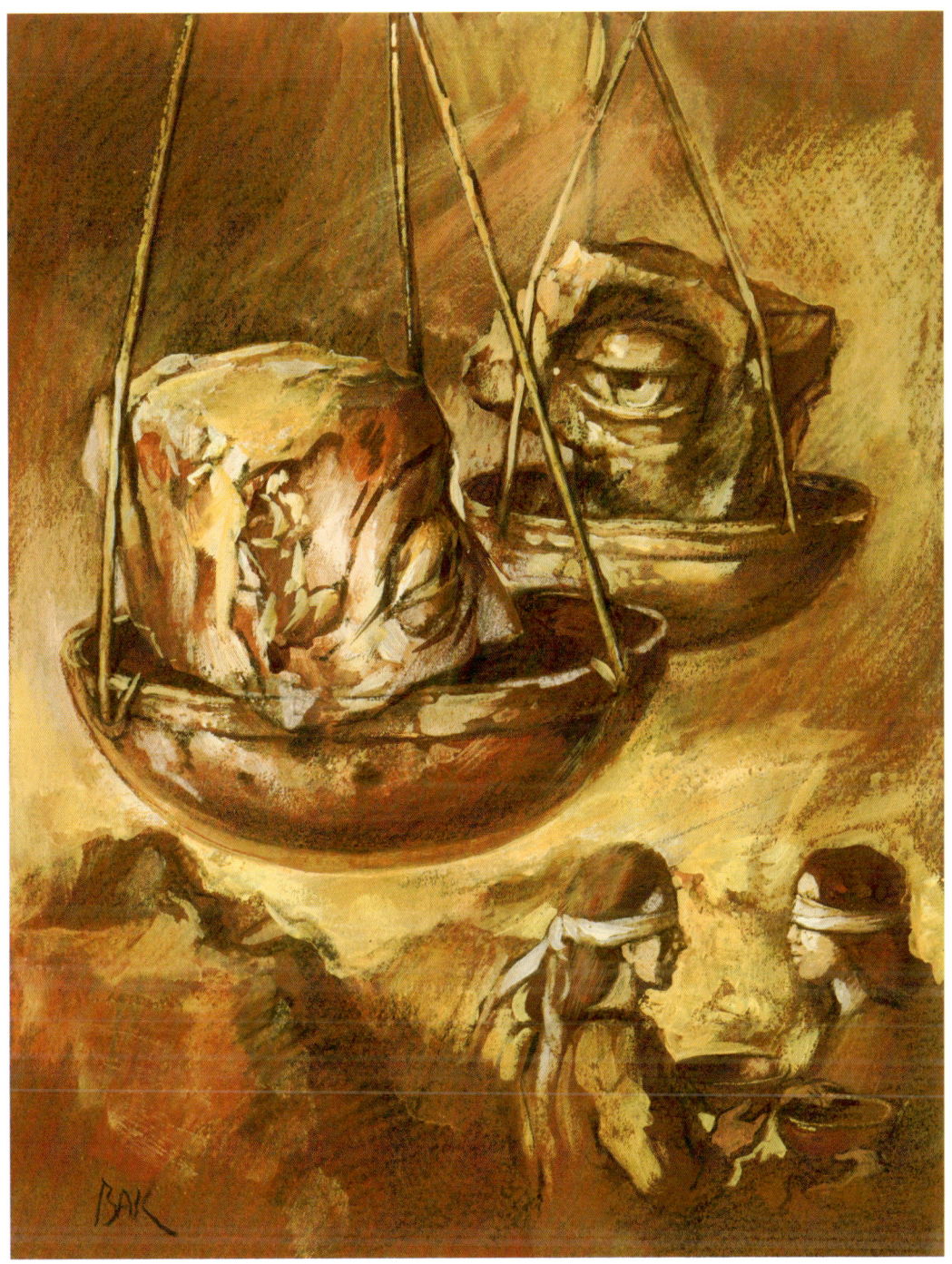

Shared Confidence
Egg tempera on paper
11 x 8.5"
BK2008

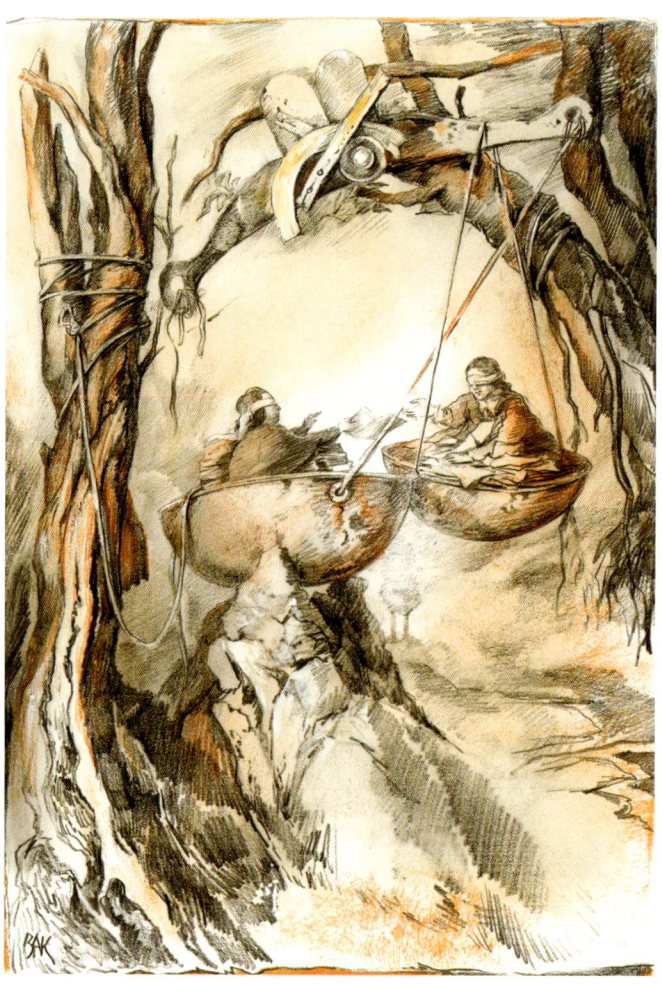

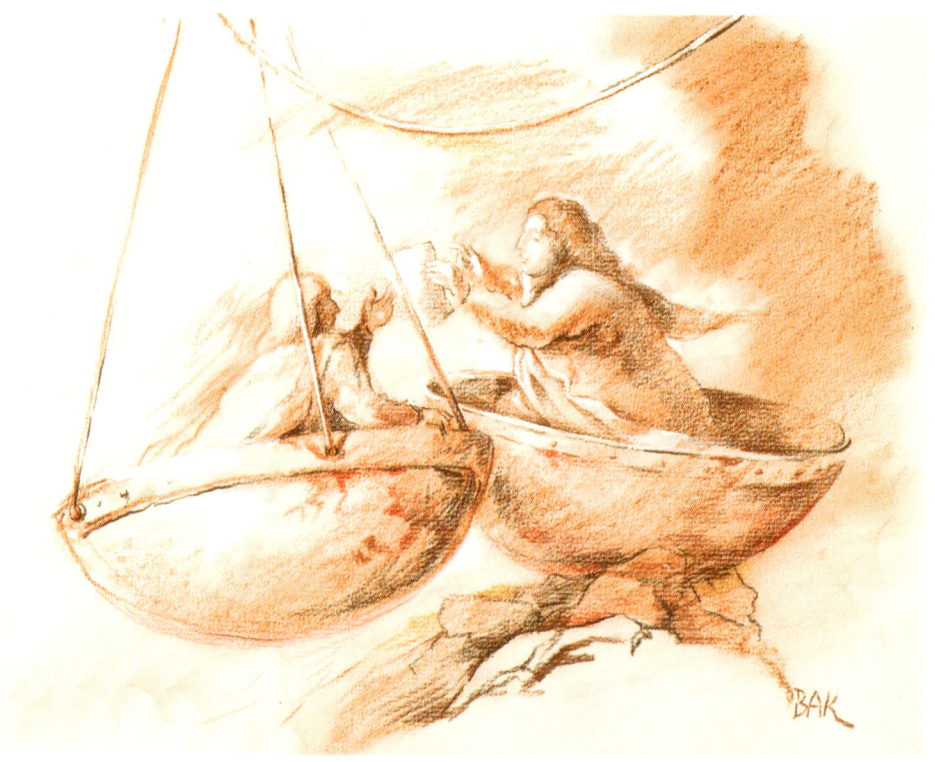

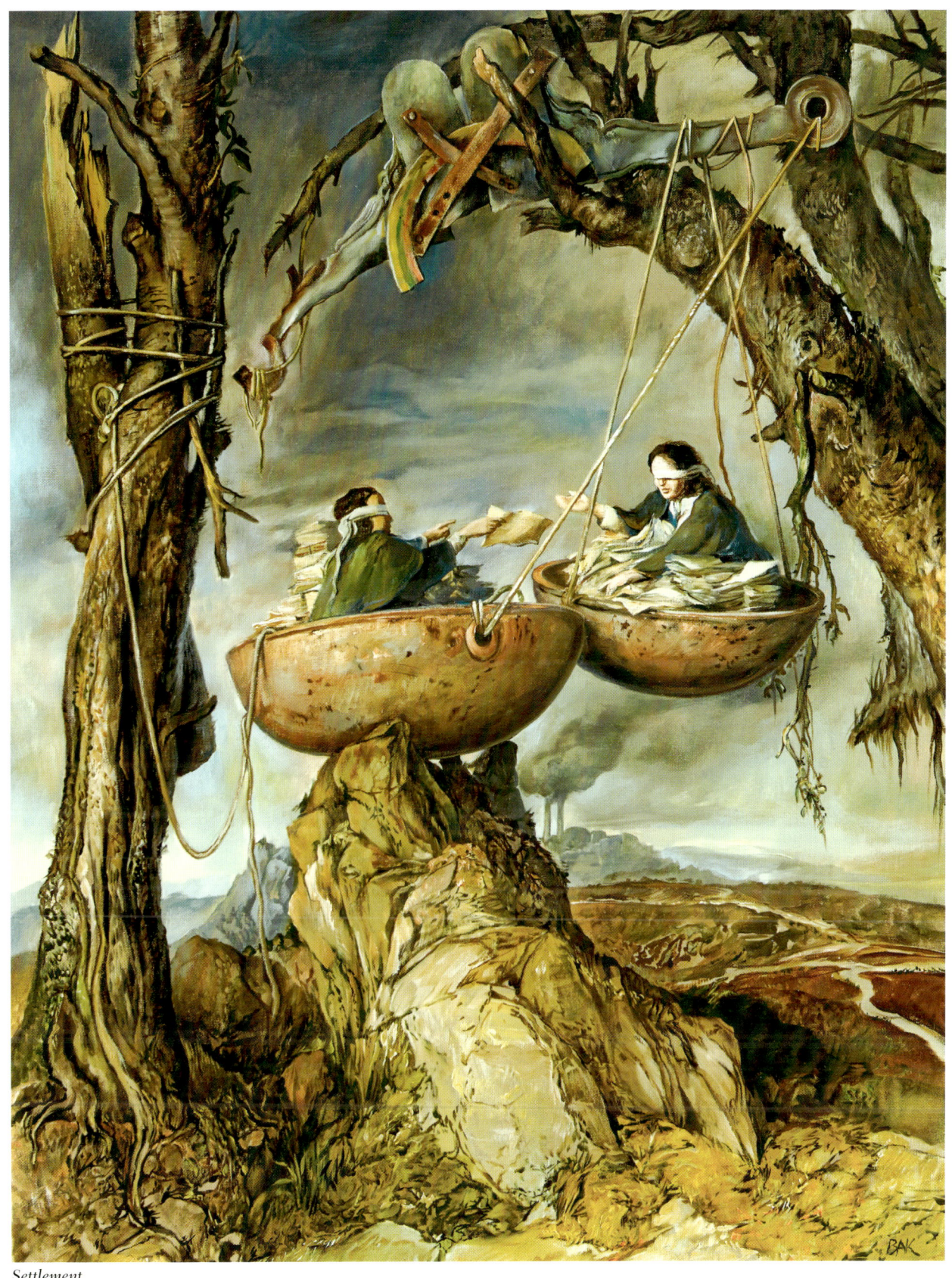

Settlement
Oil on canvas
40 x 30"
BK1937

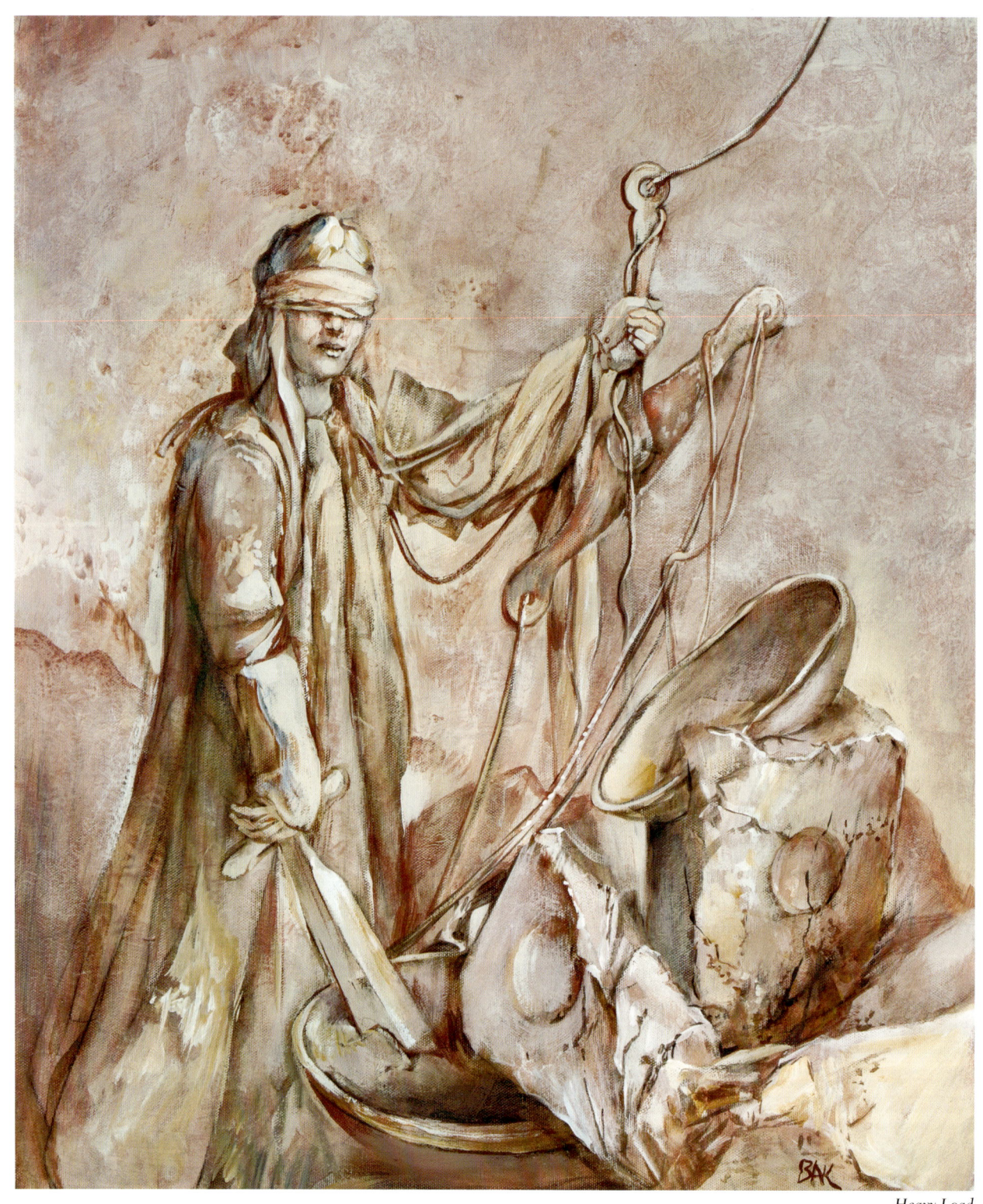

Heavy Load
Acrylic on canvas
24 x 20"
BK2000

RIGHT:
Portrait with Eyes
Oil on canvas
28 x 22"
BK1948

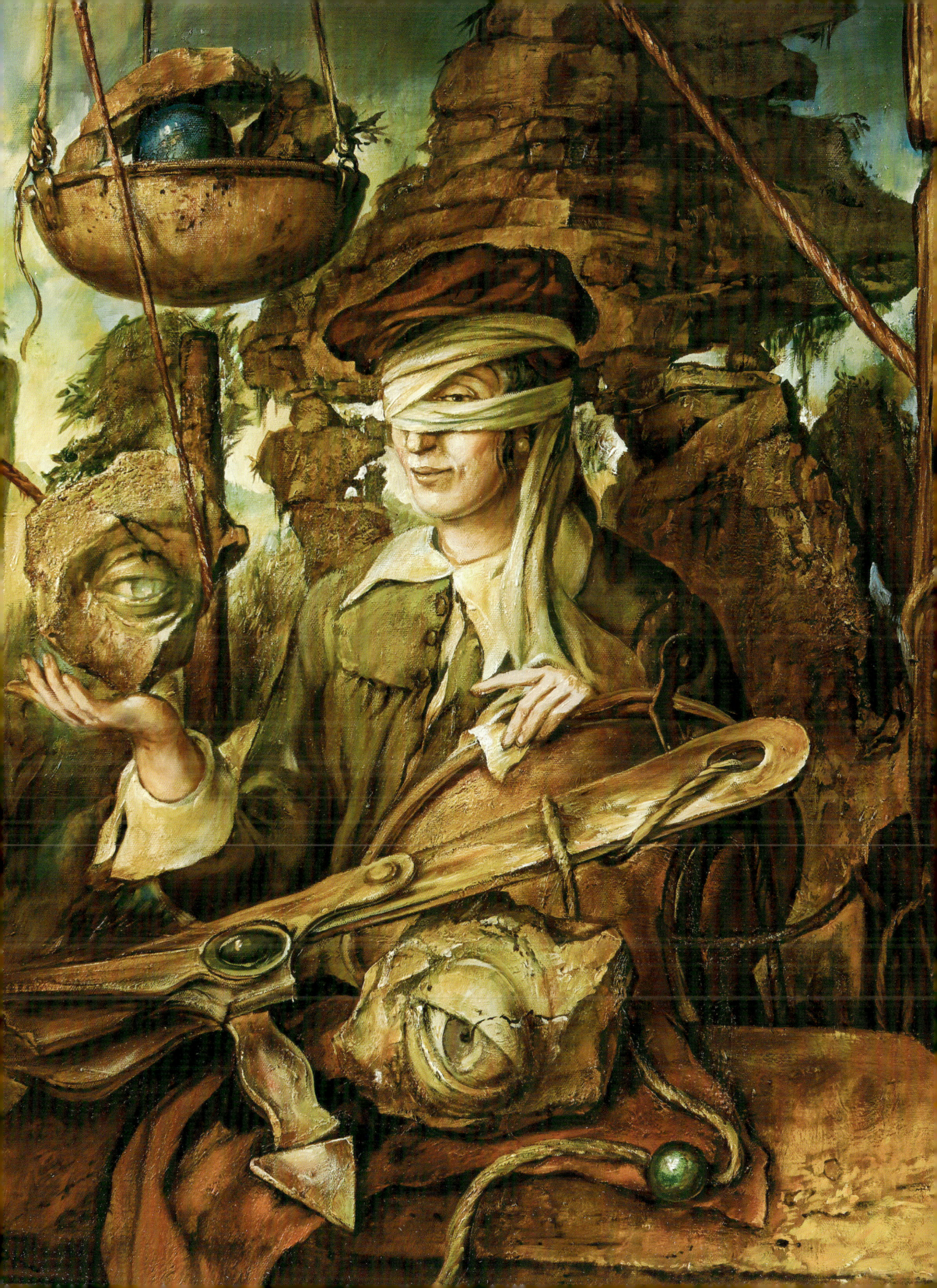

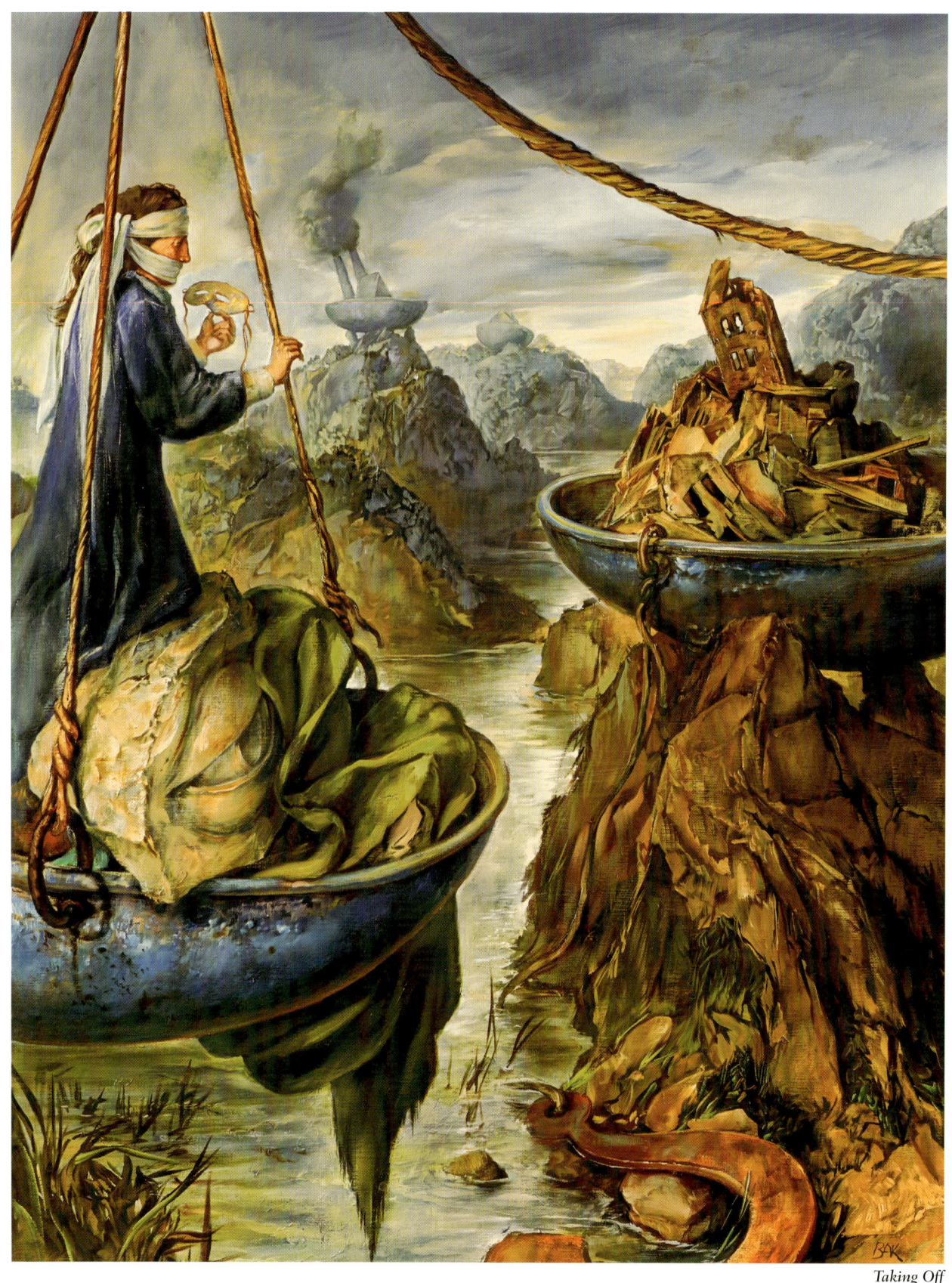

Taking Off
Oil on canvas
40 x 30"
BK1936

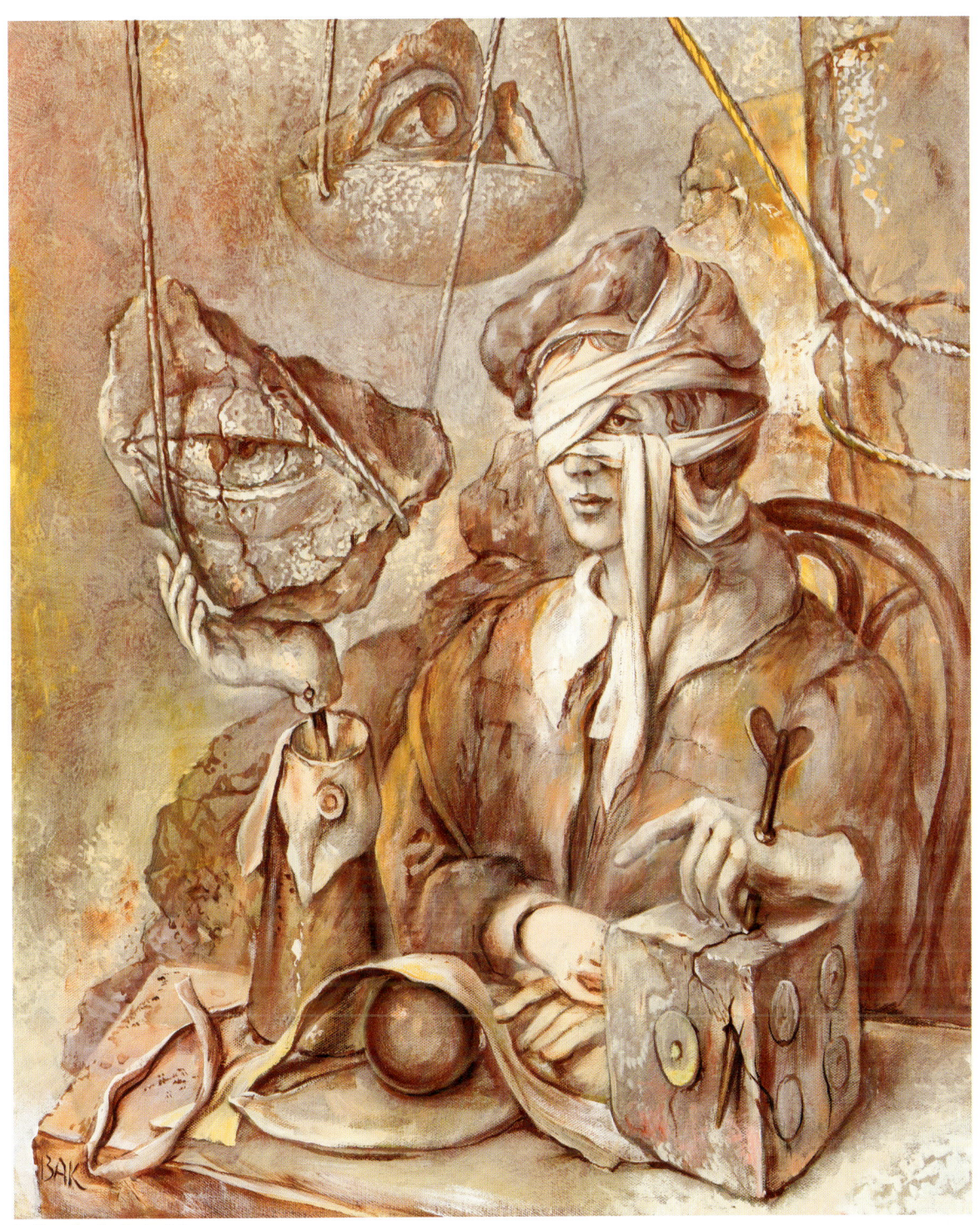

In Search of a Portrait A
Acrylic on canvas
24 x 20"
BK1999

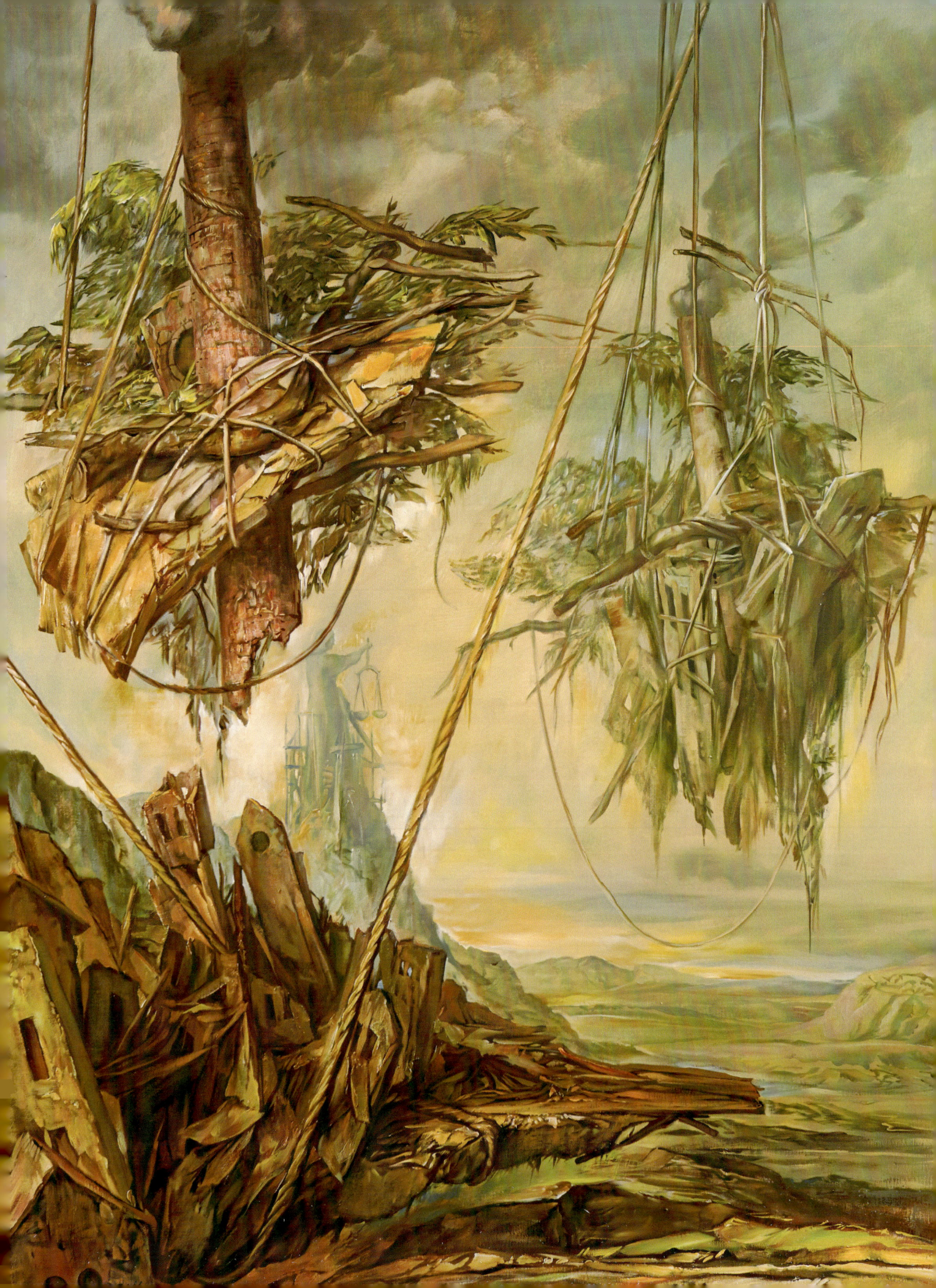

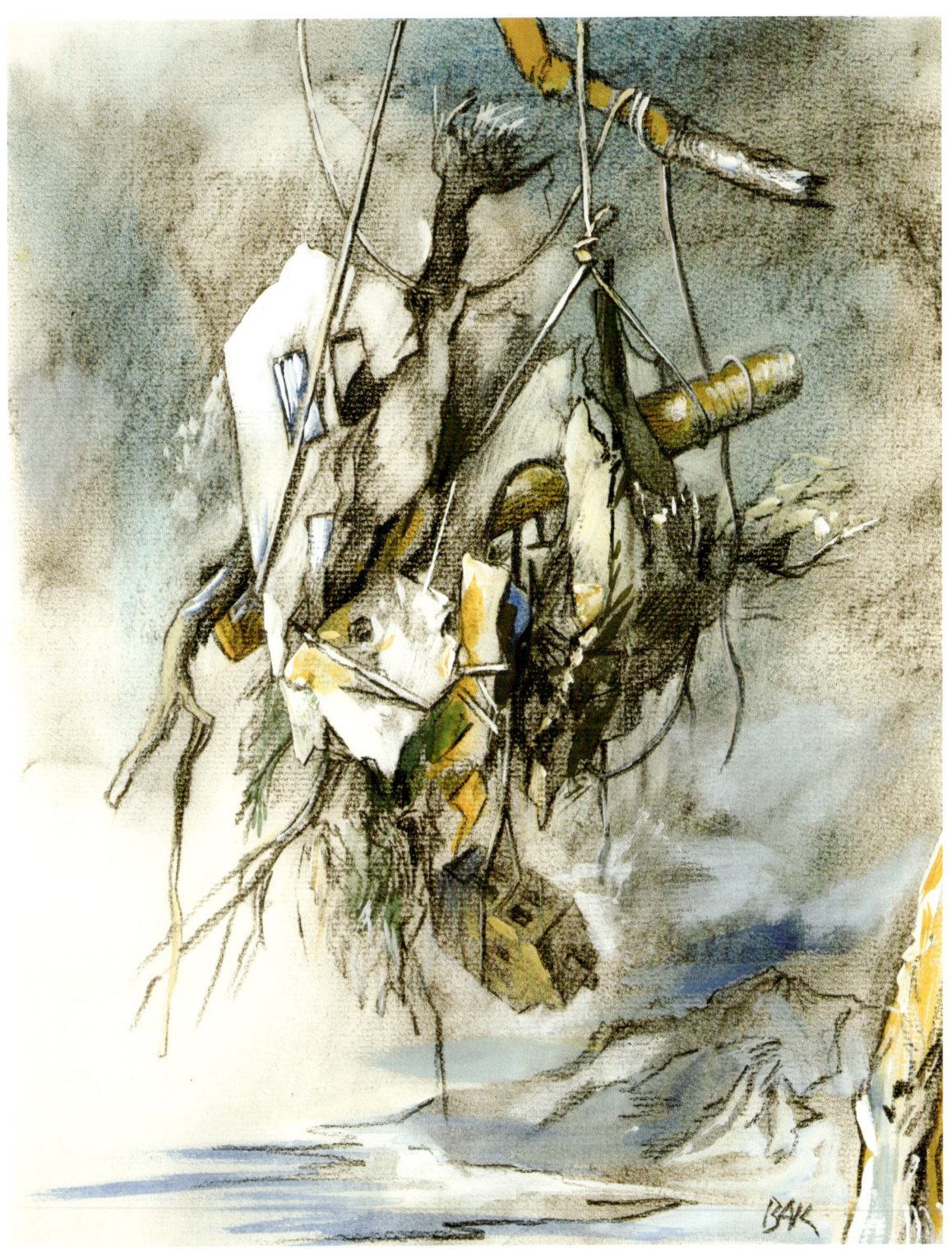

Study for The Past Present
Tempera and charcoal on paper
13 x 10.5"
BK1994

LEFT:
Inadmissible
Oil on canvas
48 x 36"
BK1931

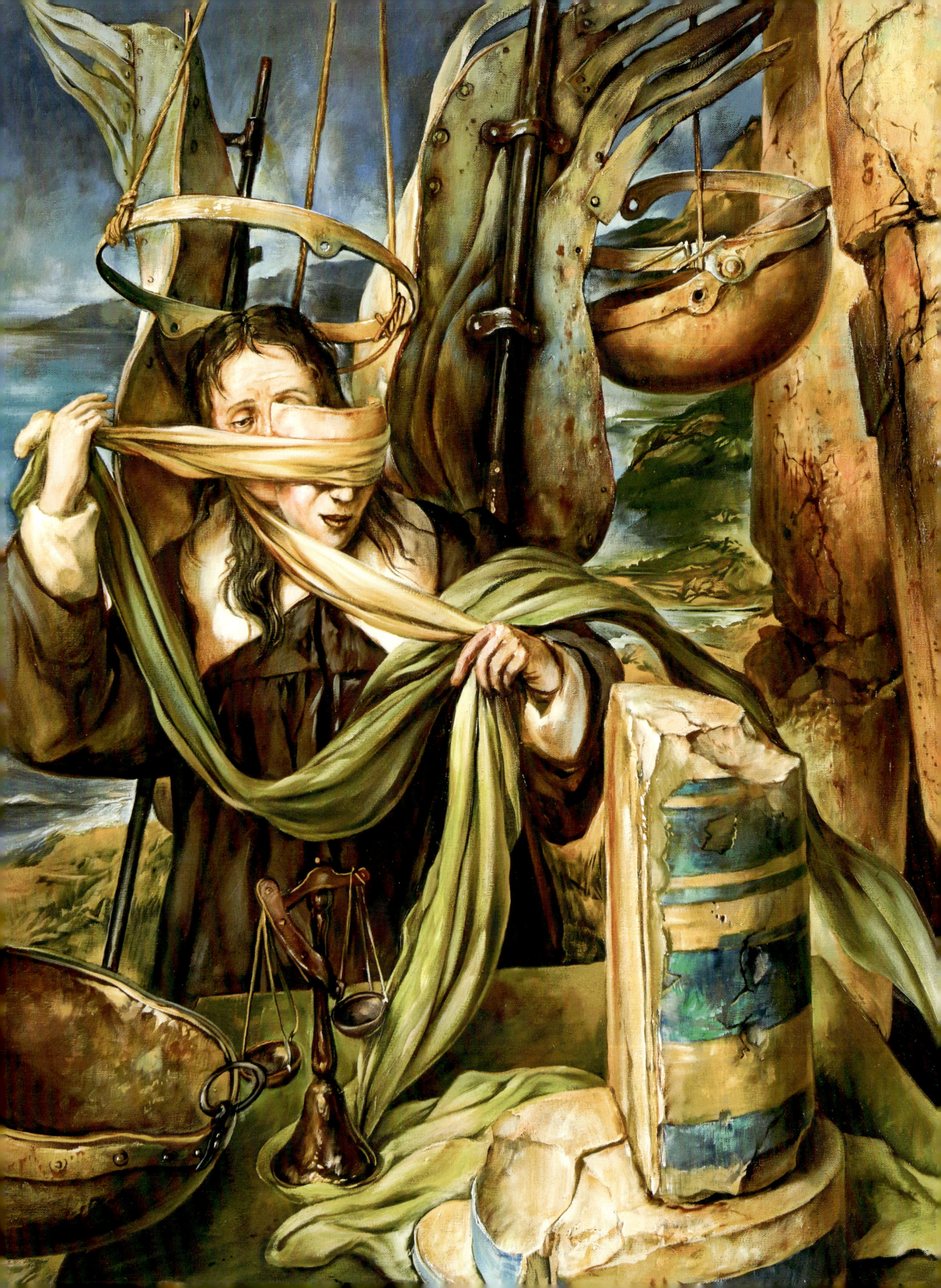

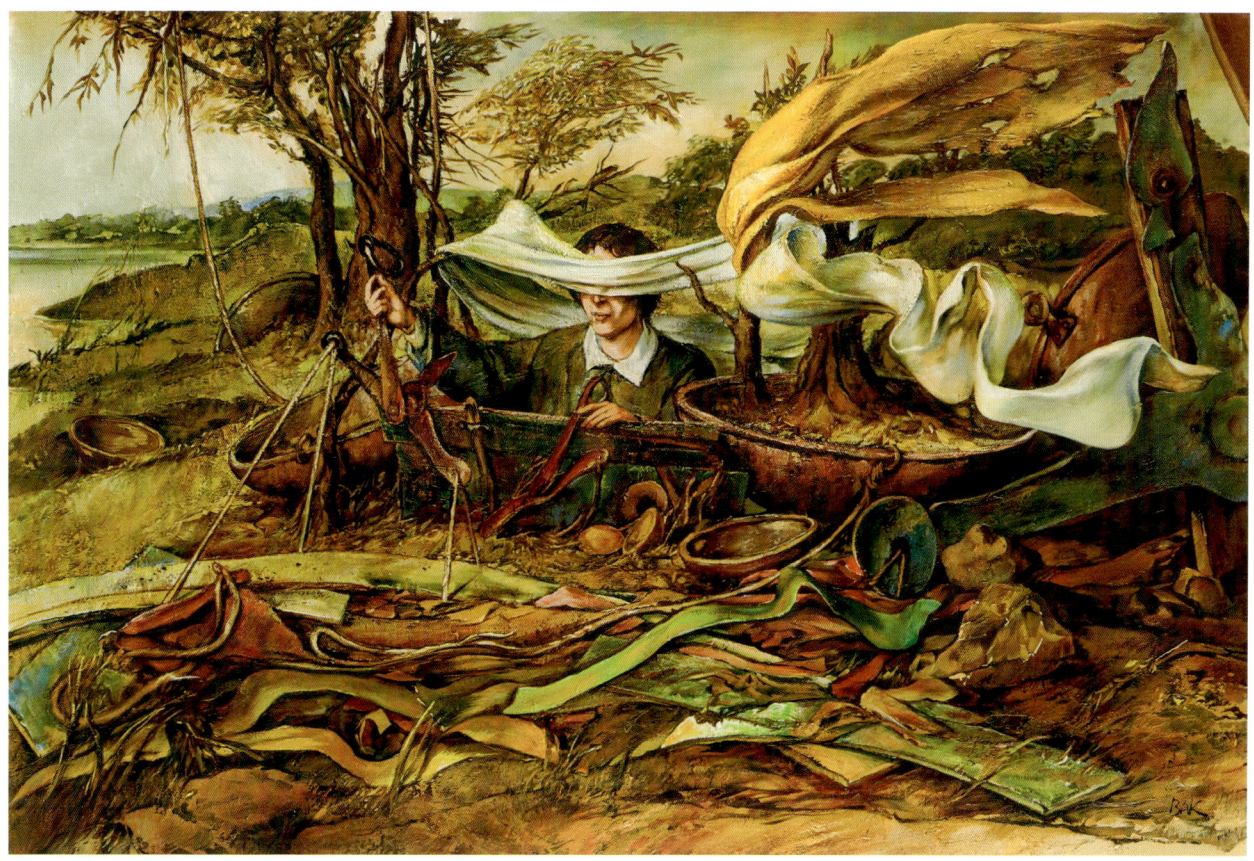

On Stable Ground
Oil on canvas
24 x 36"
BK1945

LEFT:
Close By
Oil on canvas
40 x 30"
BK1940

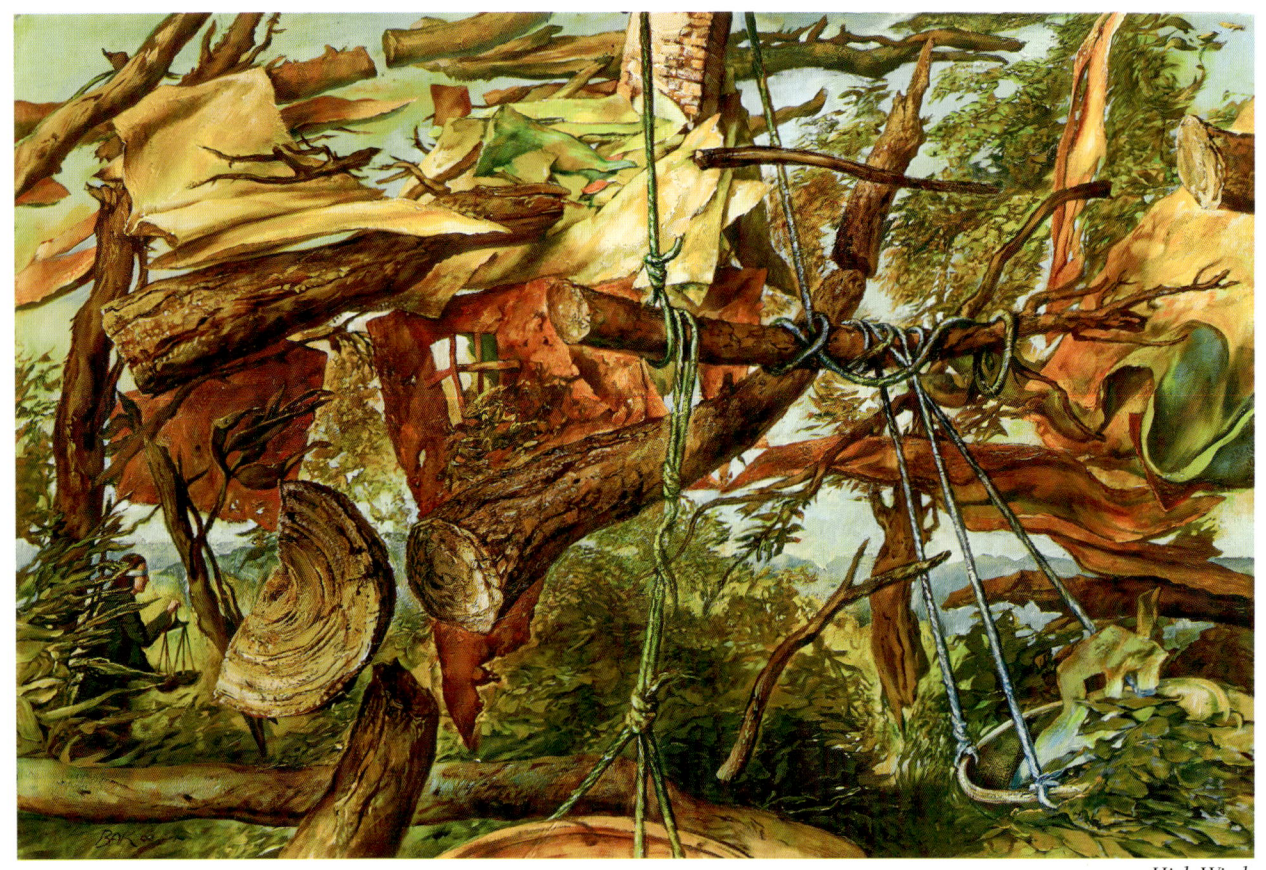

High Winds
Oil on canvas
24 x 36"
BK1944

RIGHT:
Scripture
Oil on canvas
40 x 30"
BK1938

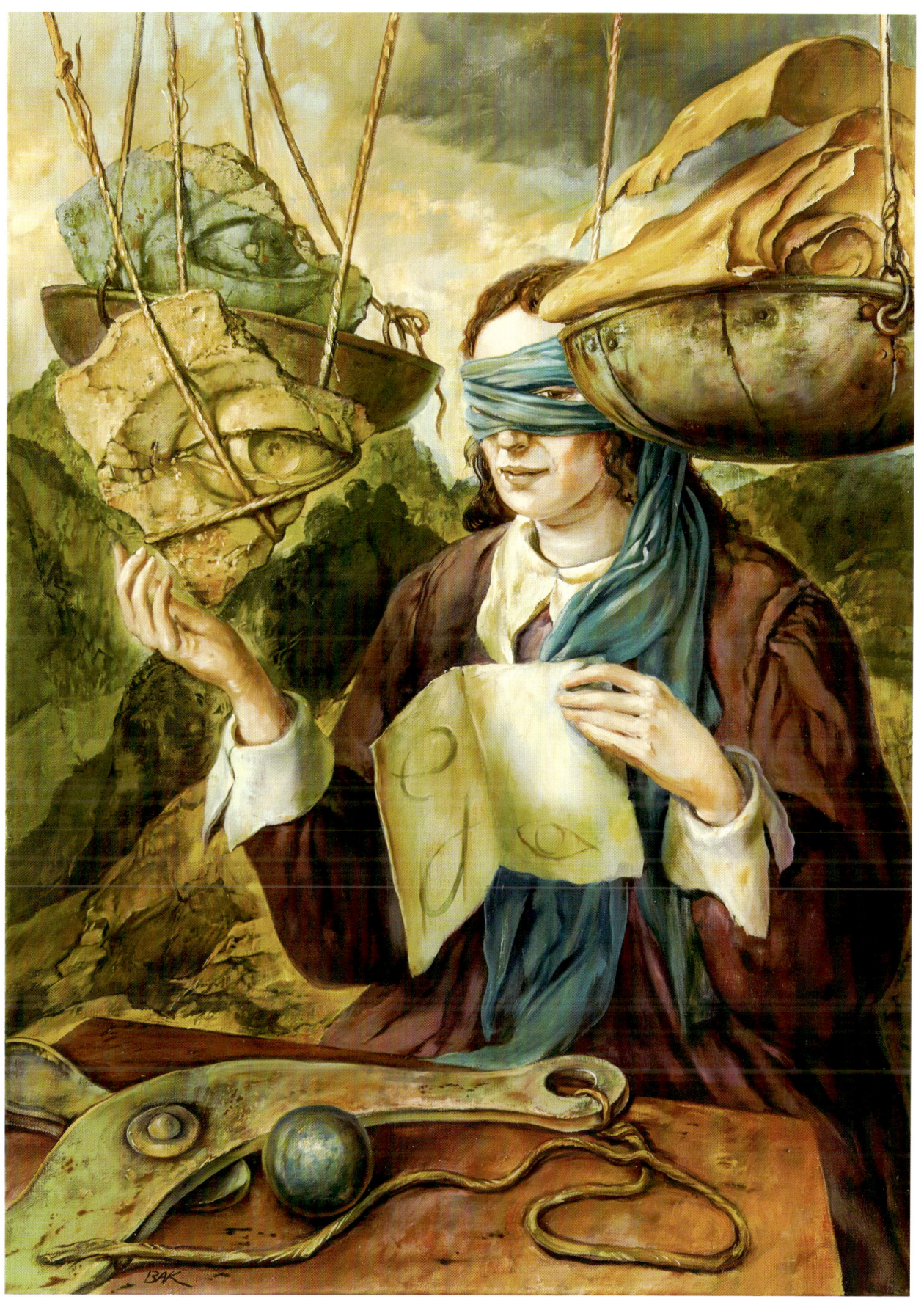

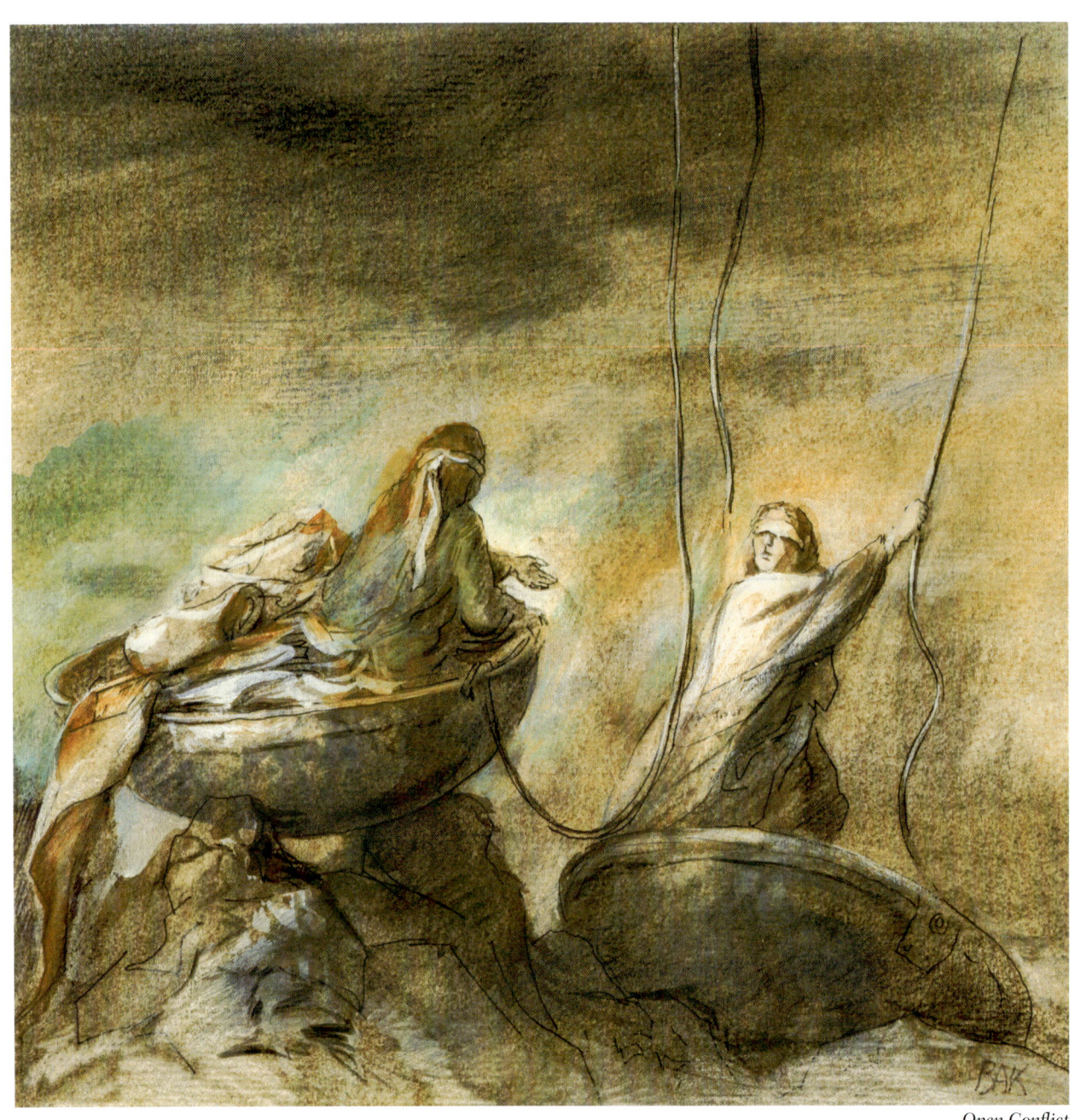

Open Conflict
Mixed media on paper
9.25 x 9.5"
BK2016

RIGHT:
By Hook
Oil on canvas
40 x 30"
BK1939

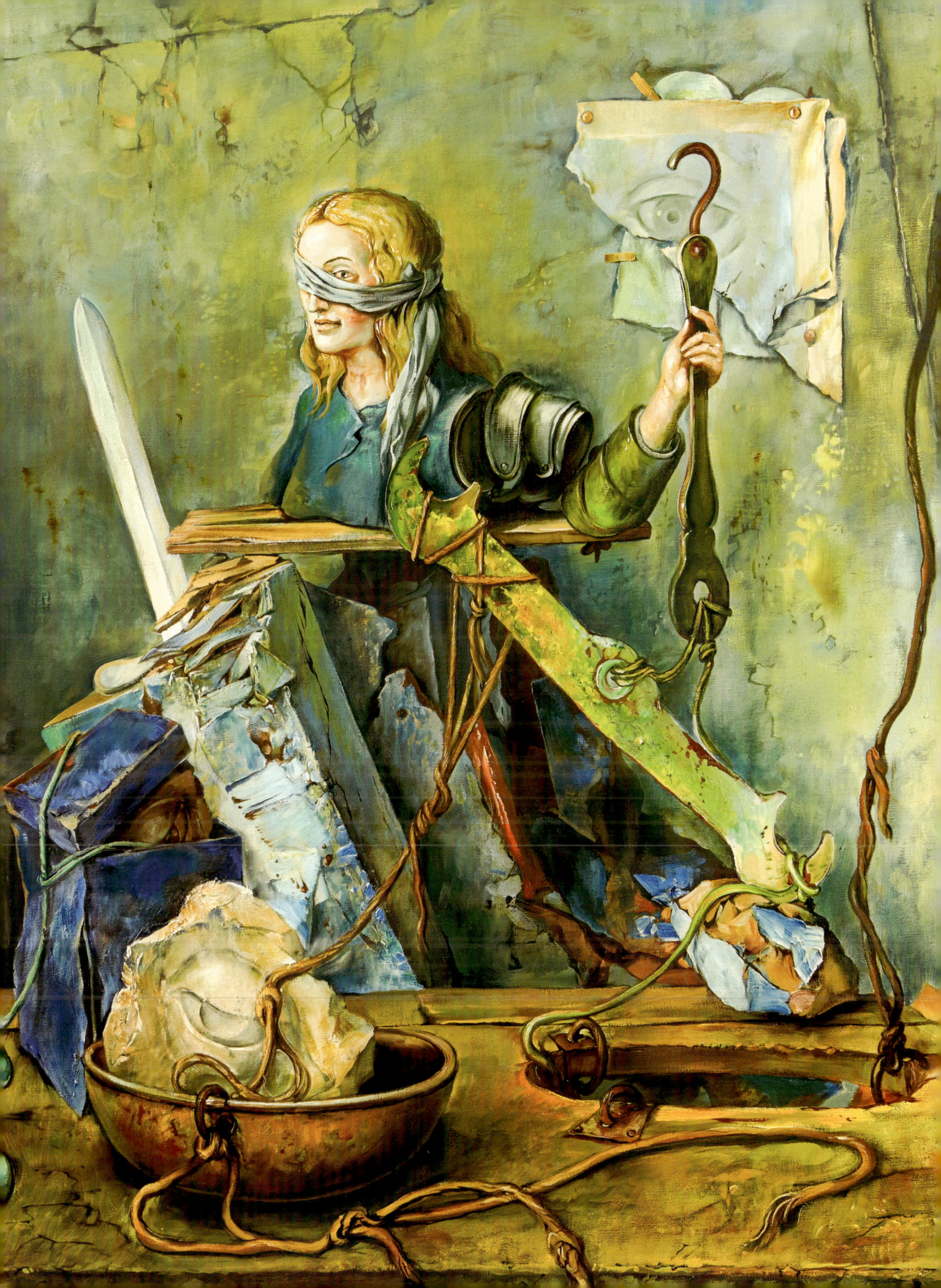

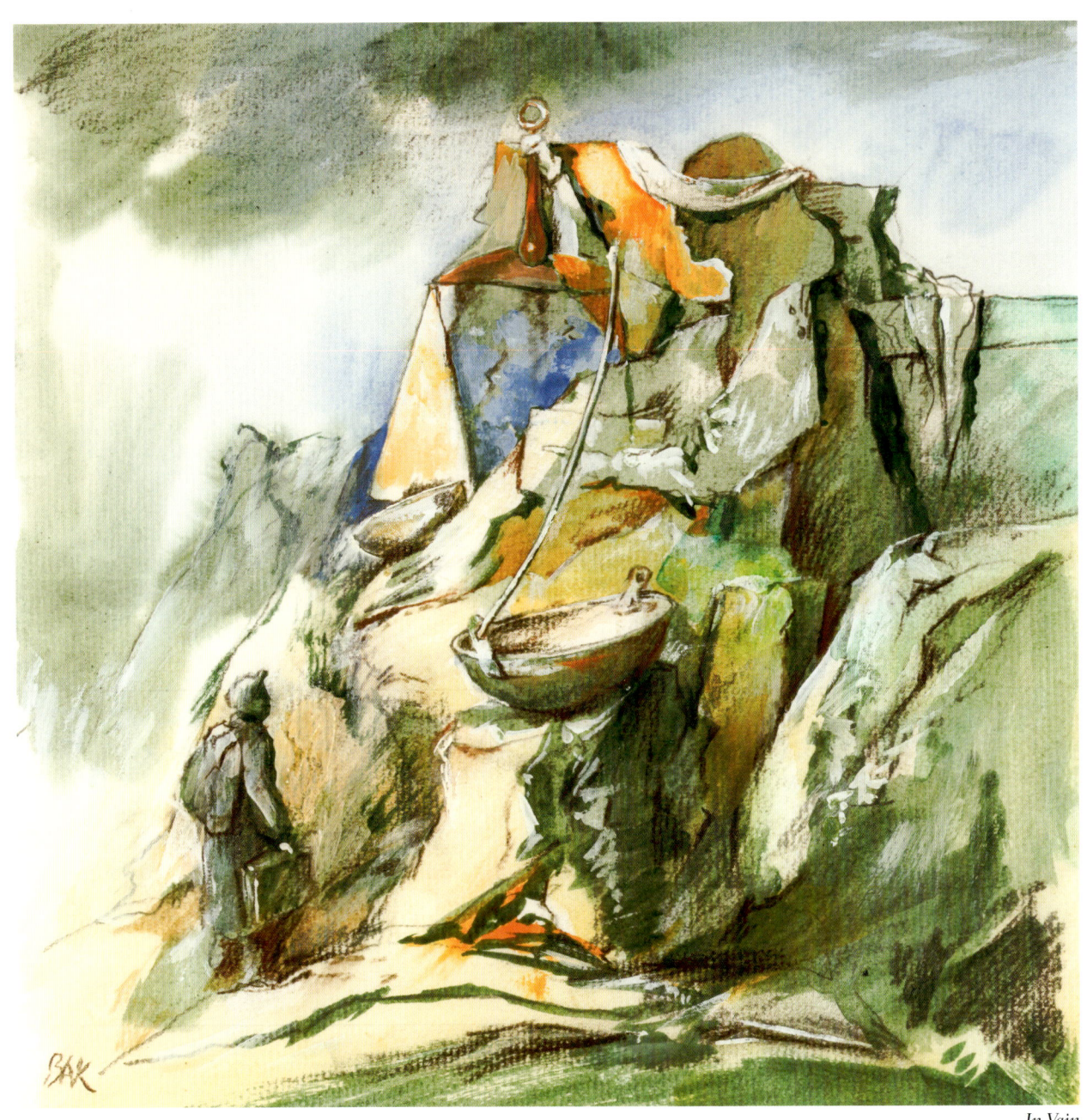

In Vain
Gouache on paper
9.25 x 9.5"
BK2009

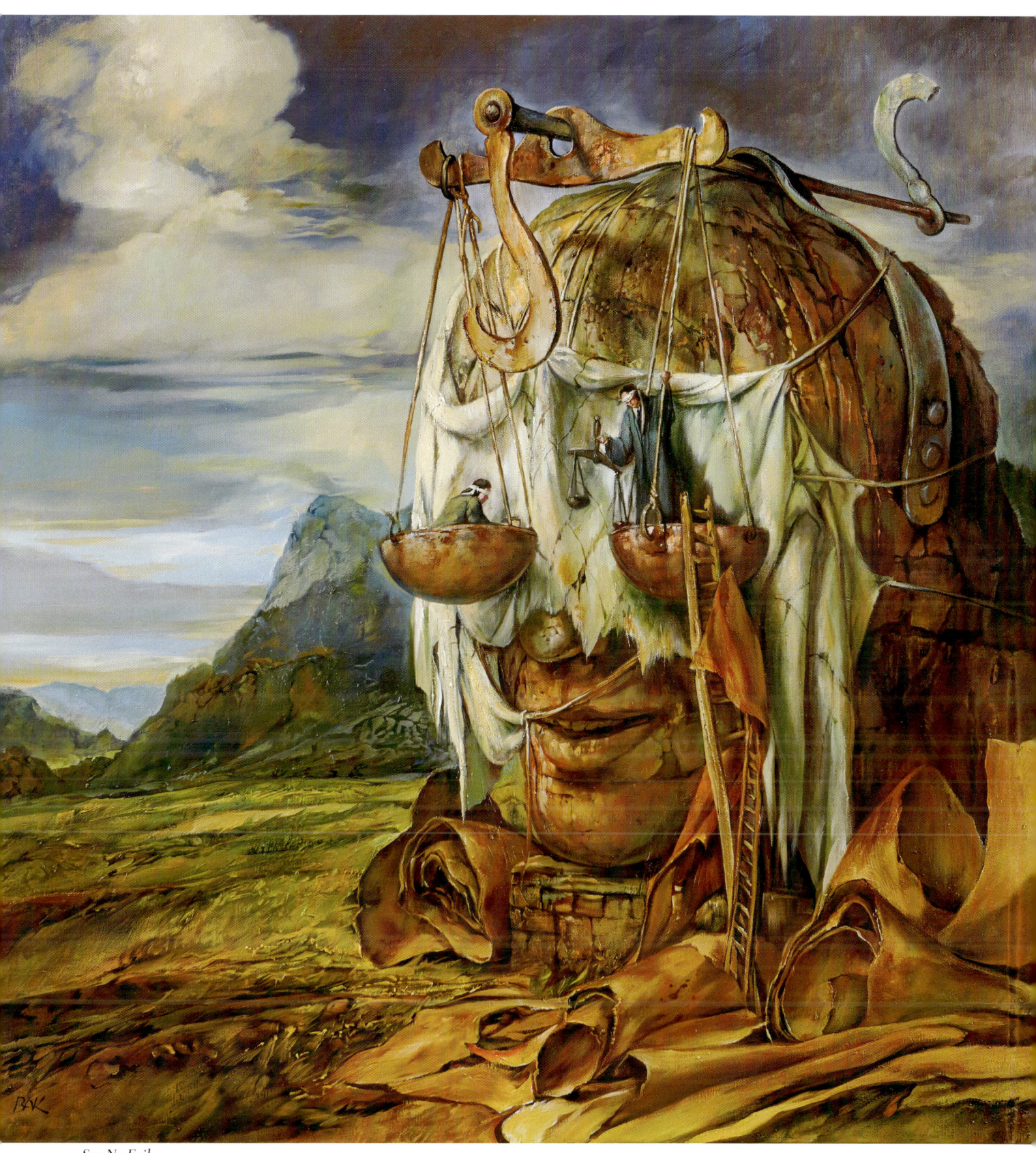

See No Evil
Oil on canvas
36 x 36"
BK1935

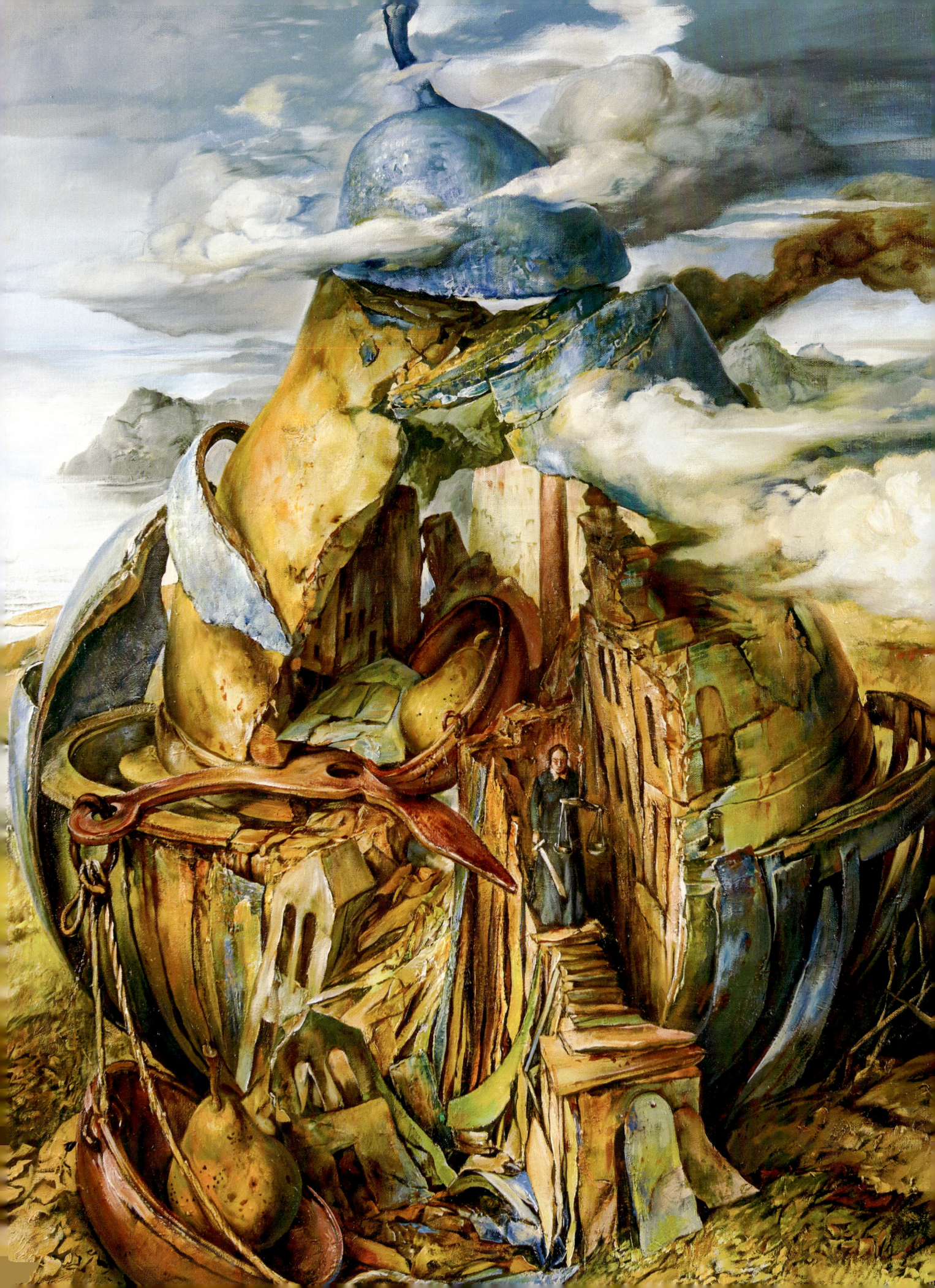

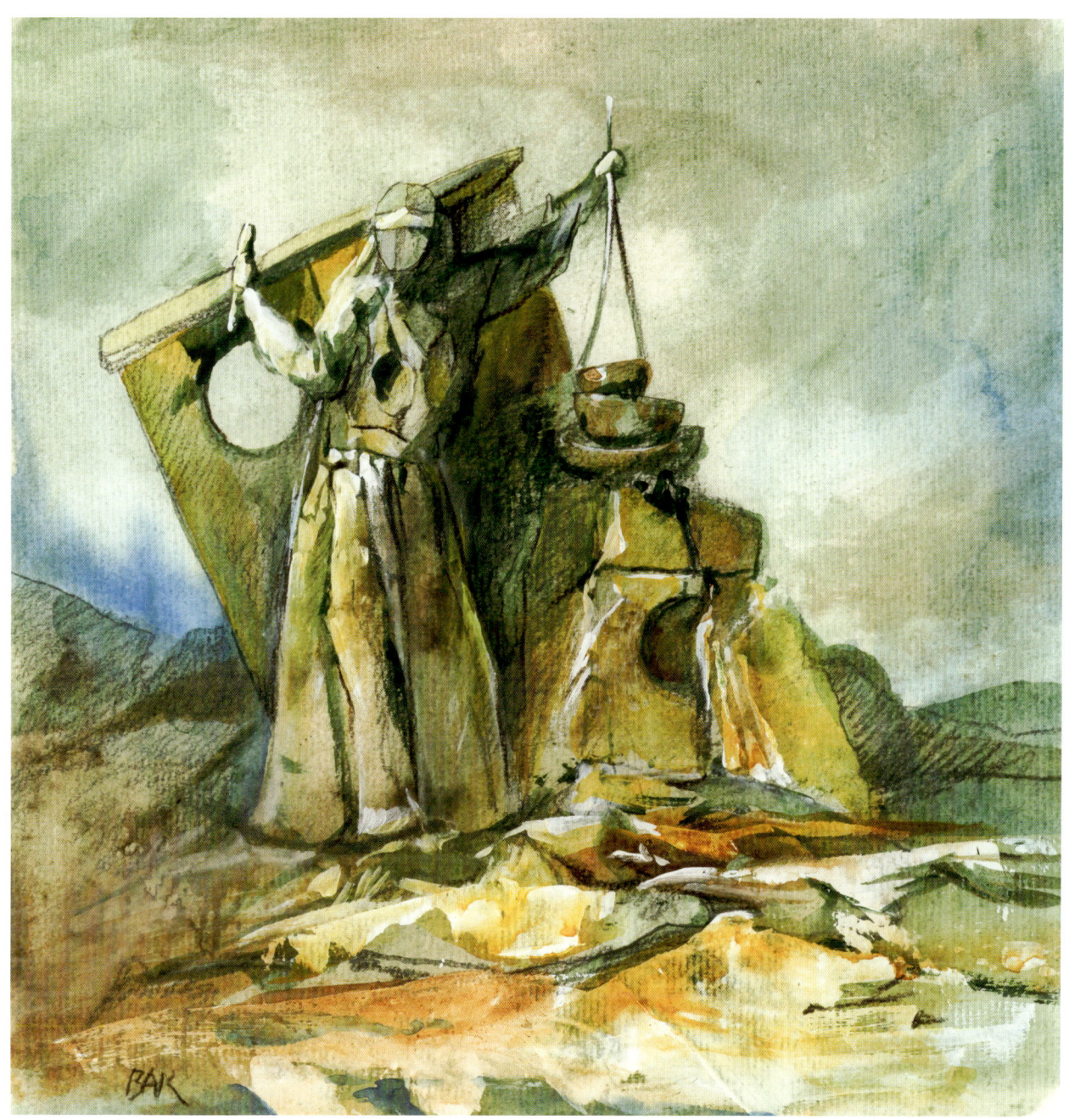

Study for Good Luck
Tempera, watercolor, and acrylic on paper
9.5 x 9.25"
BK1990

LEFT:
Long Lasting
Oil on canvas
40 x 30"
BK1941

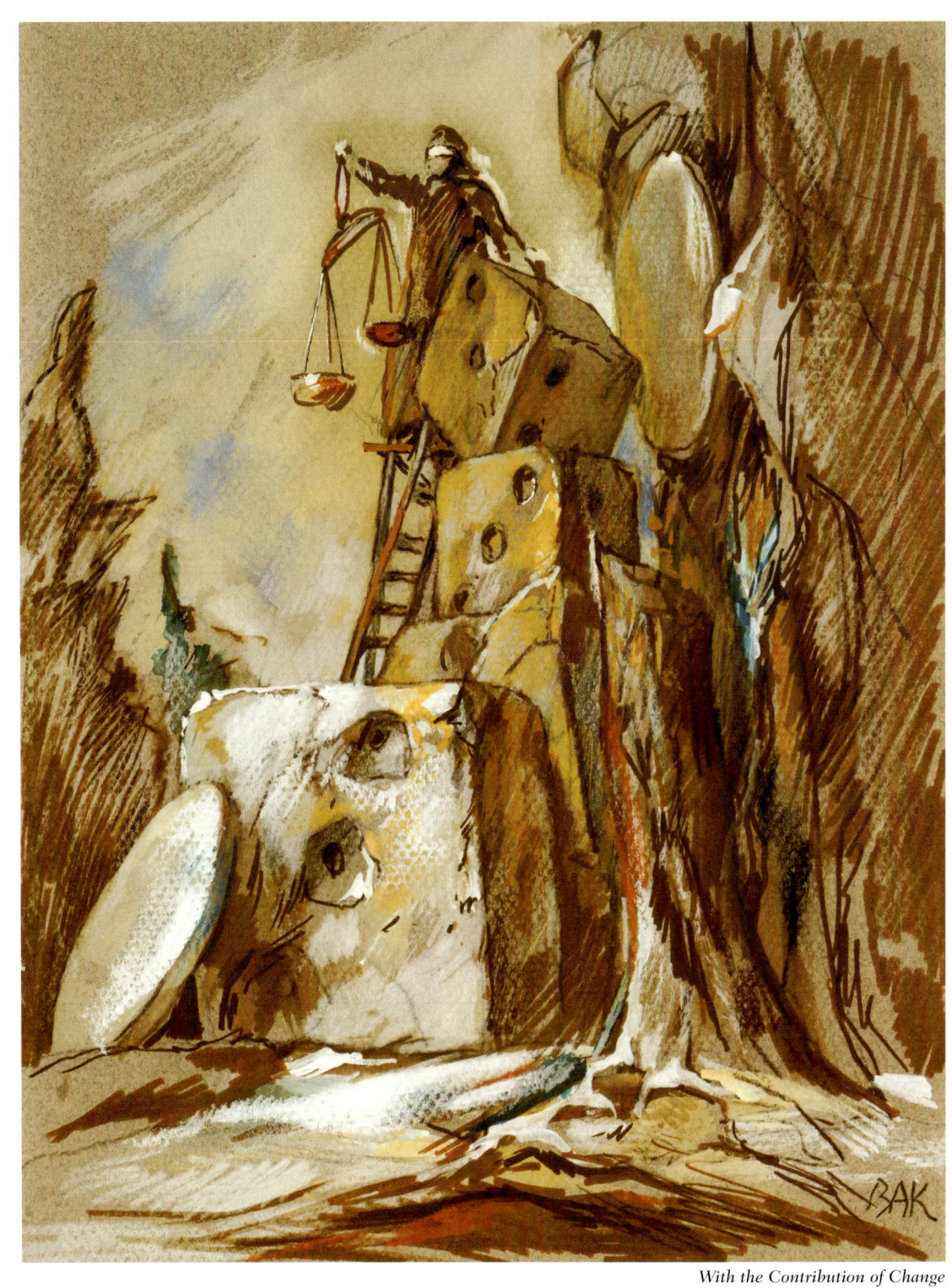

With the Contribution of Change
Gouache on paper
11 x 8.5"
BK2010

RIGHT:
Ever Ready
Oil on canvas
40 x 30"
BK1942

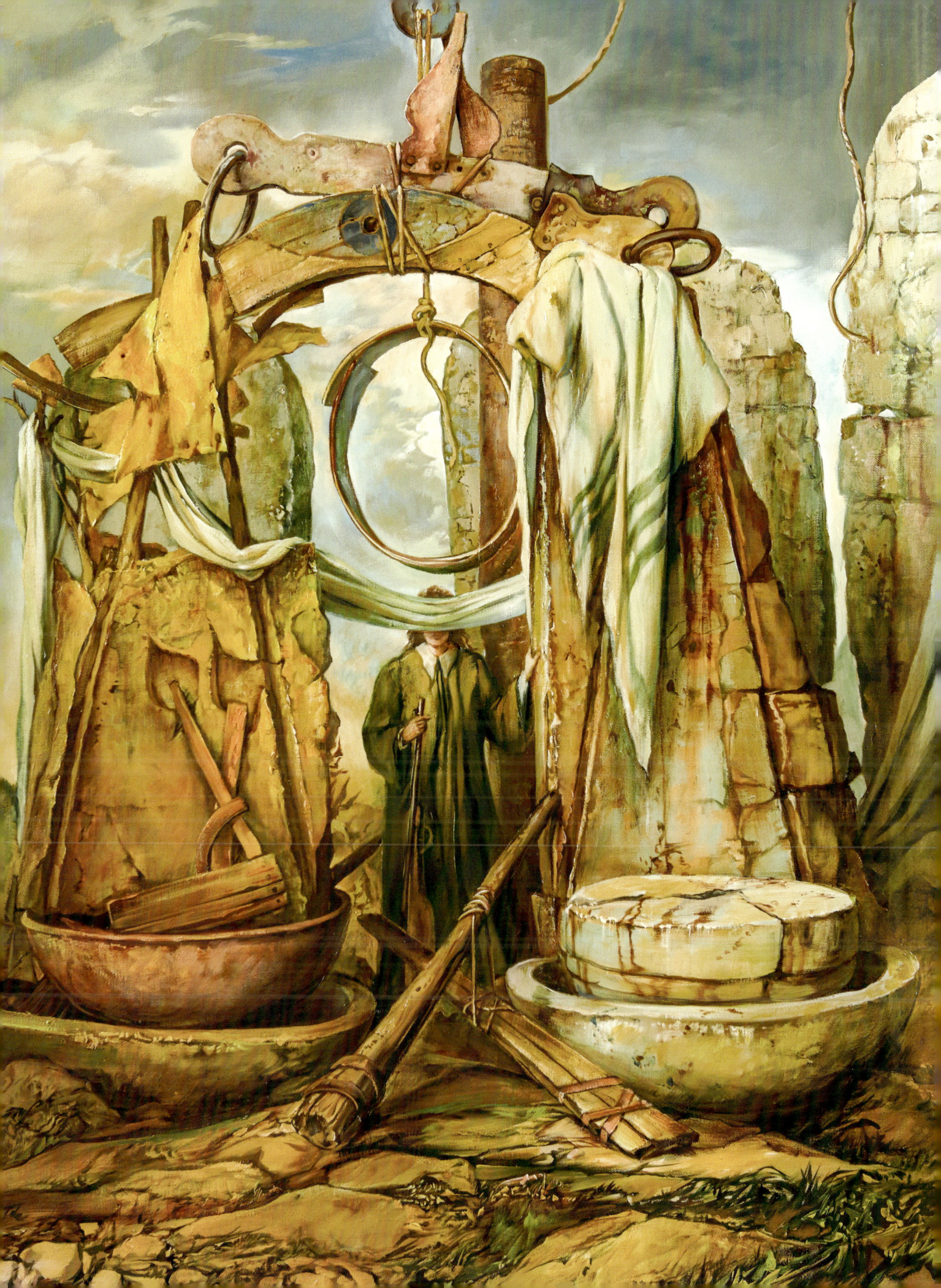

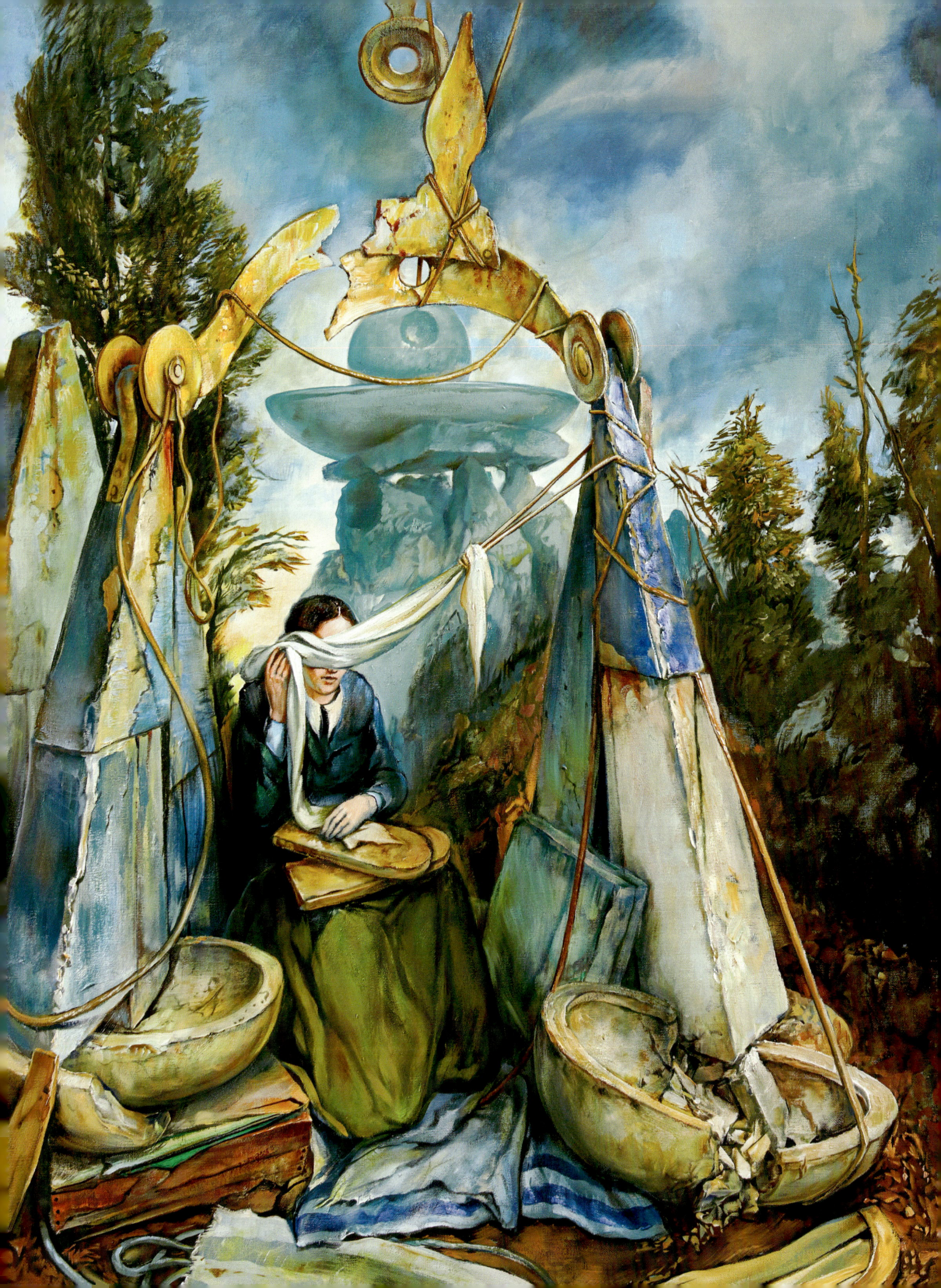

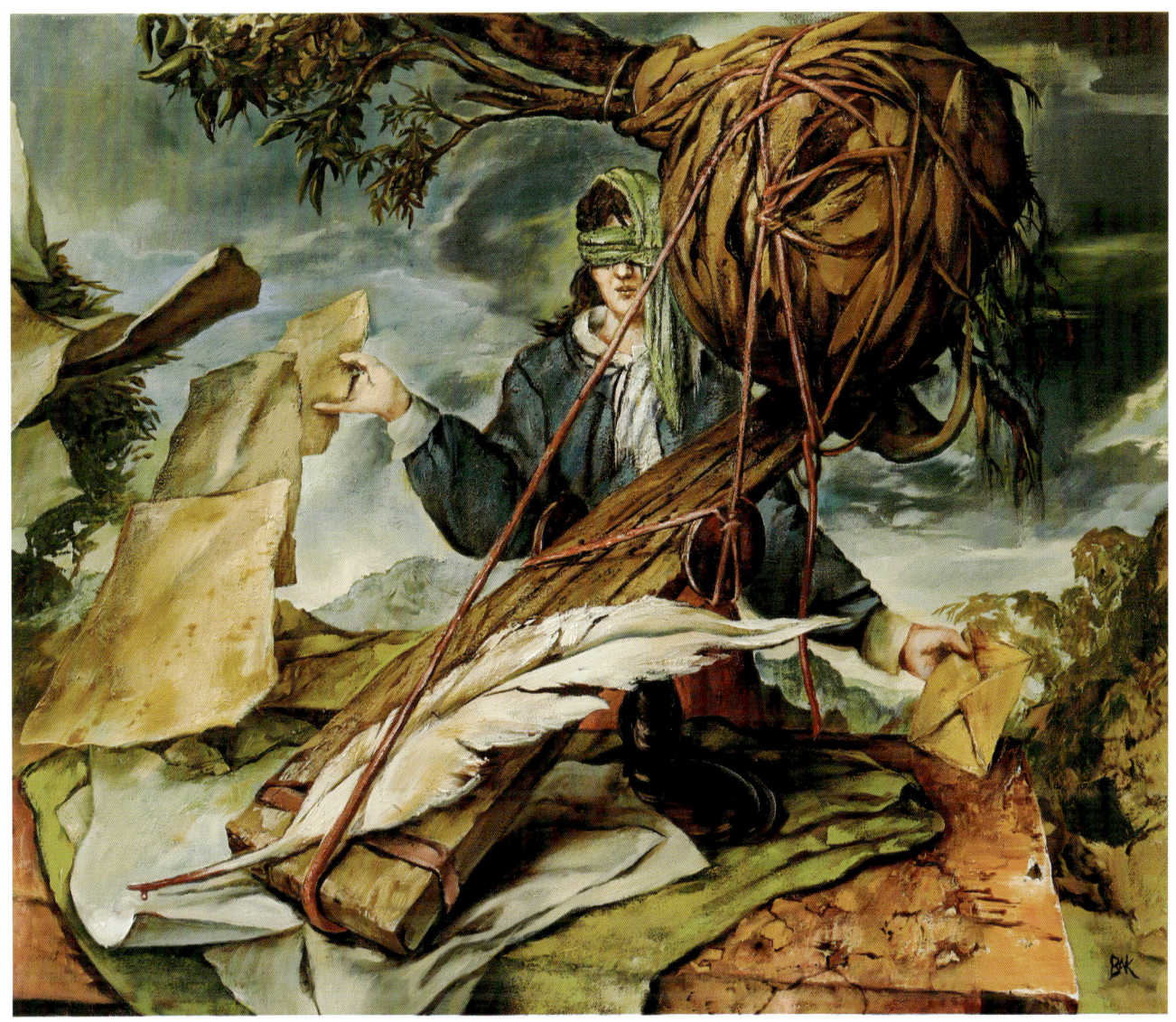

Balanced
Oil on canvas
20 x 24"
BK1954

LEFT:
Eye Witness
Oil on canvas
40 x 30"
BK1943

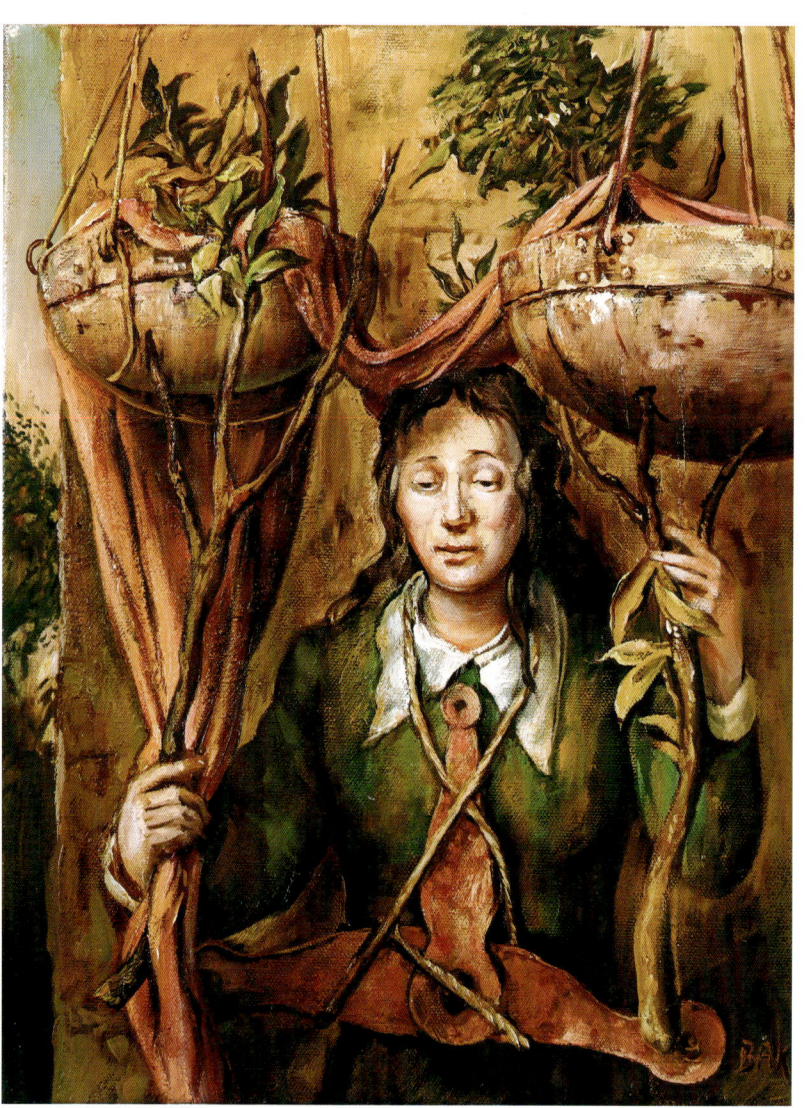

Growing
Oil on canvas
14 x 11"
BK1977

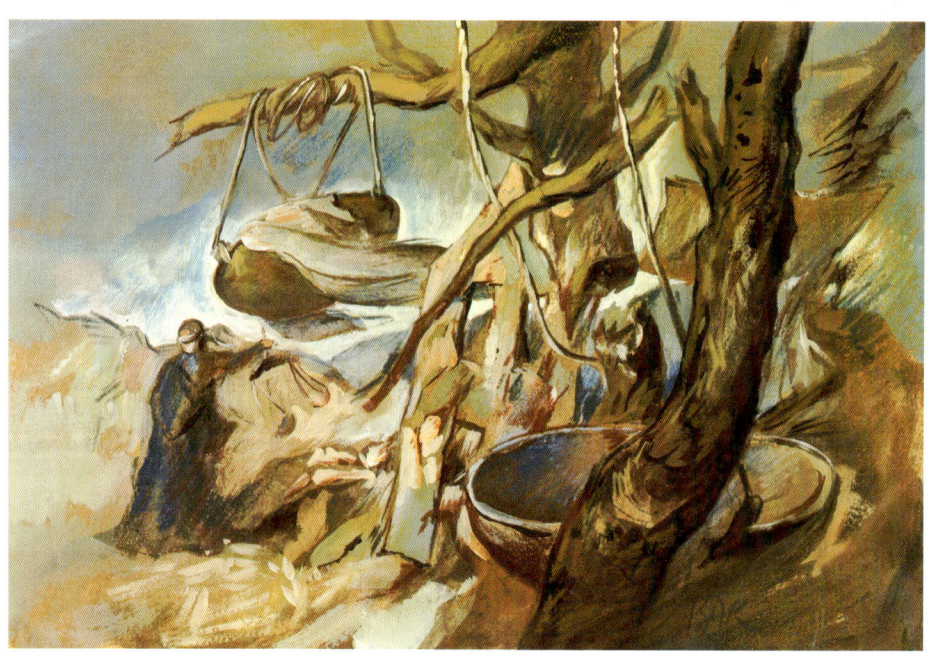

Stormy
Gouache and watercolor on paper
7.25 x 11"
BK2019

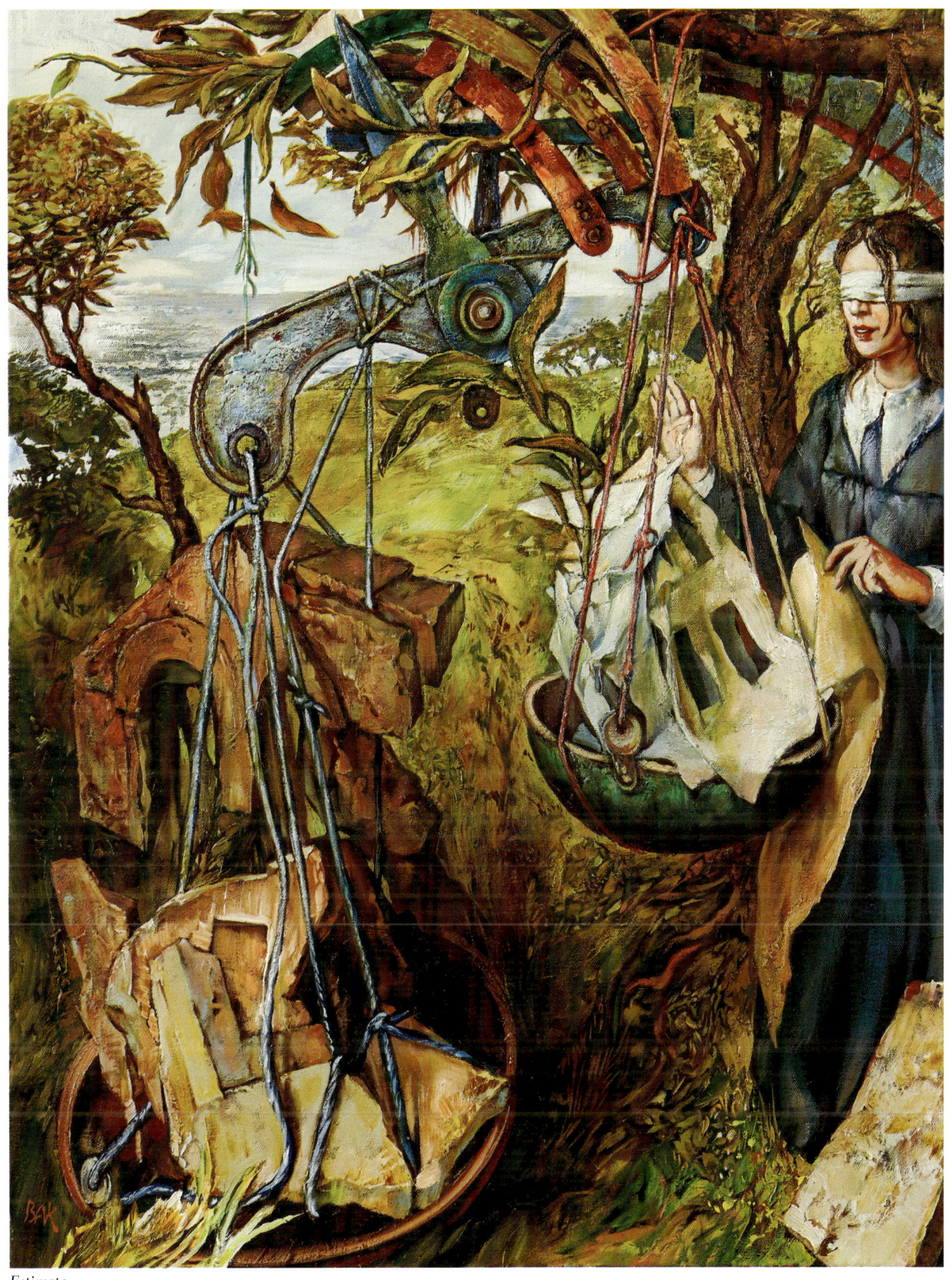

Estimate
Oil on canvas
22 x 28"
BK1946

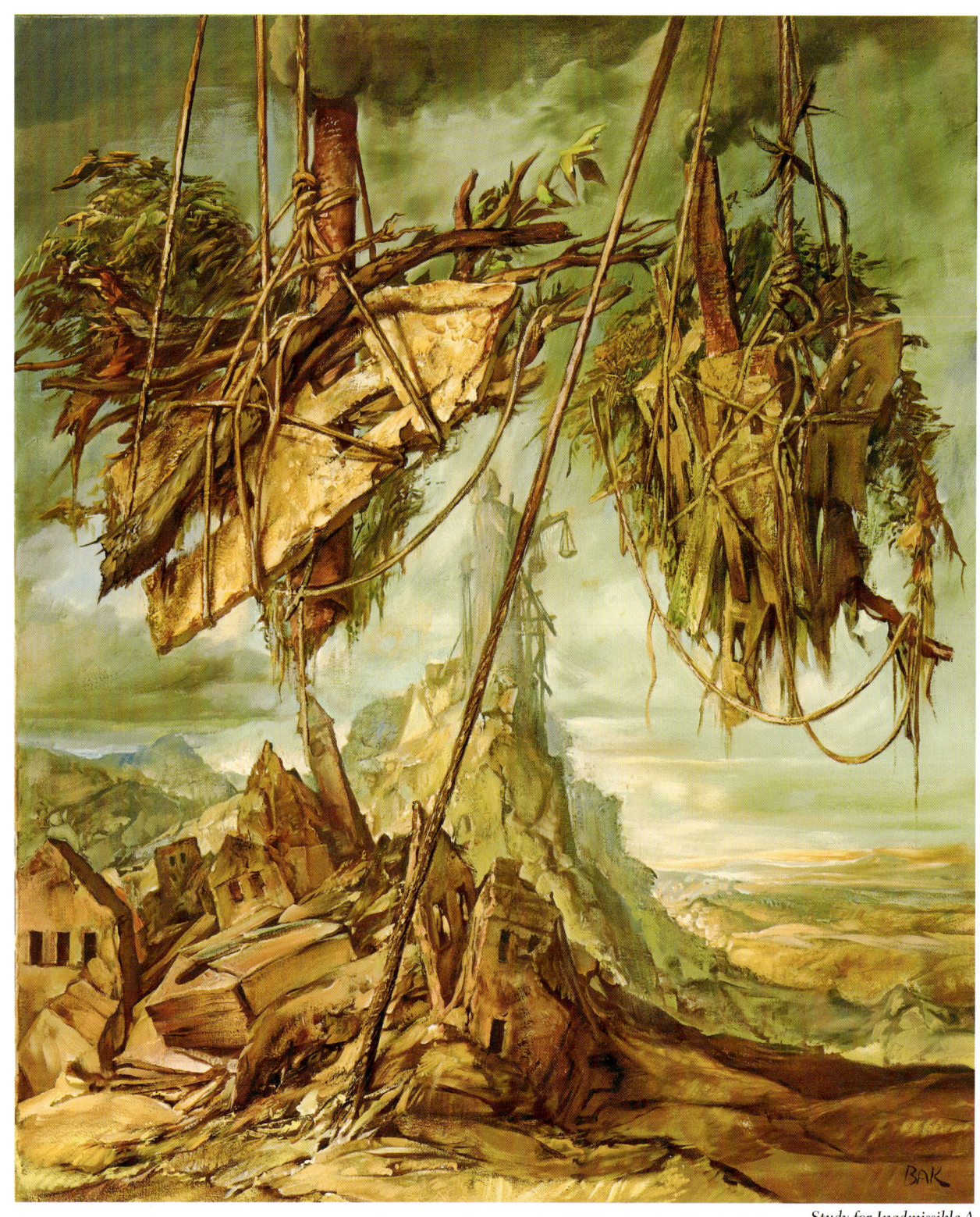

Study for Inadmissible A
Oil on canvas
24 x 20"
BK1959

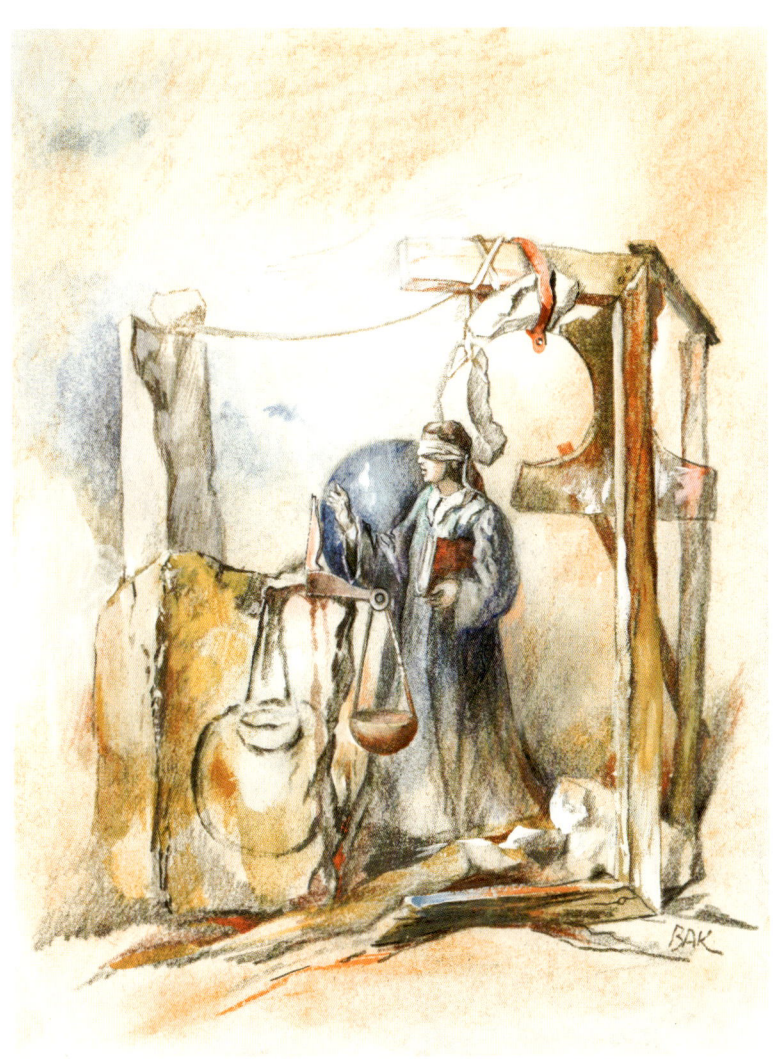

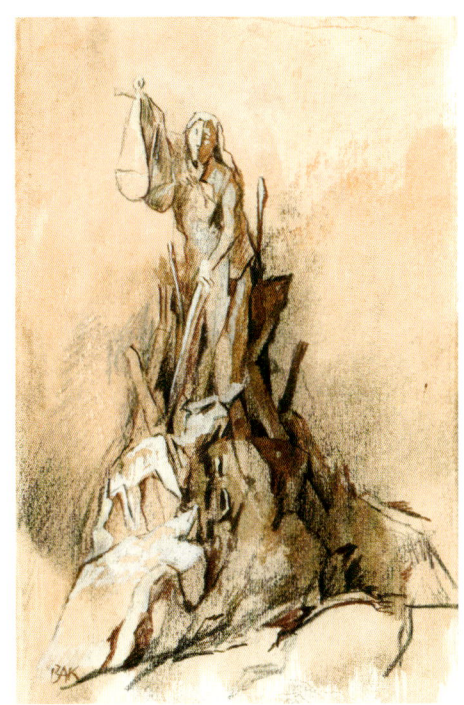

Reminder
Gouache on paper
8.75 x 5.75"
BK2004

Factors of Chance
Watercolor and gouache on paper
14.5 x 11"
BK2012

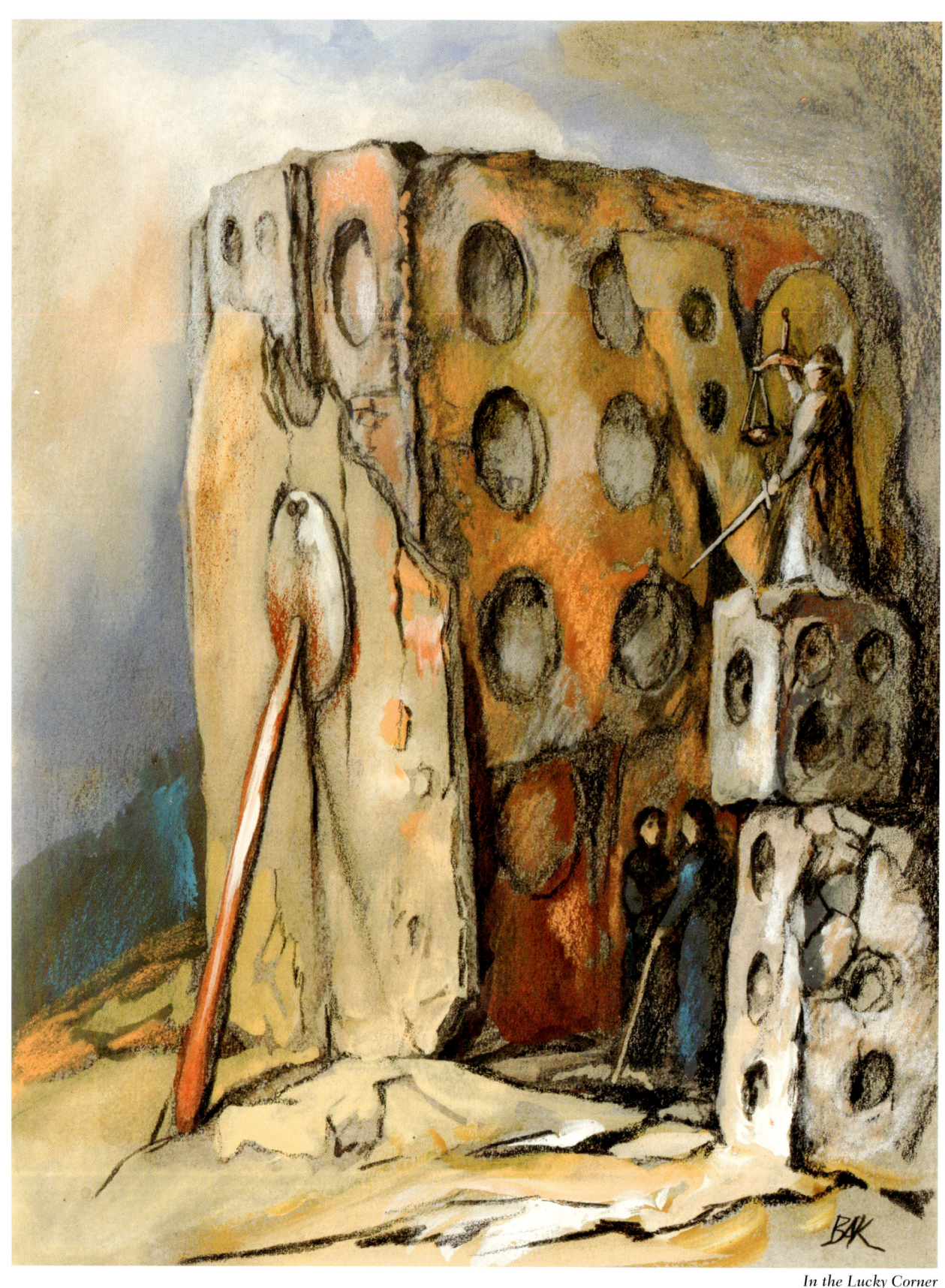

In the Lucky Corner
Crayon and oil on paper
11 x 8.5"
BK2013

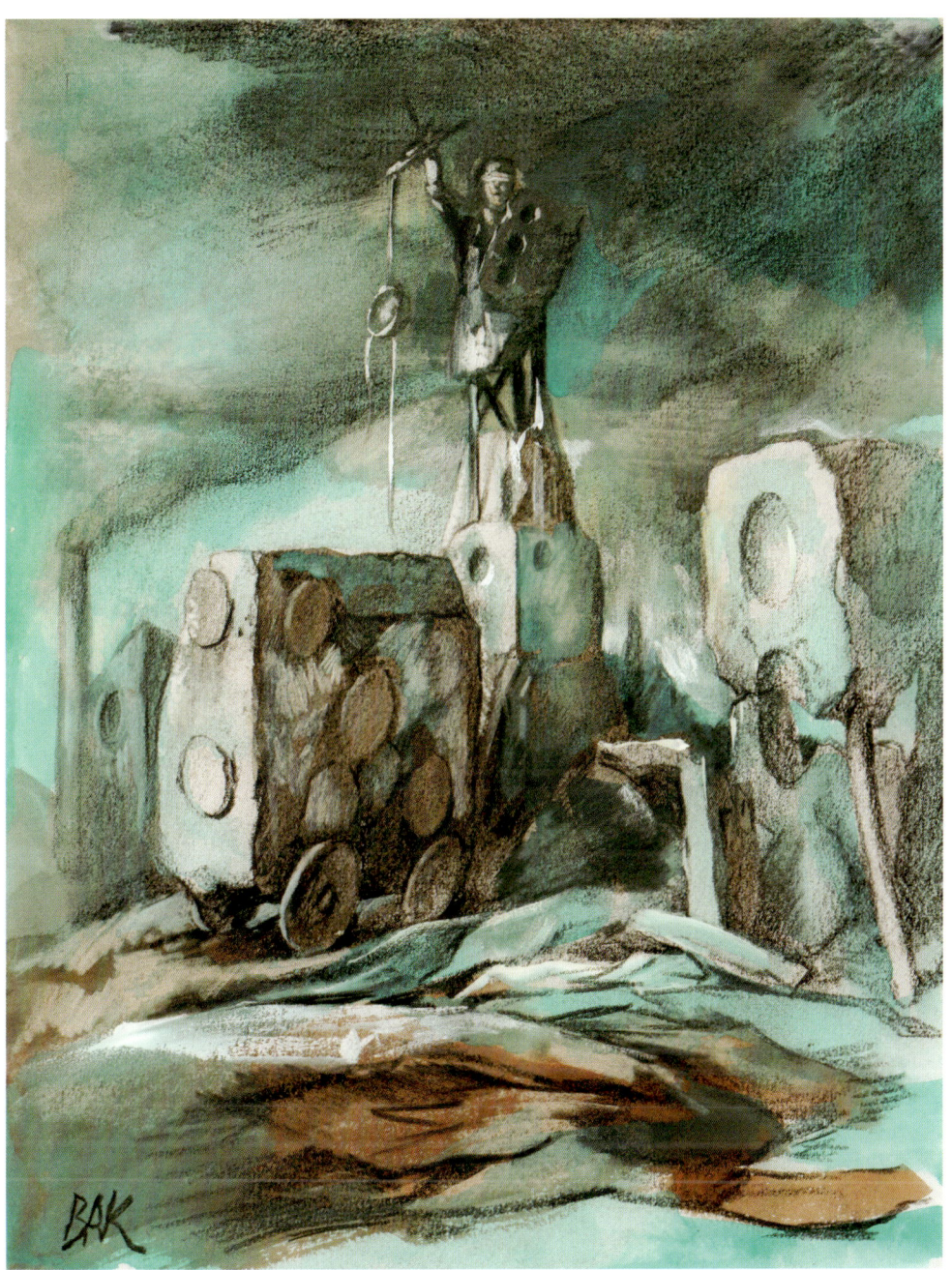

In the Monument Passage
Crayon and tempera on paper
11 x 8.5"
BK2003

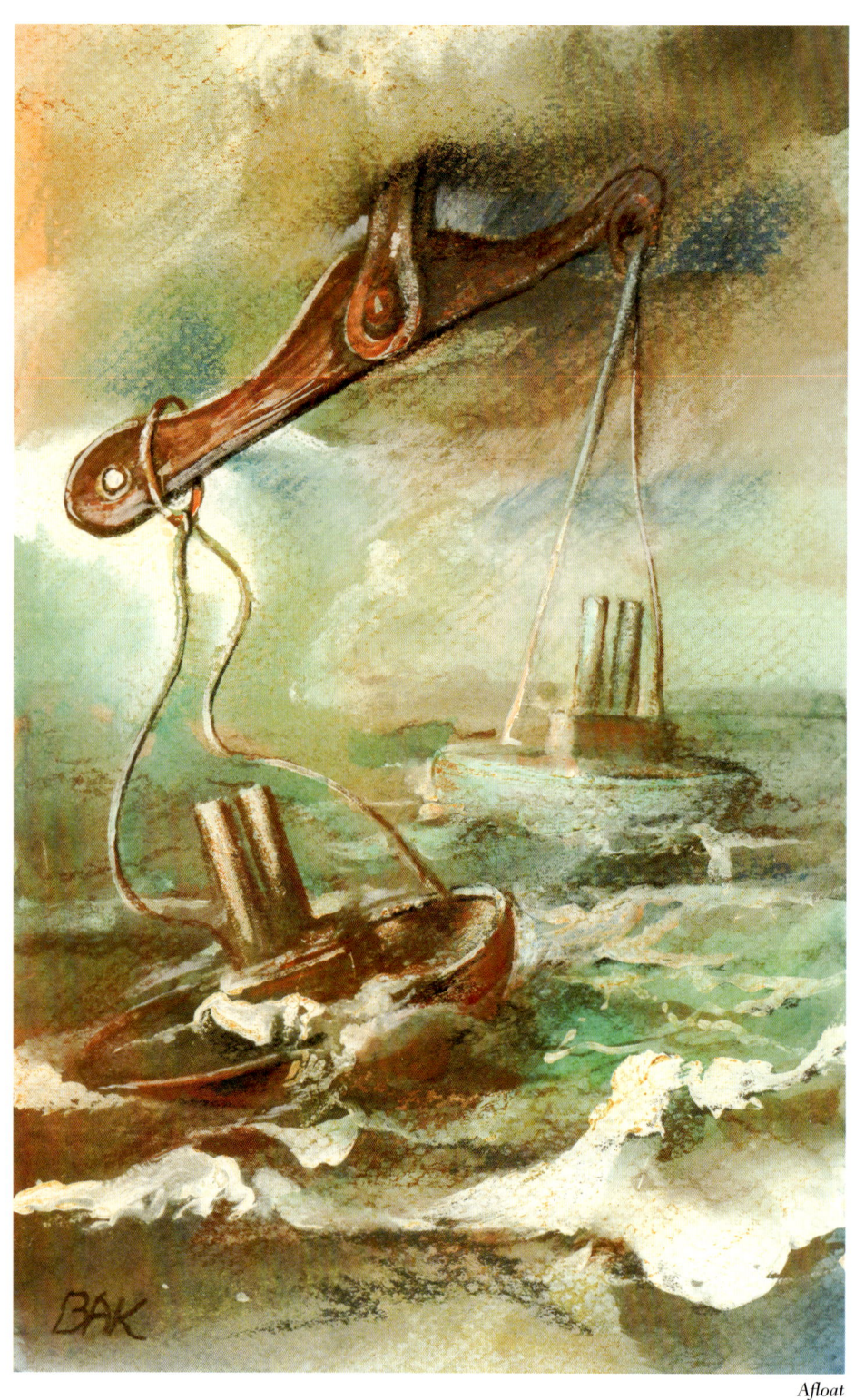

Afloat
Gouache on paper
8.5 x 5.5"
BK2001

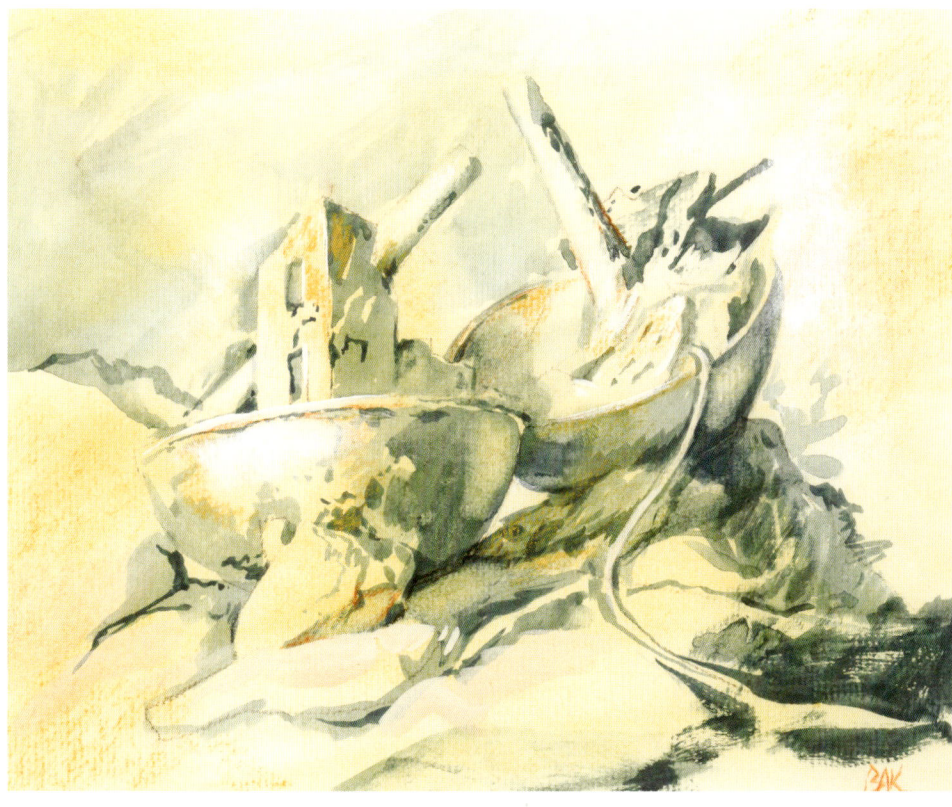

Study for Heritage
Watercolor on paper
7.5 x 9.5"
BK1993

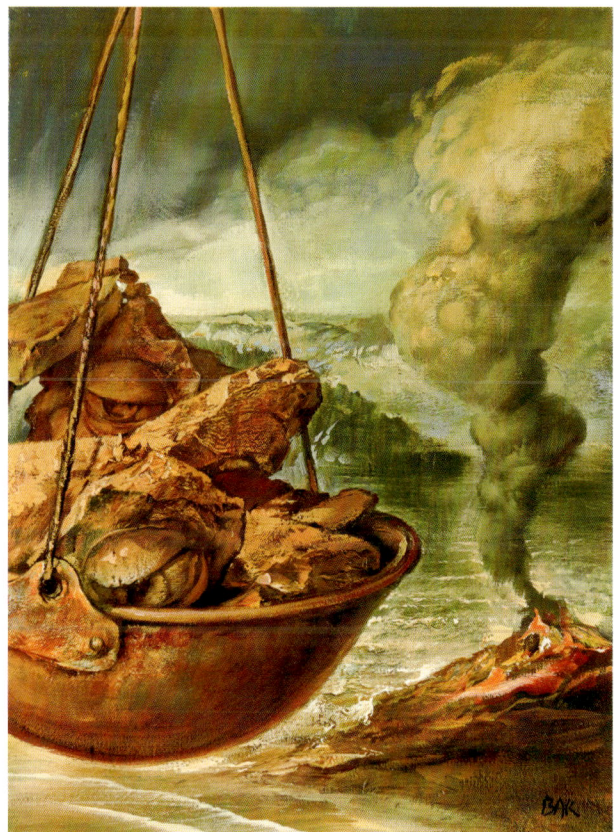

Common Destiny
Oil on canvas
12 x 9"
BK1985

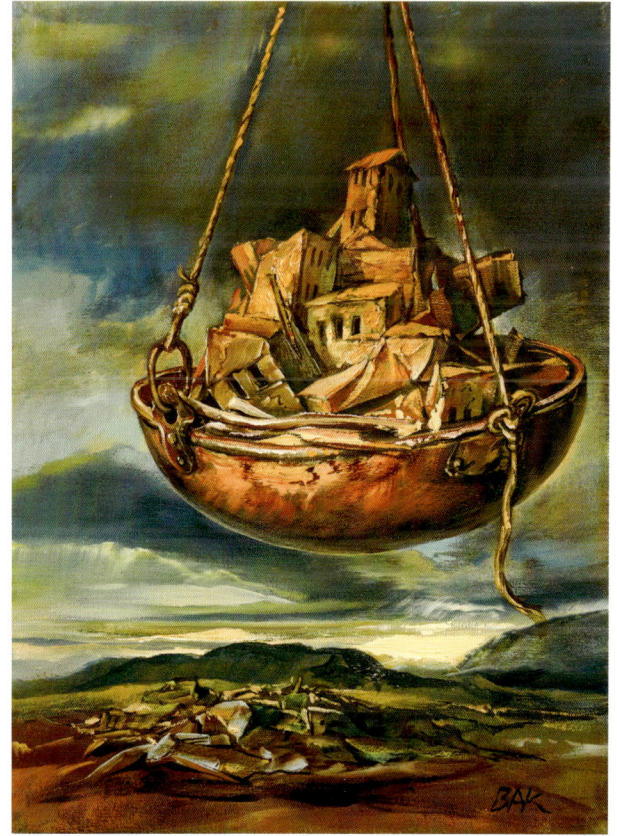

One of Two A
Oil on canvas
12 x 9"
BK1983

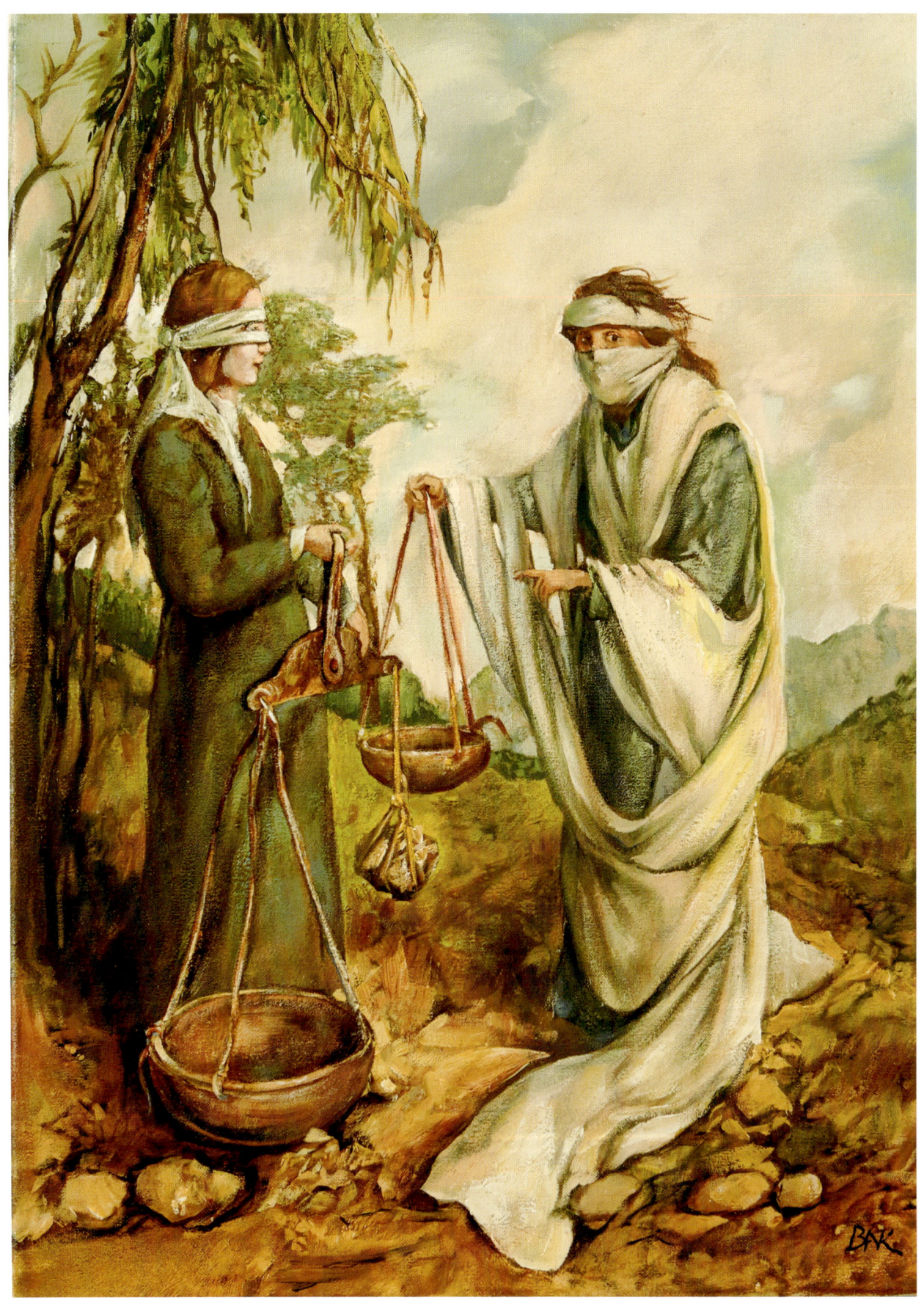

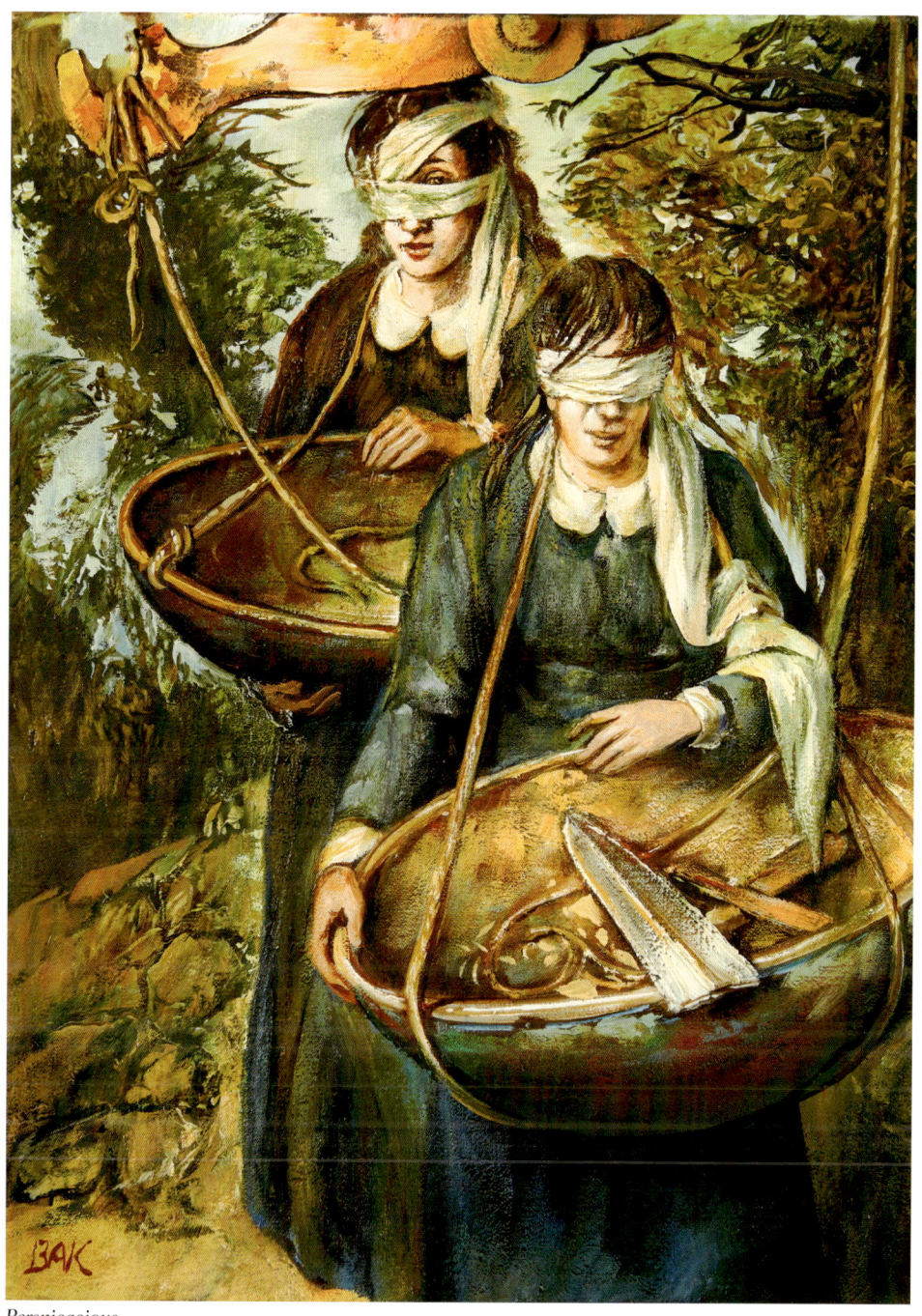

Perspicacious
Oil on canvas
12 x 9"
BK1986

LEFT:
Clearly
Oil on canvas
16 x 12"
BK1974

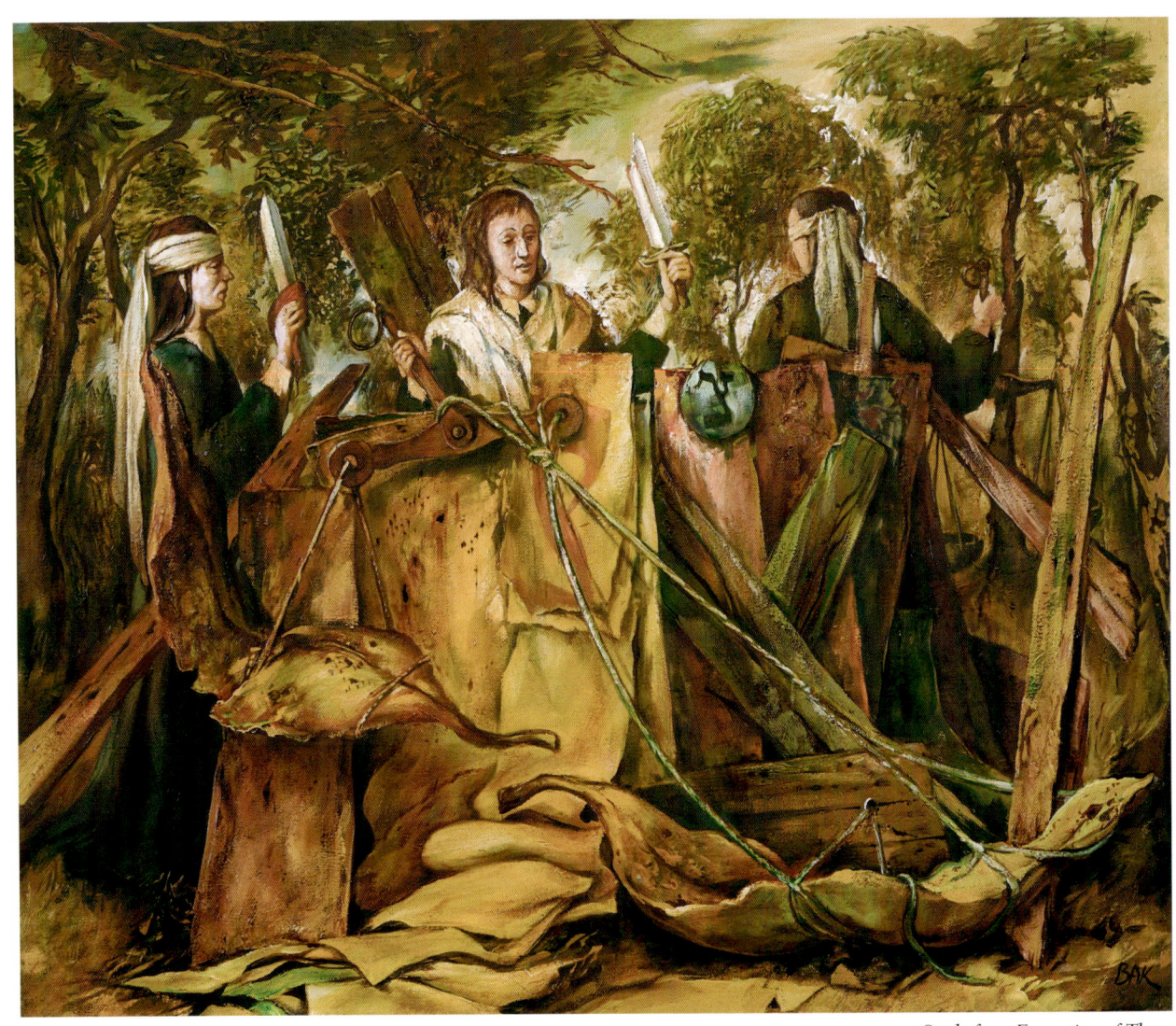

Study for a Formation of Three
Oil on canvas
20 x 24"
BK1956

RIGHT:
Holding On
Oil on canvas
22 x 28"
BK1950

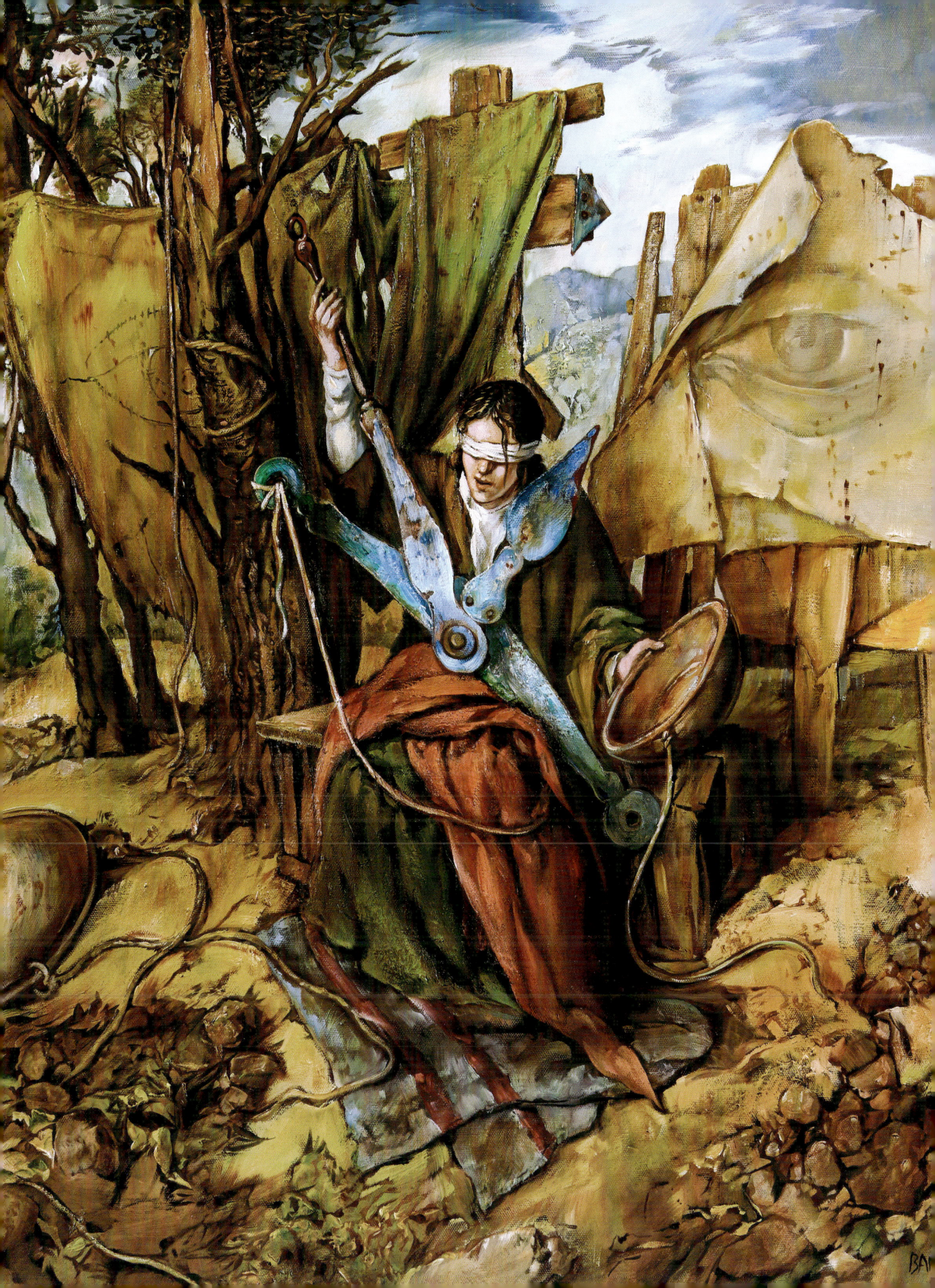

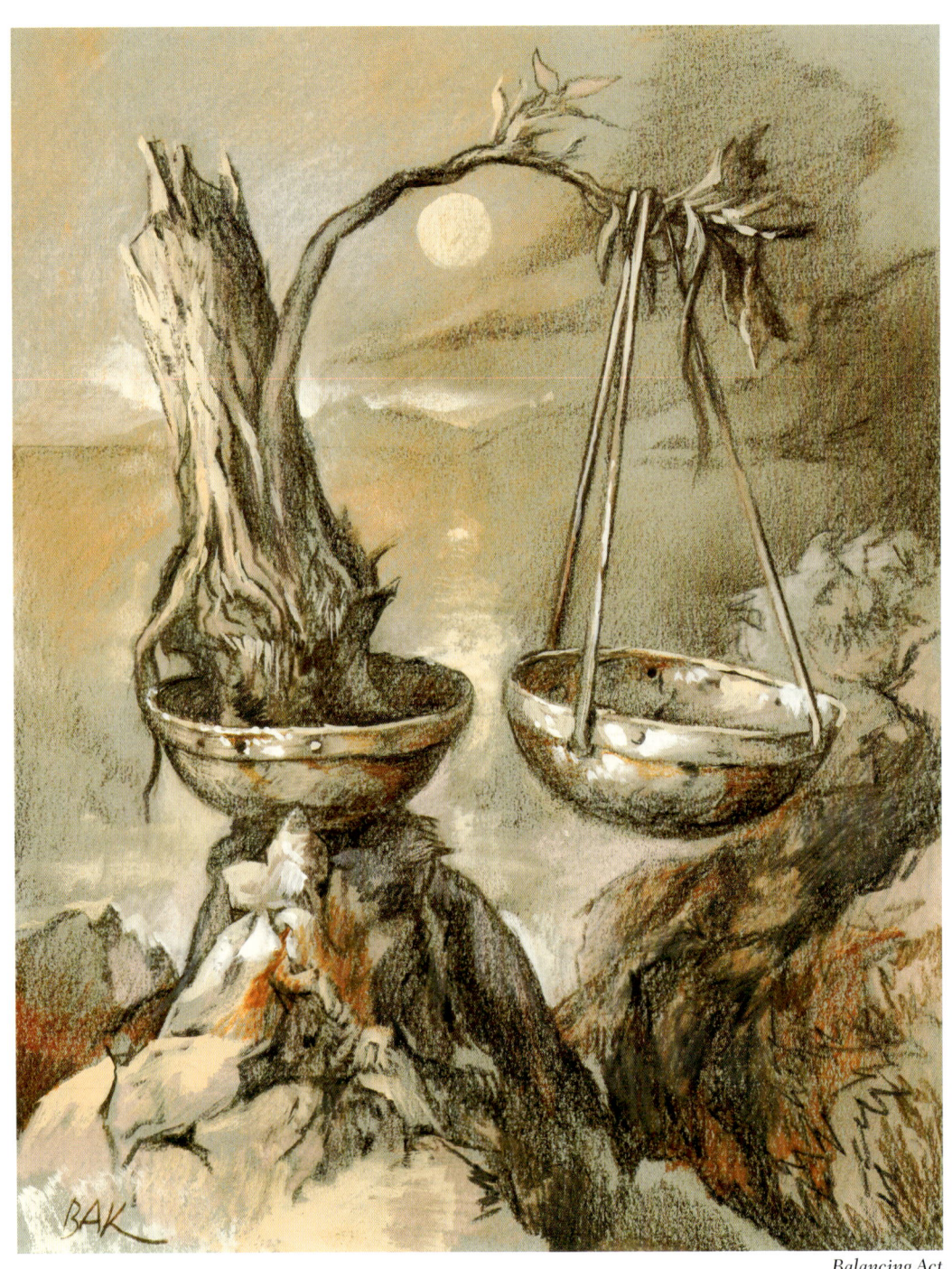

Balancing Act
Crayon and gouache on paper
11 x 8.5"
BK2007

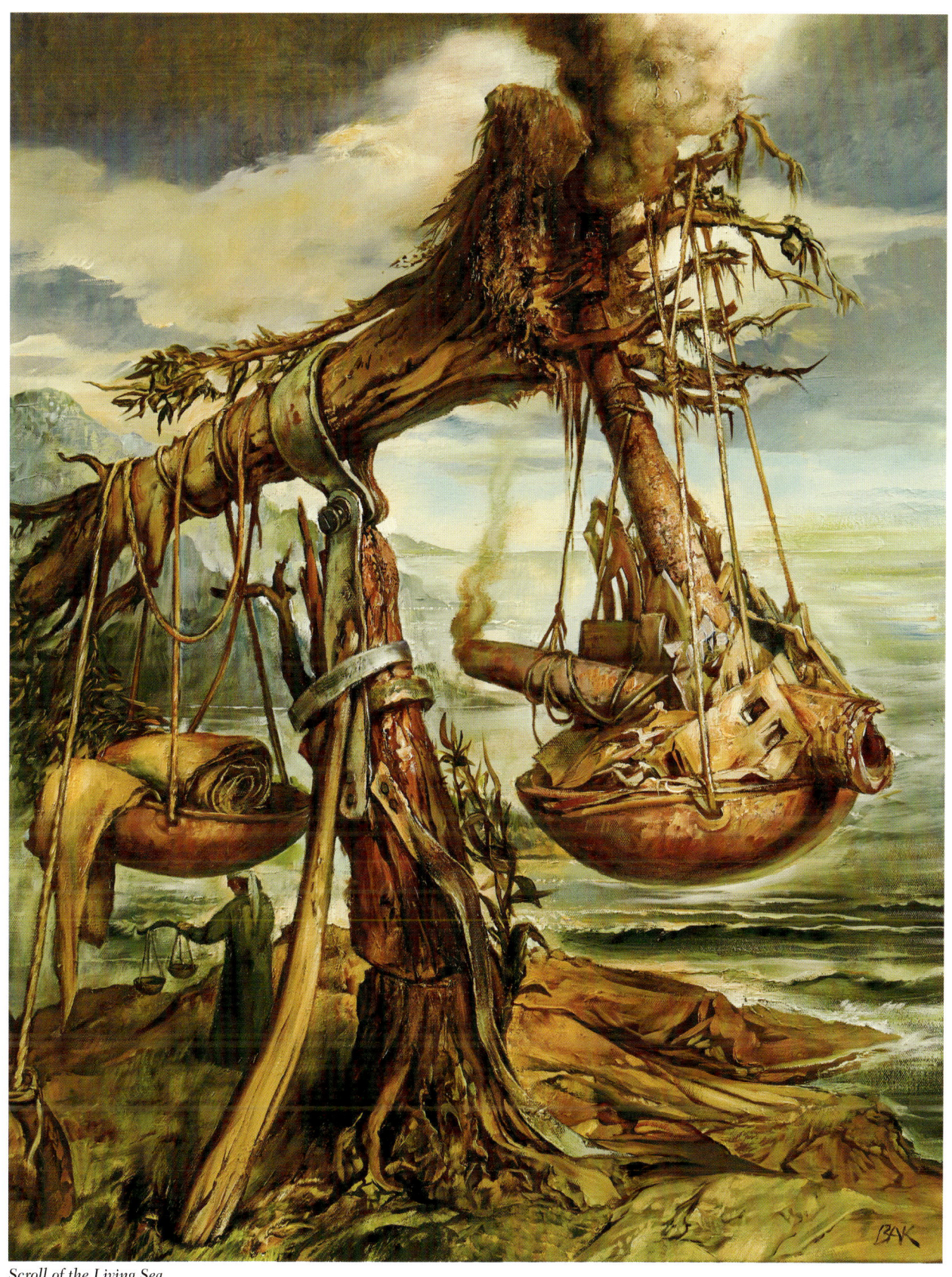

Scroll of the Living Sea
Oil on canvas
22 x 28"
BK1949

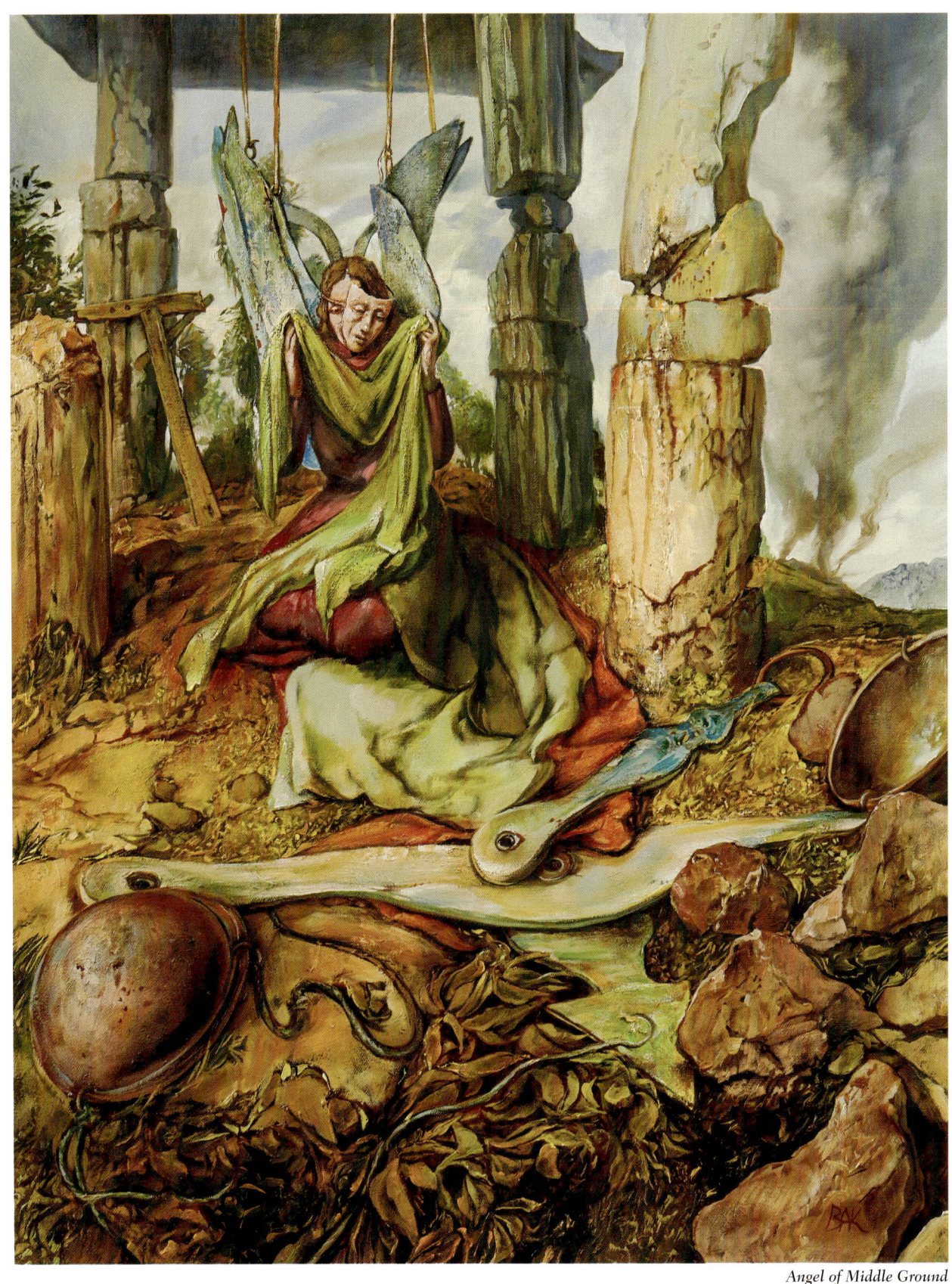

Angel of Middle Ground
Oil on canvas
22 x 28"
BK1947

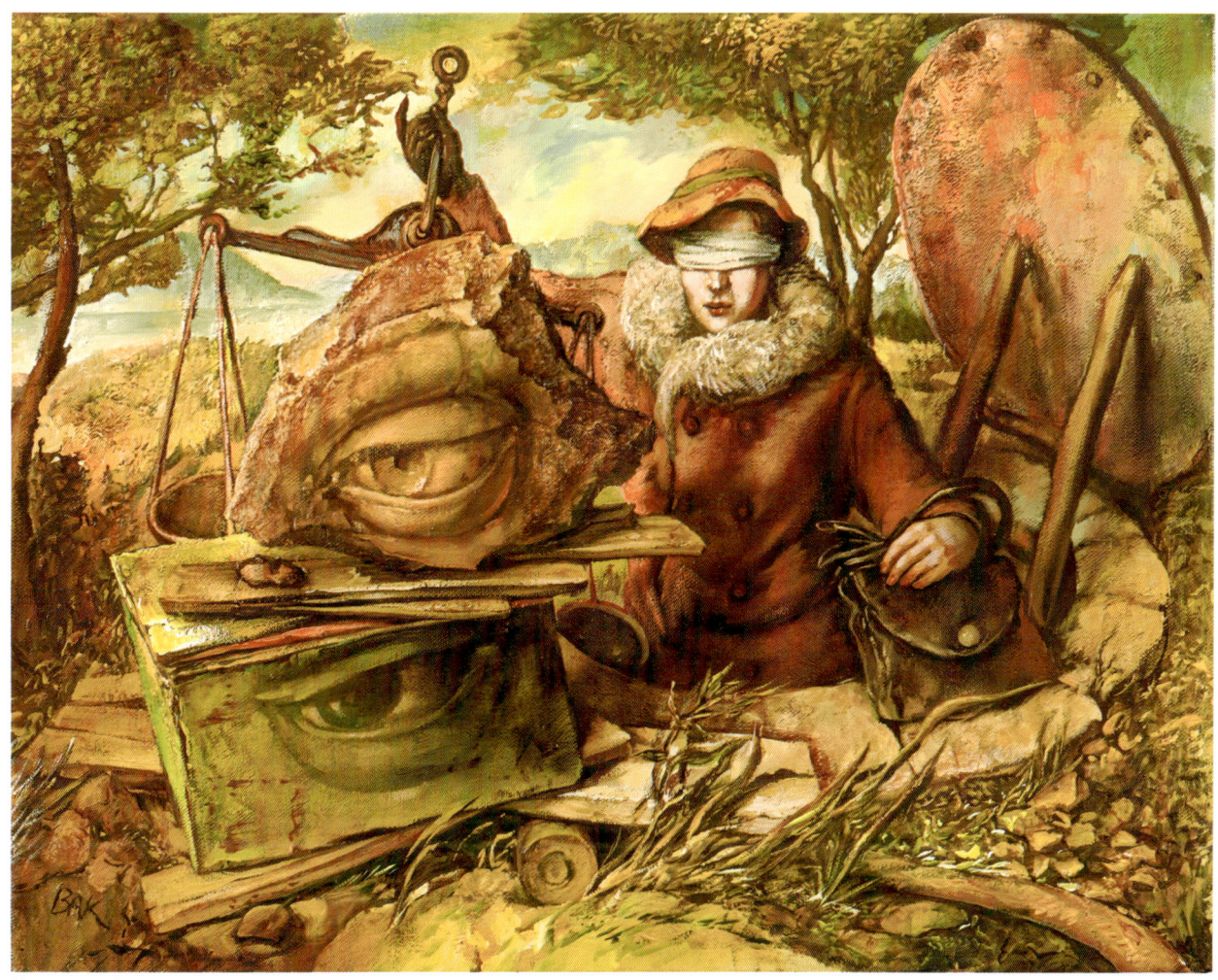

Emergence A
Oil on canvas
14 x 18"
BK1967

Study for Open-Eyed
Crayon and tempera on paper
11 x 8.5"
BK1989

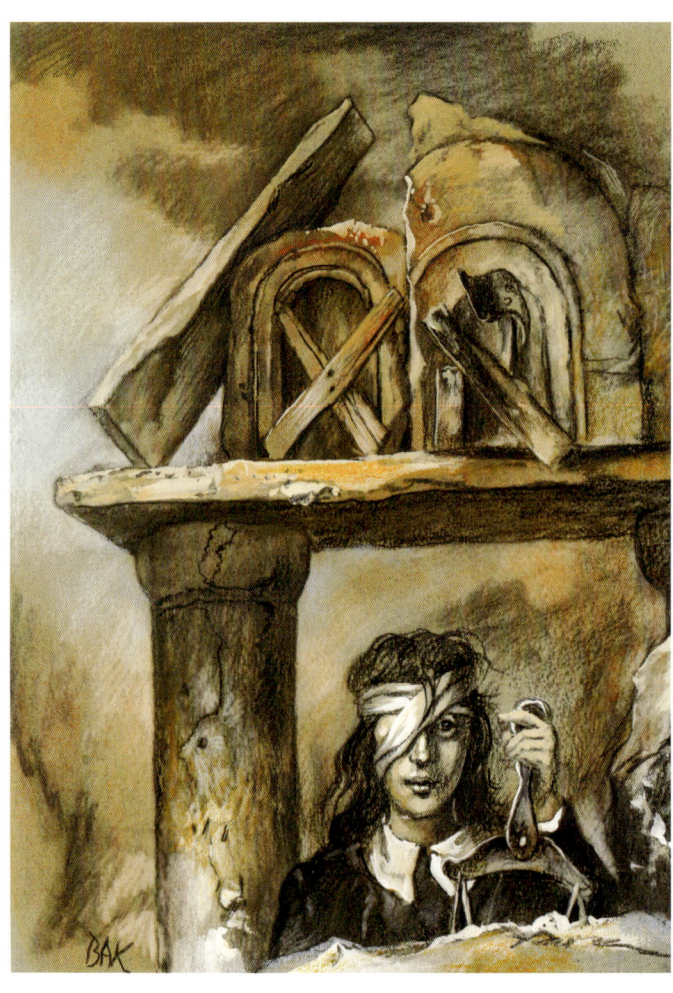

Study for Observation
Crayon and gouache on paper
8.5 x 11"
BK1987

FAR RIGHT:
Study for a Almost
Oil on canvas
16 x 12"
BK1969

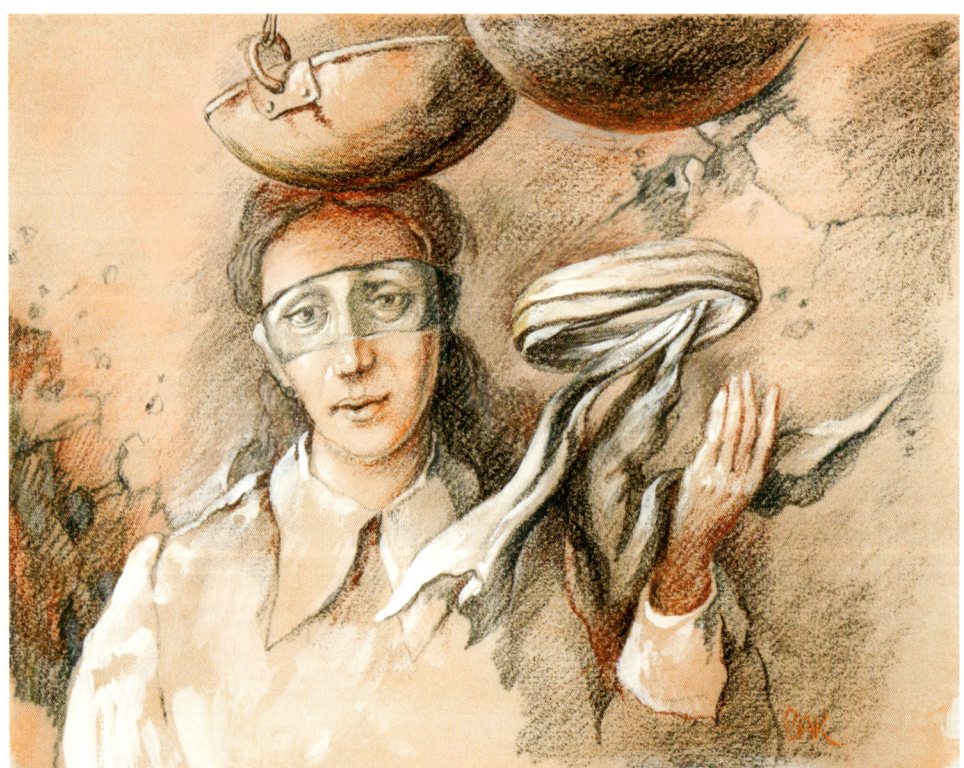

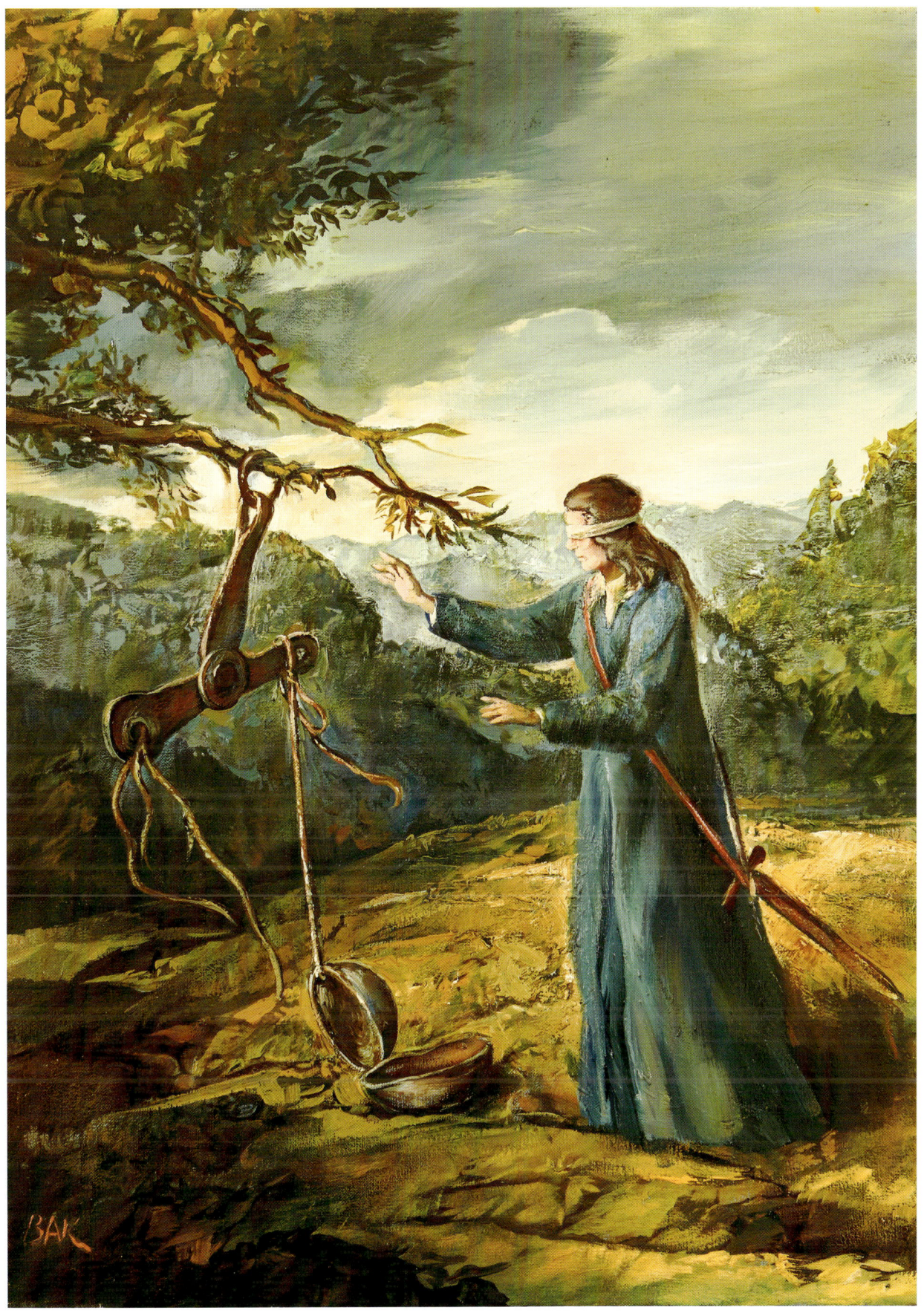

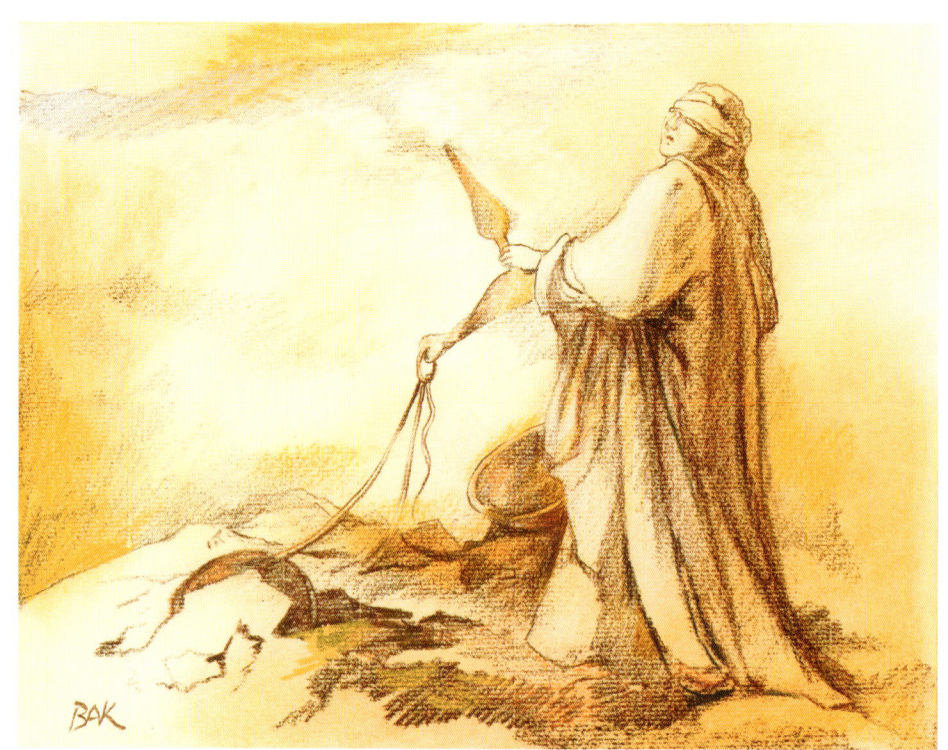

Early Stage
Pastel on paper
9.5 x 12.25"
BK2006

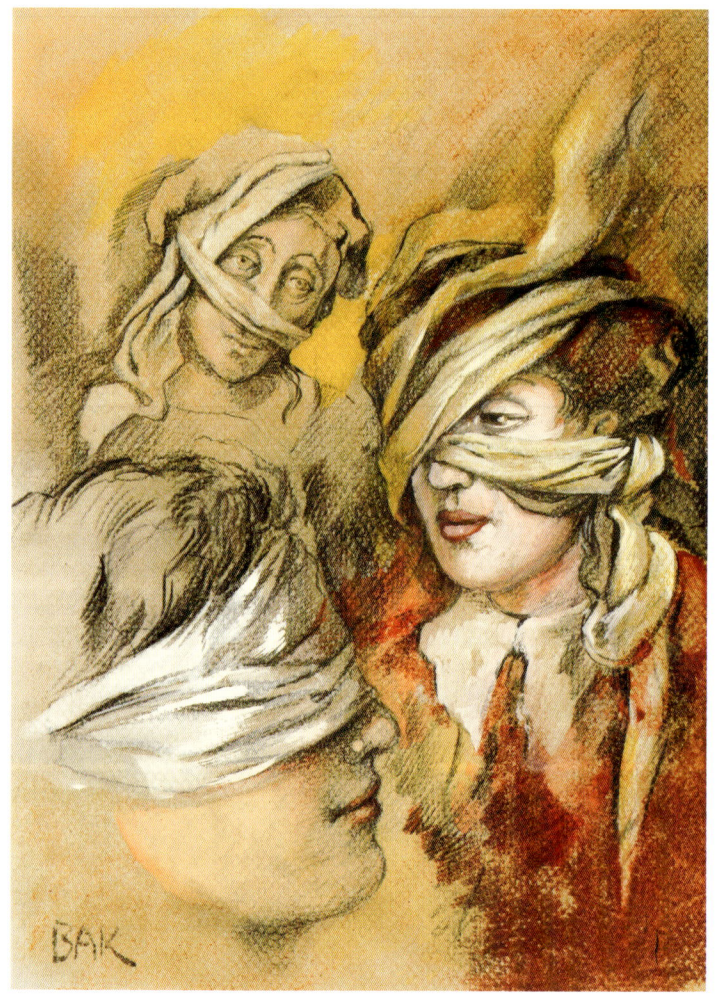

Blindfolds
Crayon and tempera on paper
11 x 8.5"
BK1991

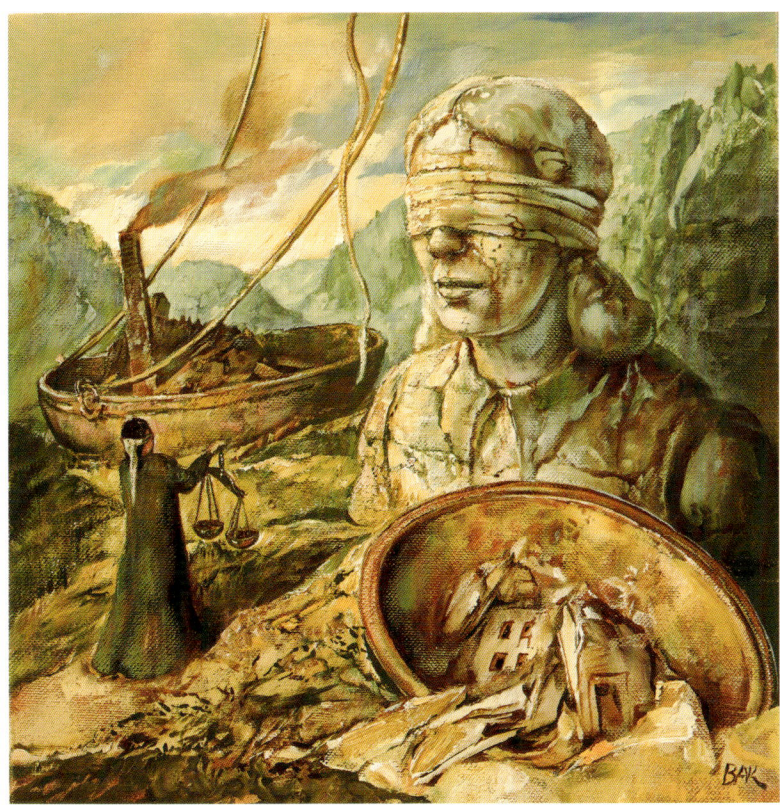

Study for Low and High
Oil on canvas
12 x 12"
BK1979

Eye with Eye
Oil on canvas
9 x 12"
BK1984

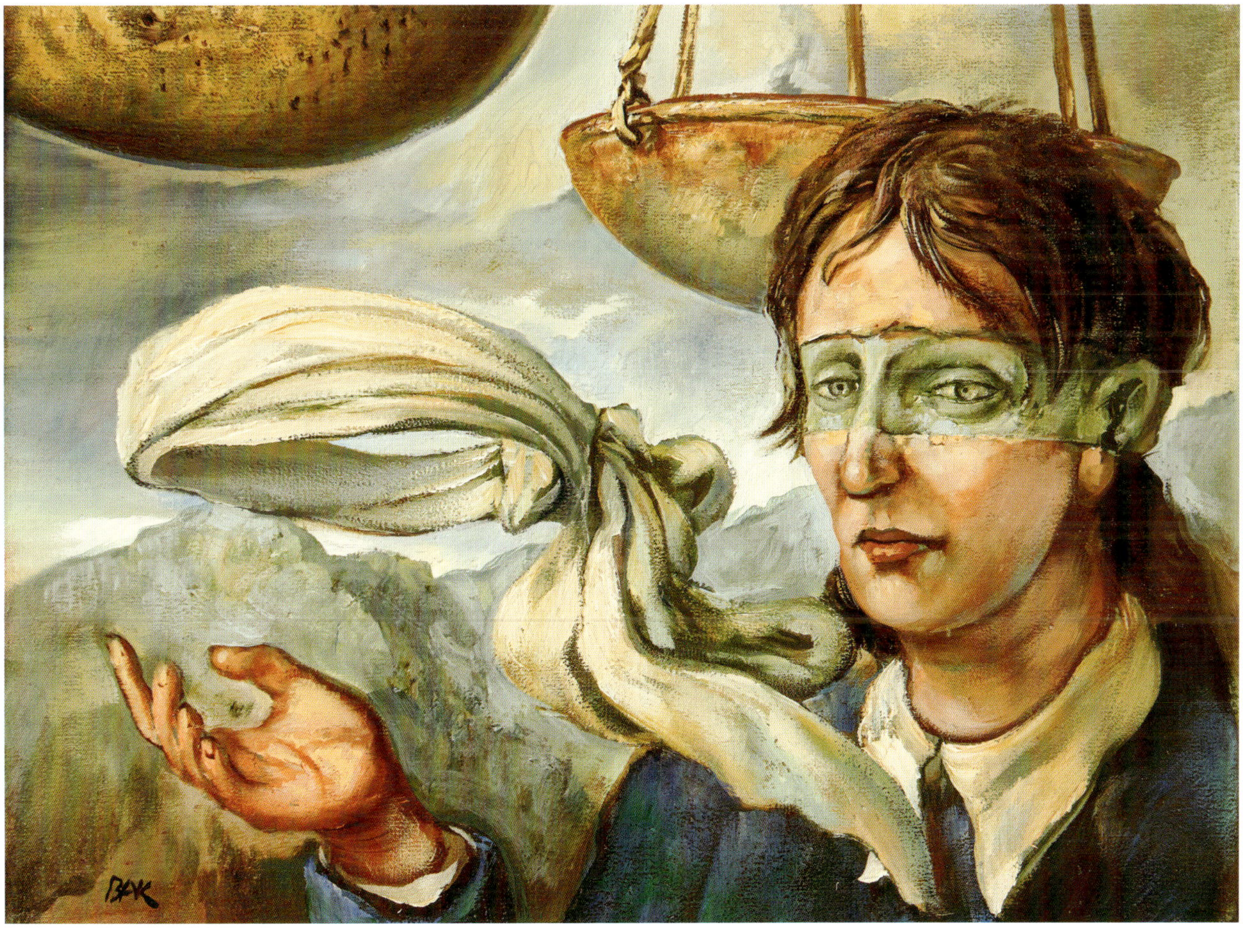

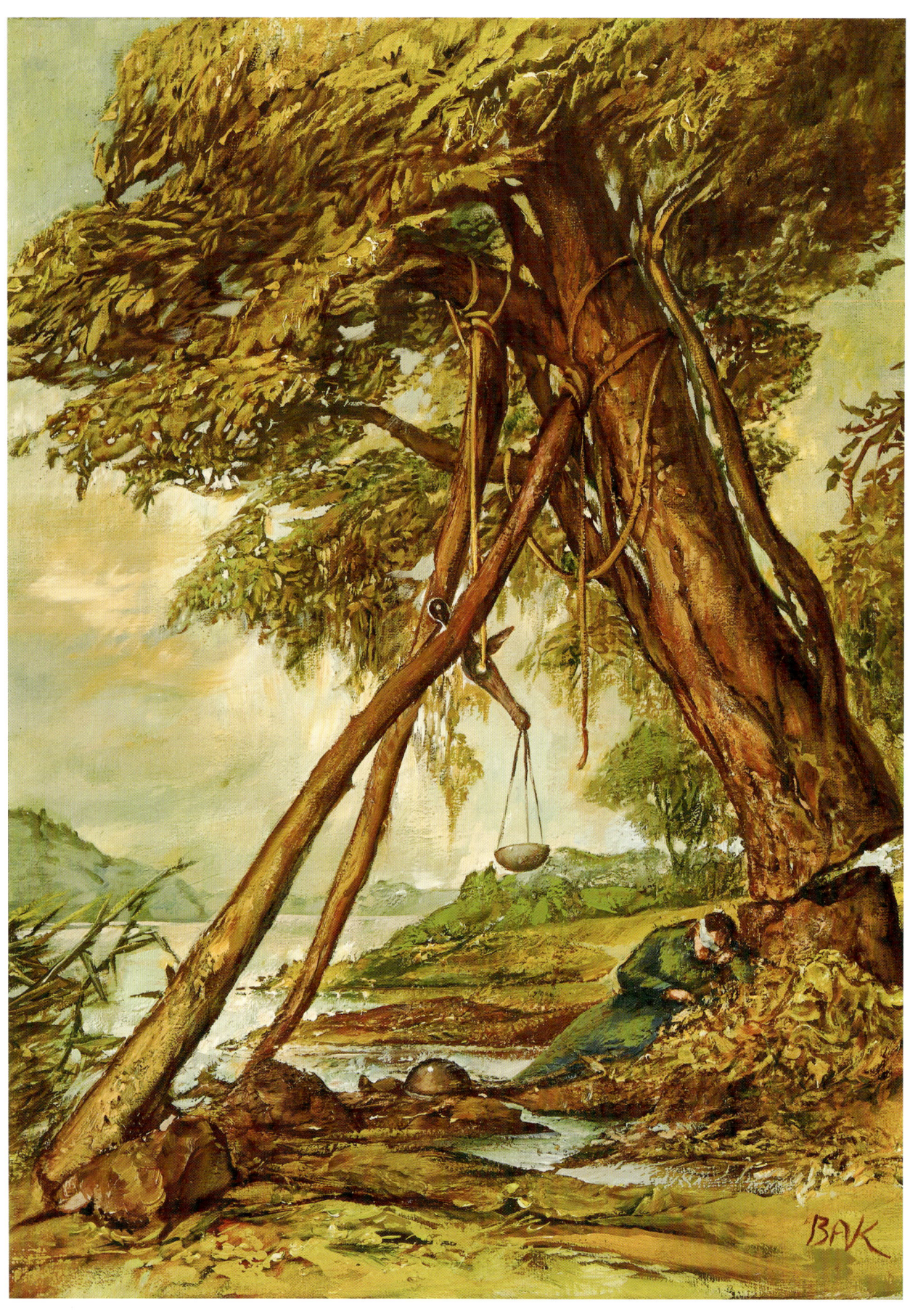

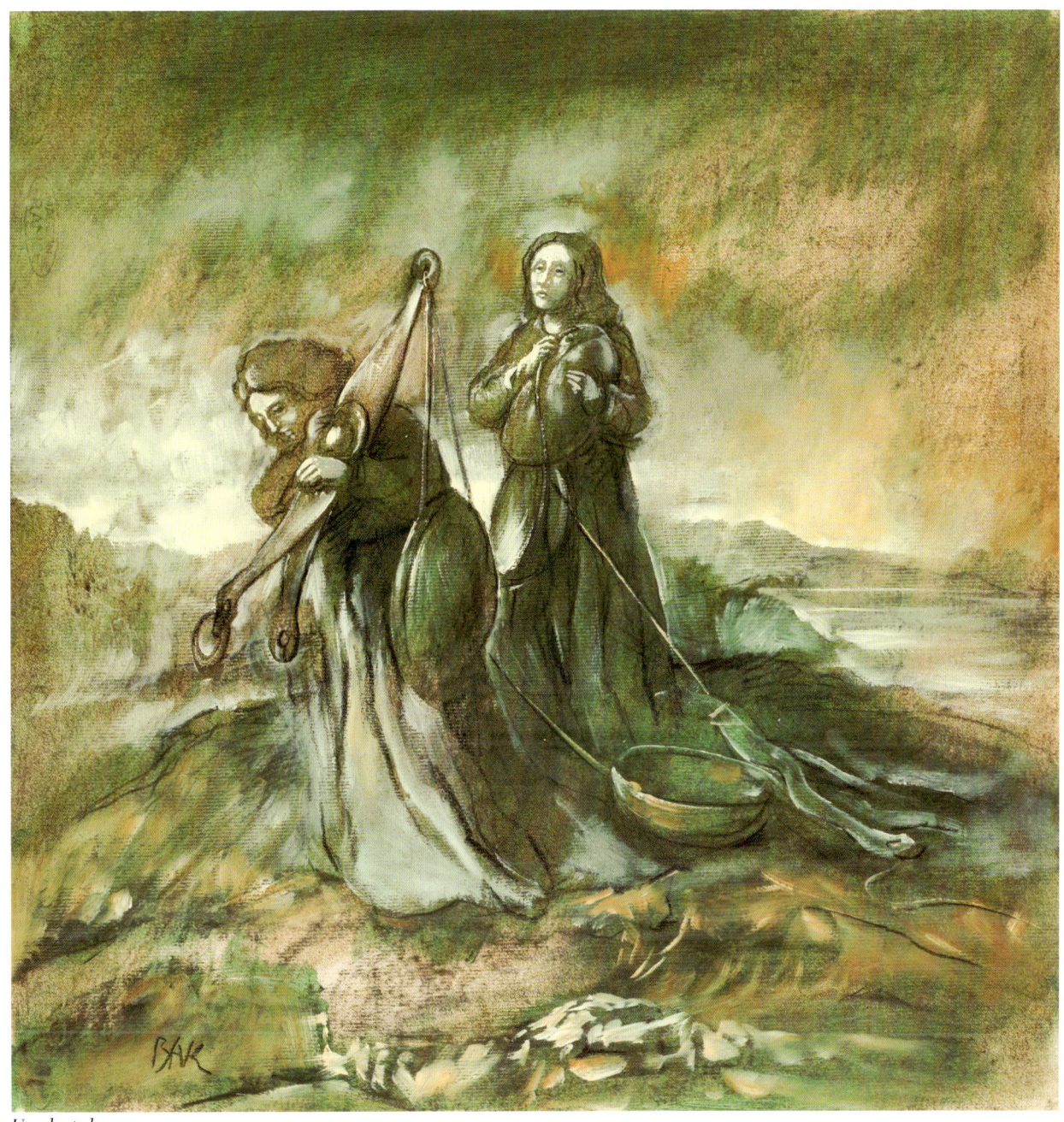

Unrelented
Charcoal and oil on paper
19 x 19"
BK2025

LEFT:
Study for a Nap
Oil on canvas
16 x 12"
BK1970

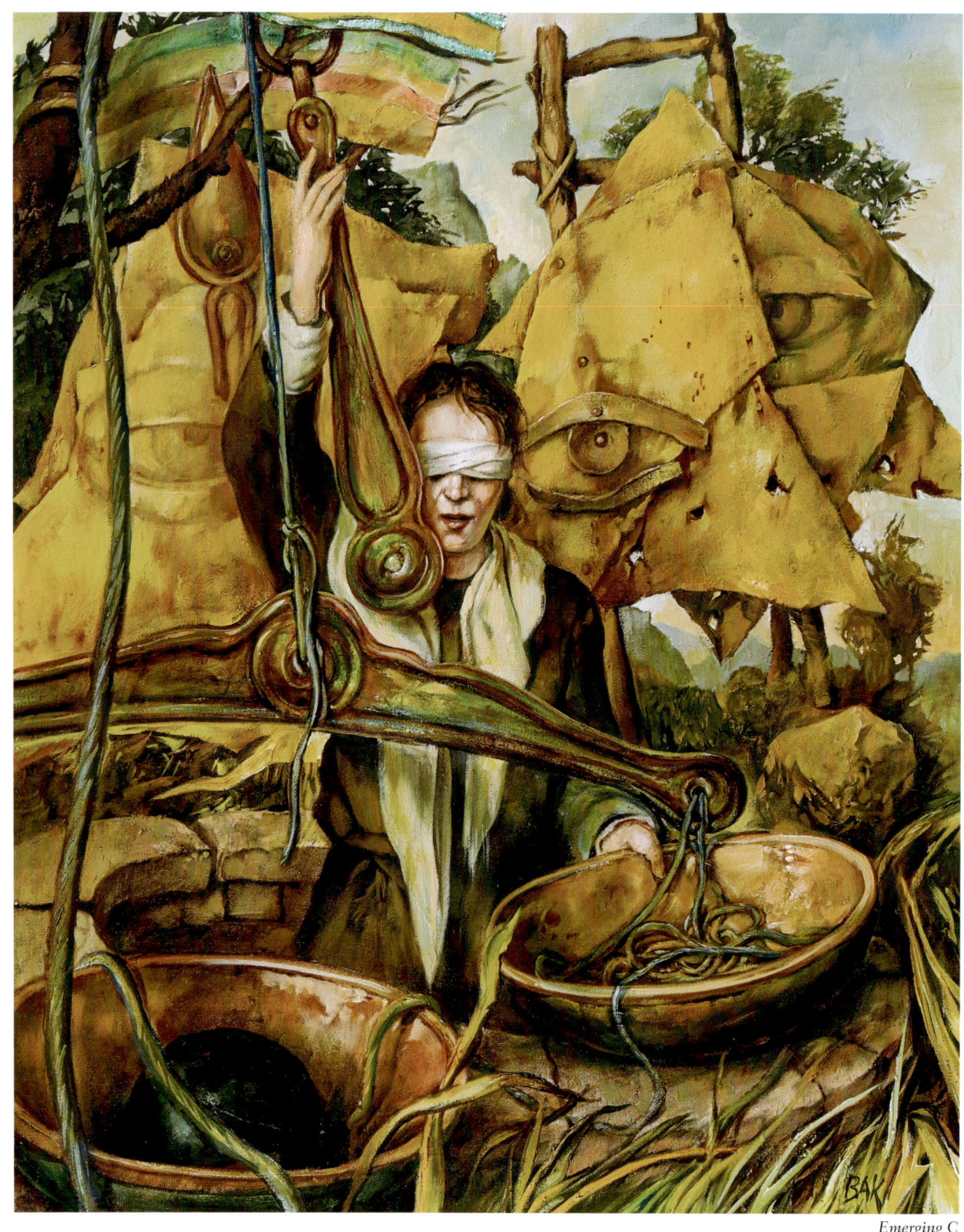

Emerging C
Oil on canvas
24 x 20"
BK1955

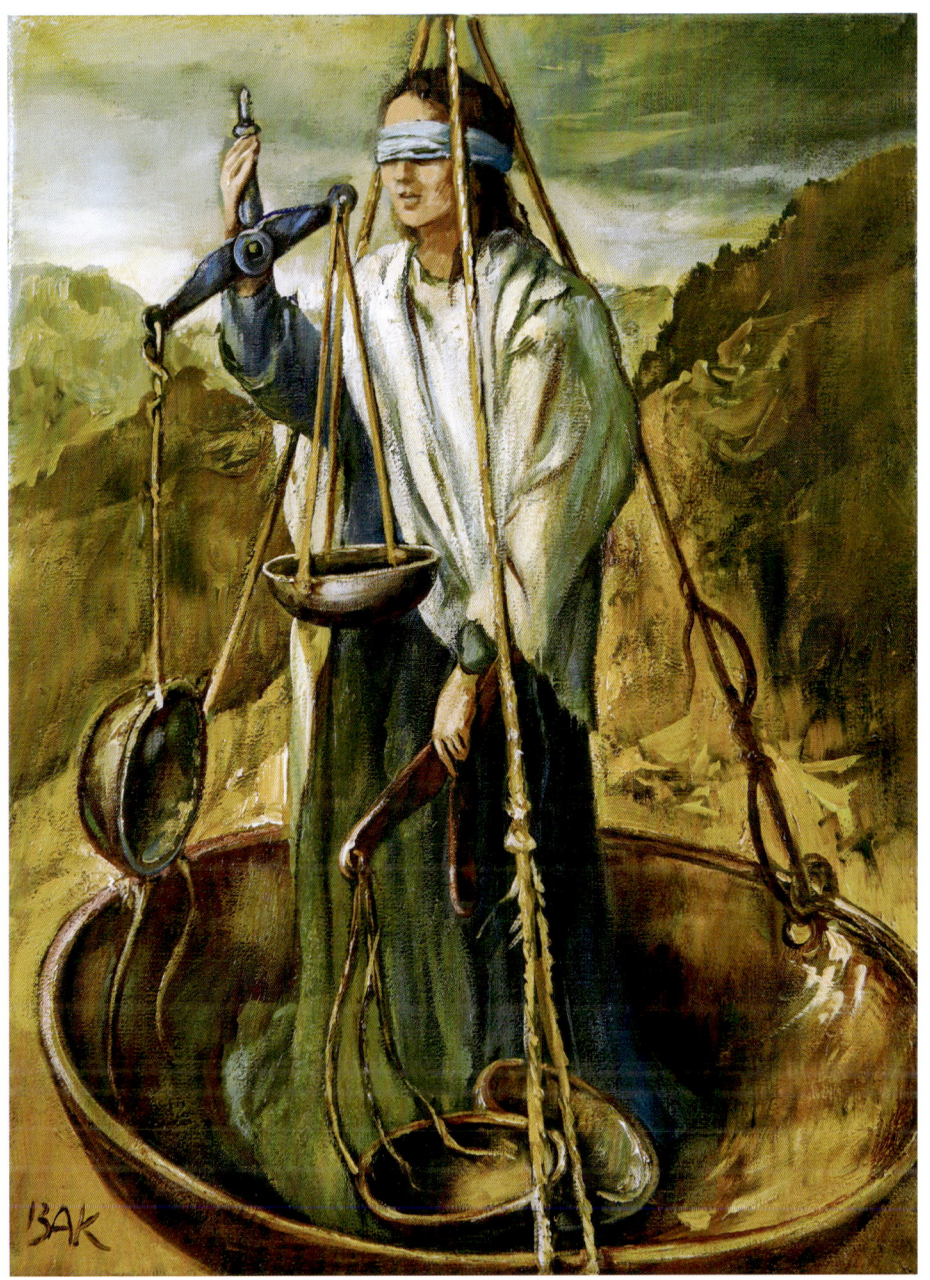

Emblem
Oil on canvas
12 x 9"
BK1982

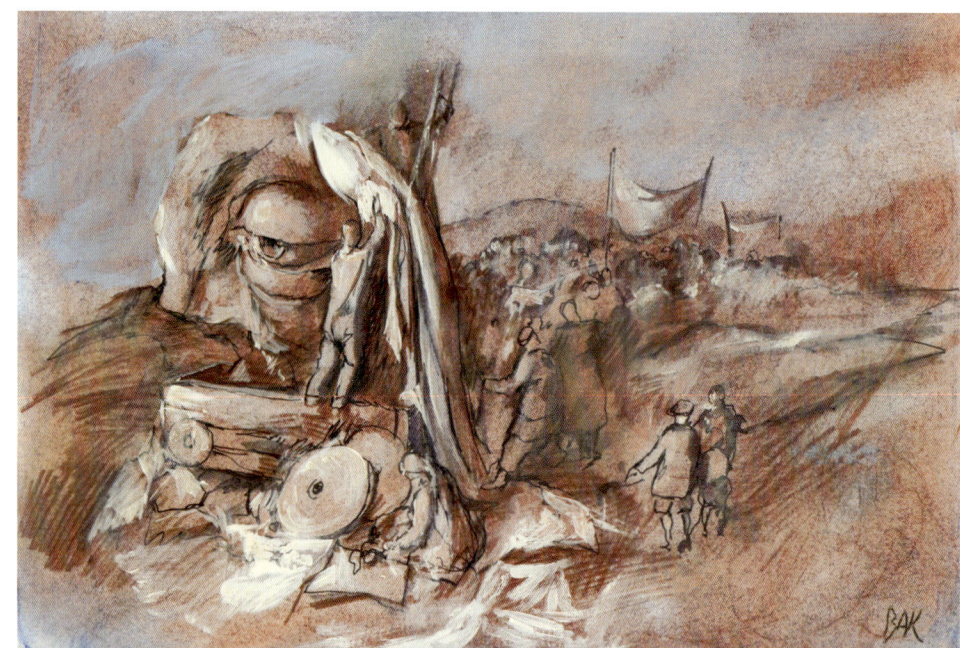

After the Before
Egg tempera on paper
8 x 11.75"
BK2005

BELOW:
Collective Memory
Oil on canvas
16 x 20"
BK1968

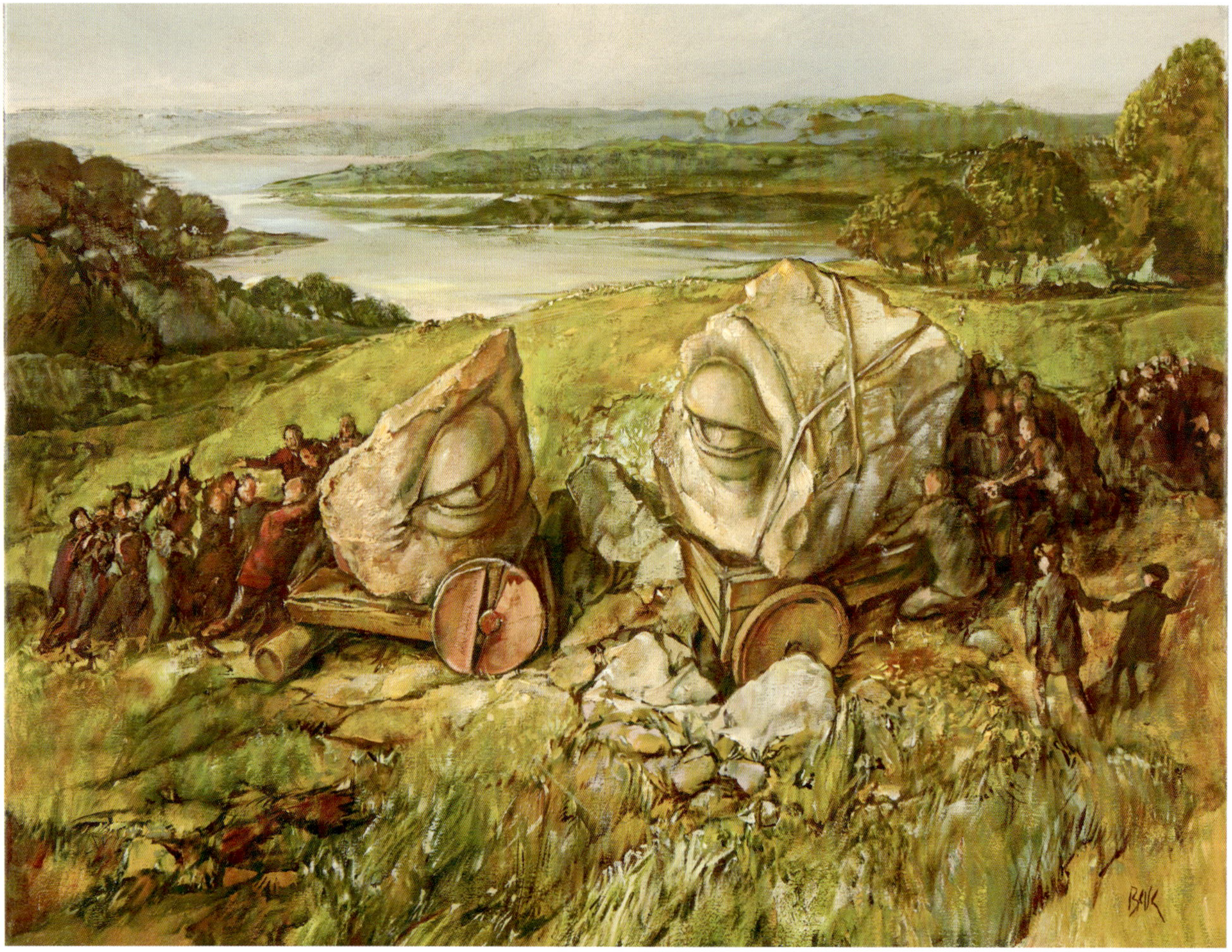

RIGHT:
N Eye for N Eye
Oil on canvas
16 x 12"
BK1971

112

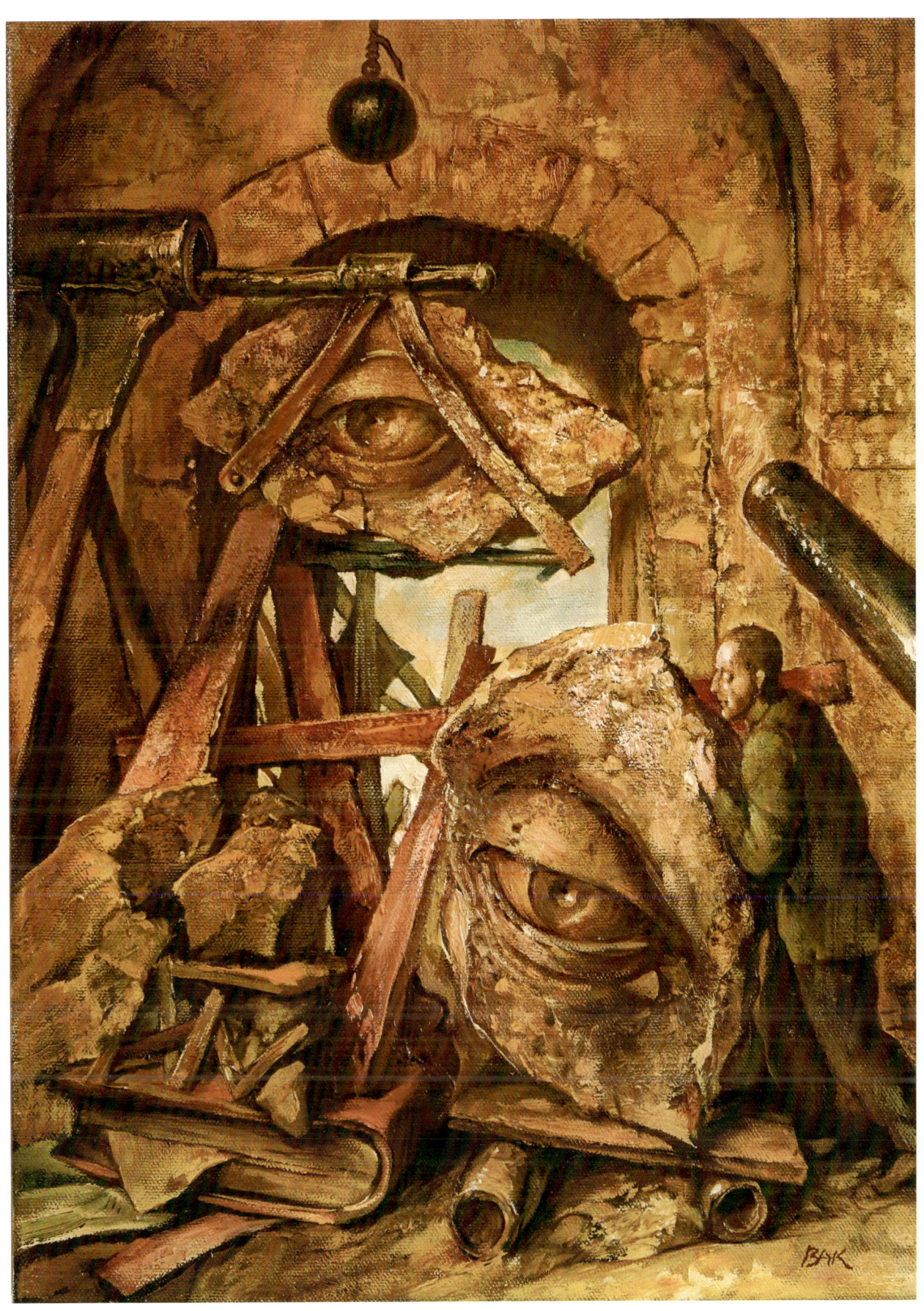

113

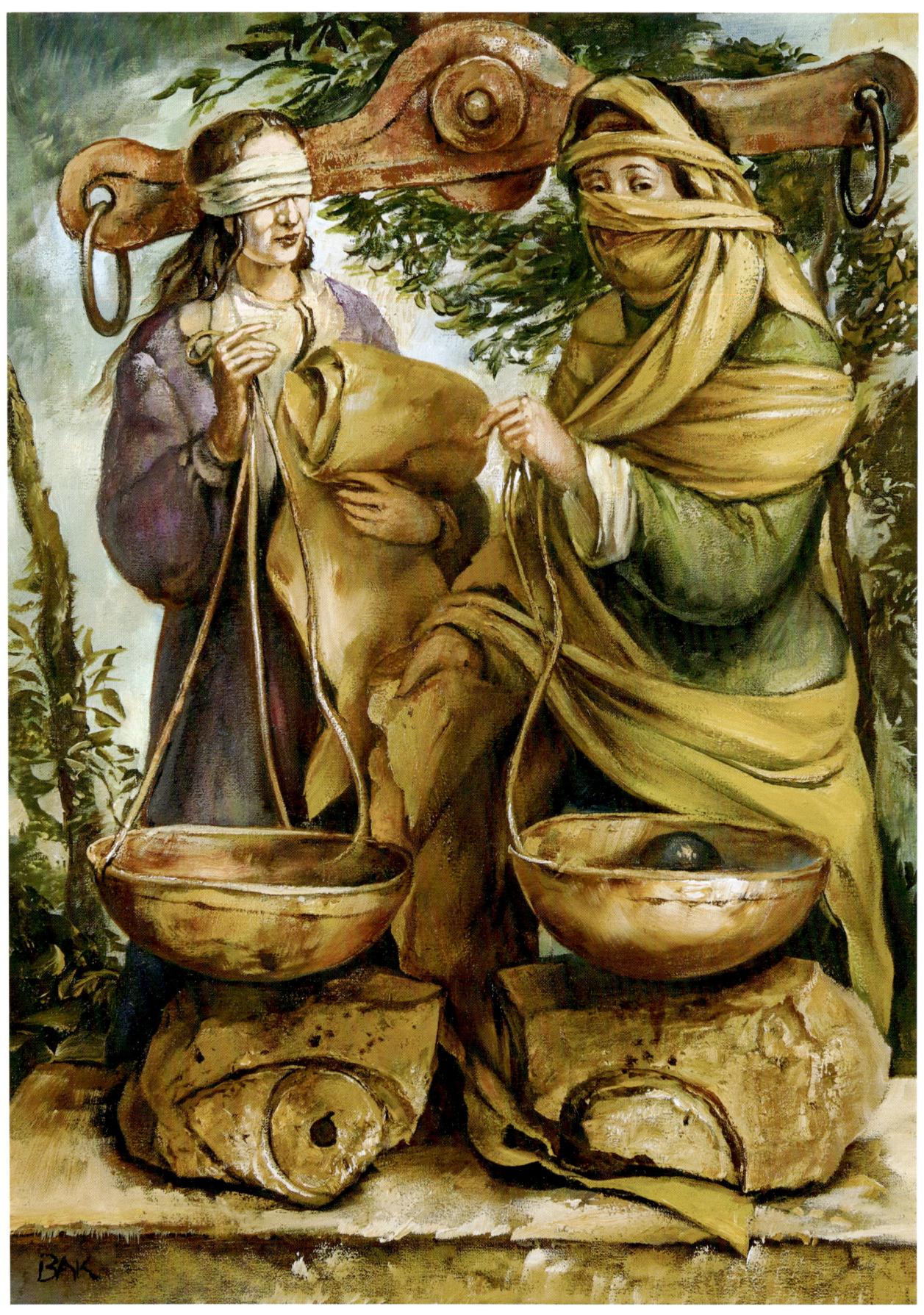

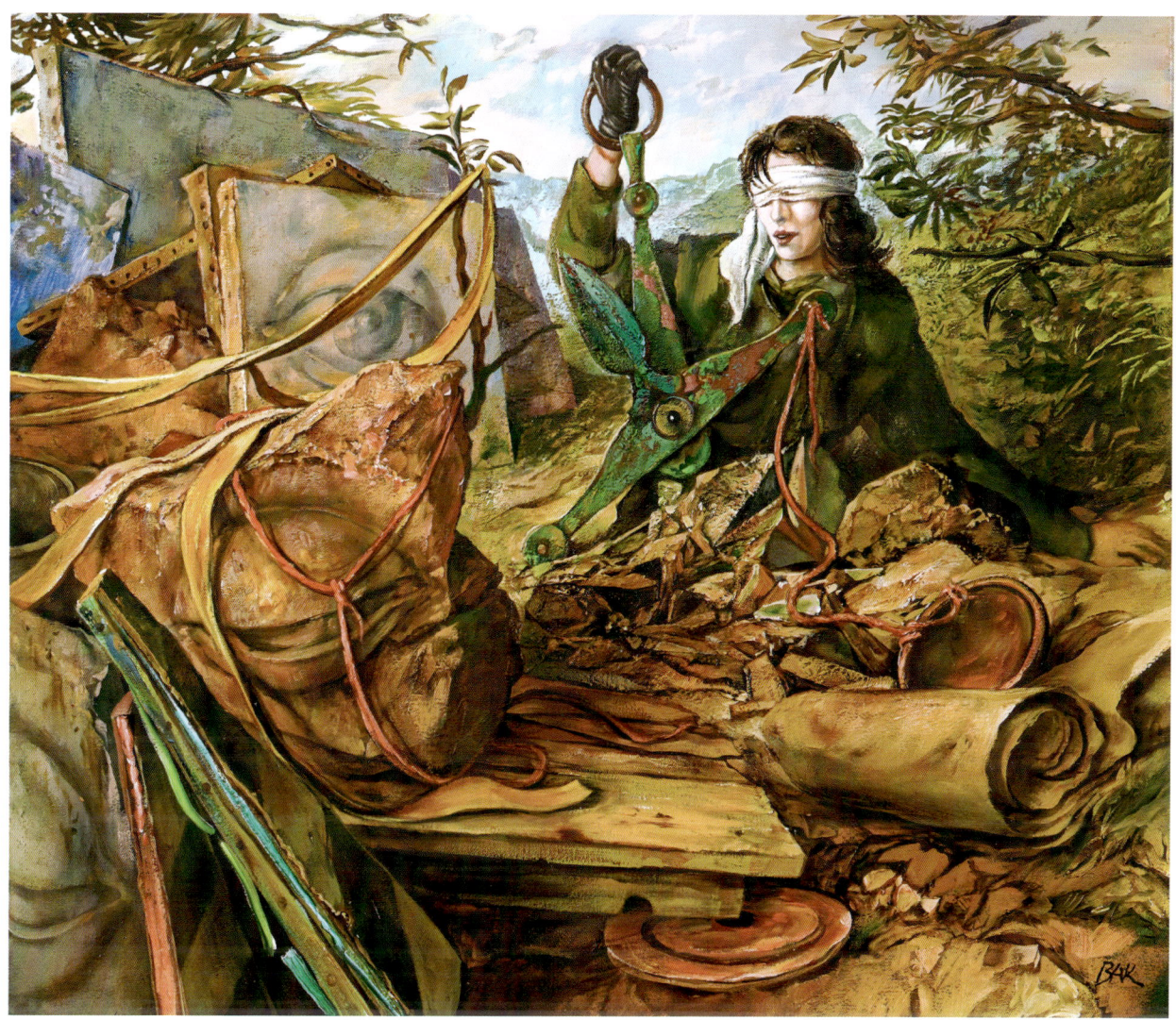

Under Investigation
Oil on canvas
20 x 24"
BK1960

LEFT:
Study for Keeping an Eye
Oil on canvas
16 x 12"
BK1976

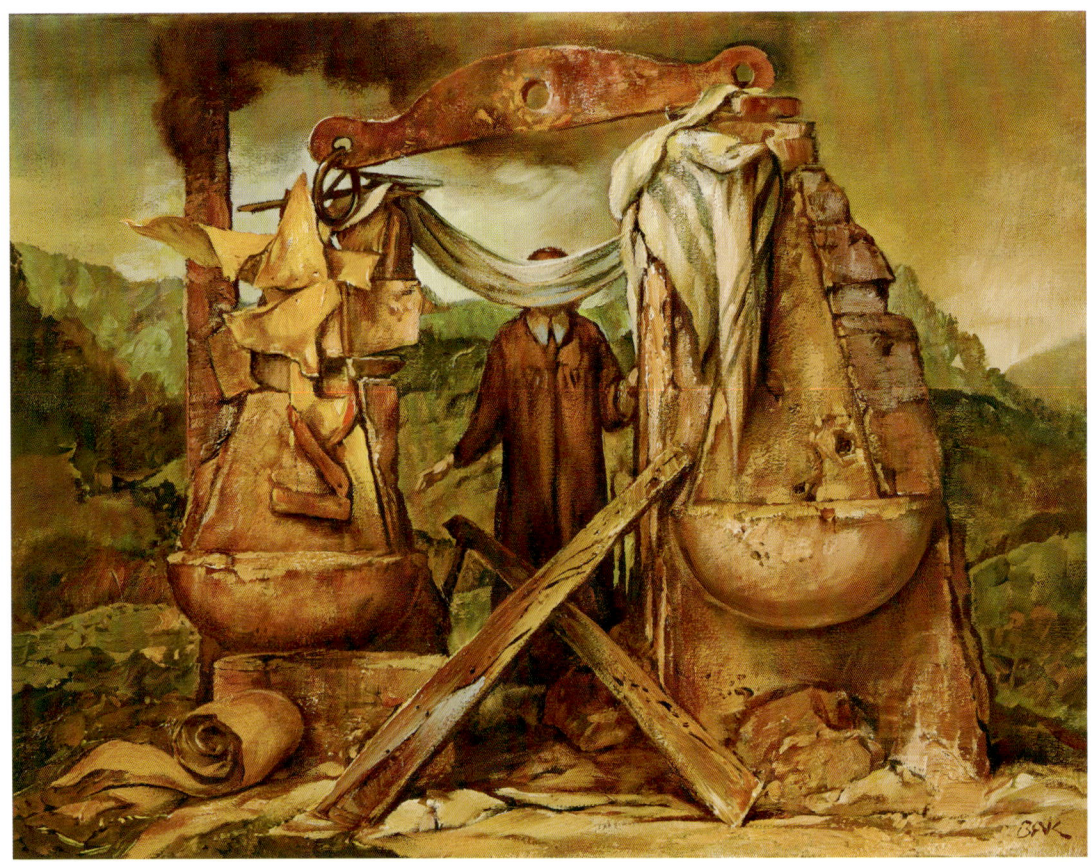

*Study in Search
of a Title A*
Oil on canvas
12 x 16"
BK1972

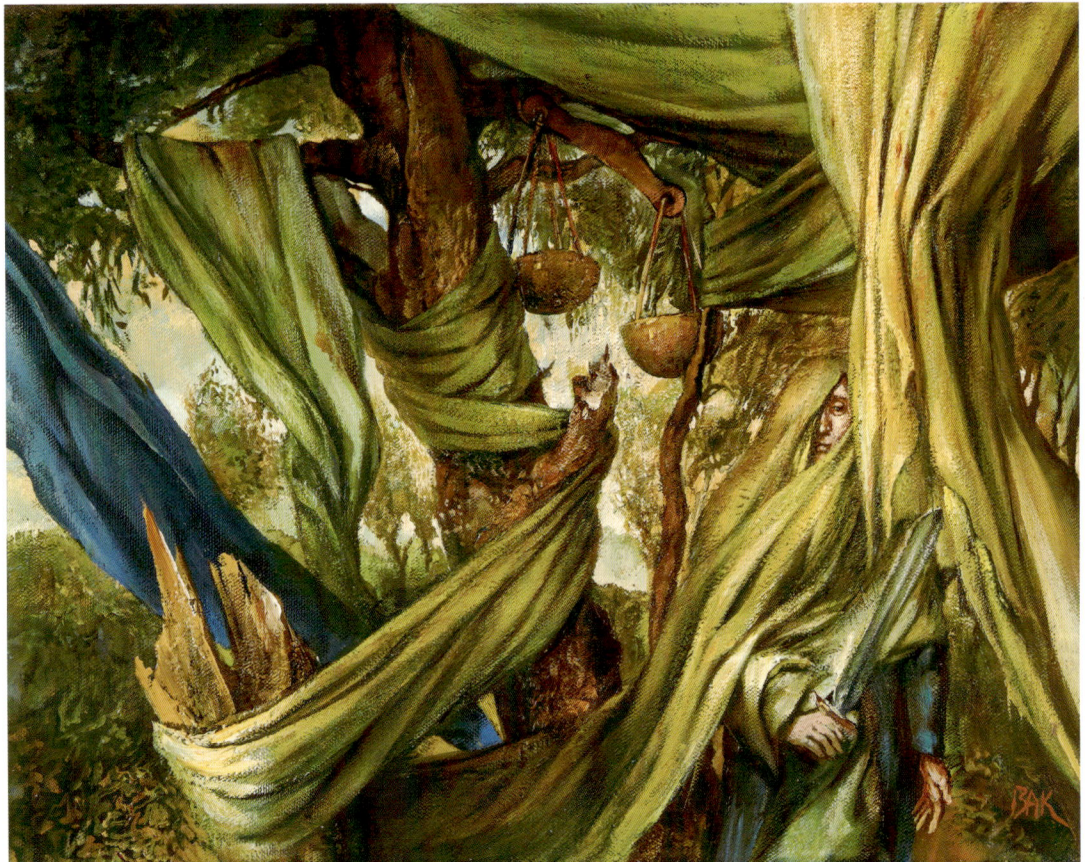

Ever Present
Oil on canvas
12 x 16"
BK1973

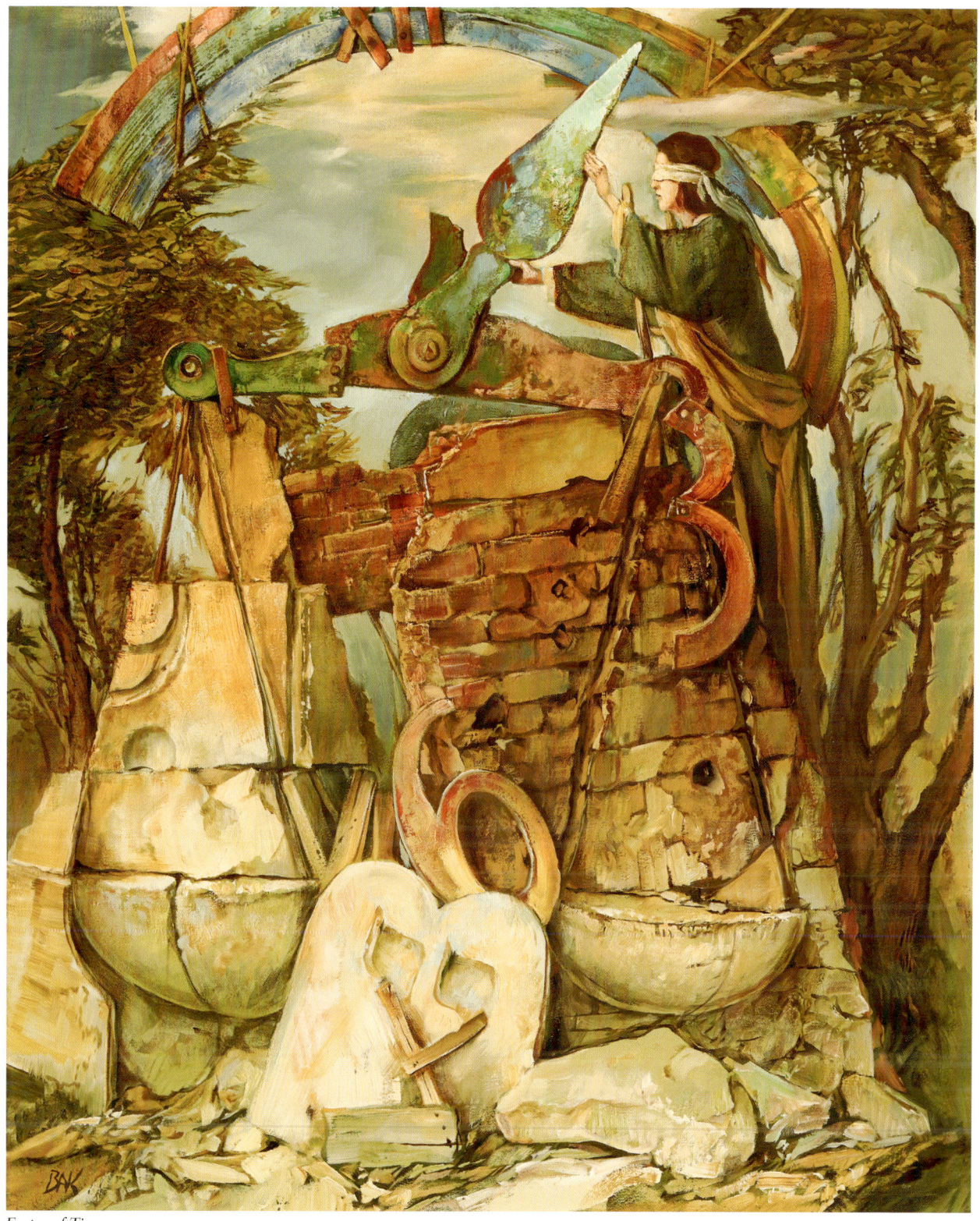

Factor of Time
Oil on canvas
24 x 20"
BK1957

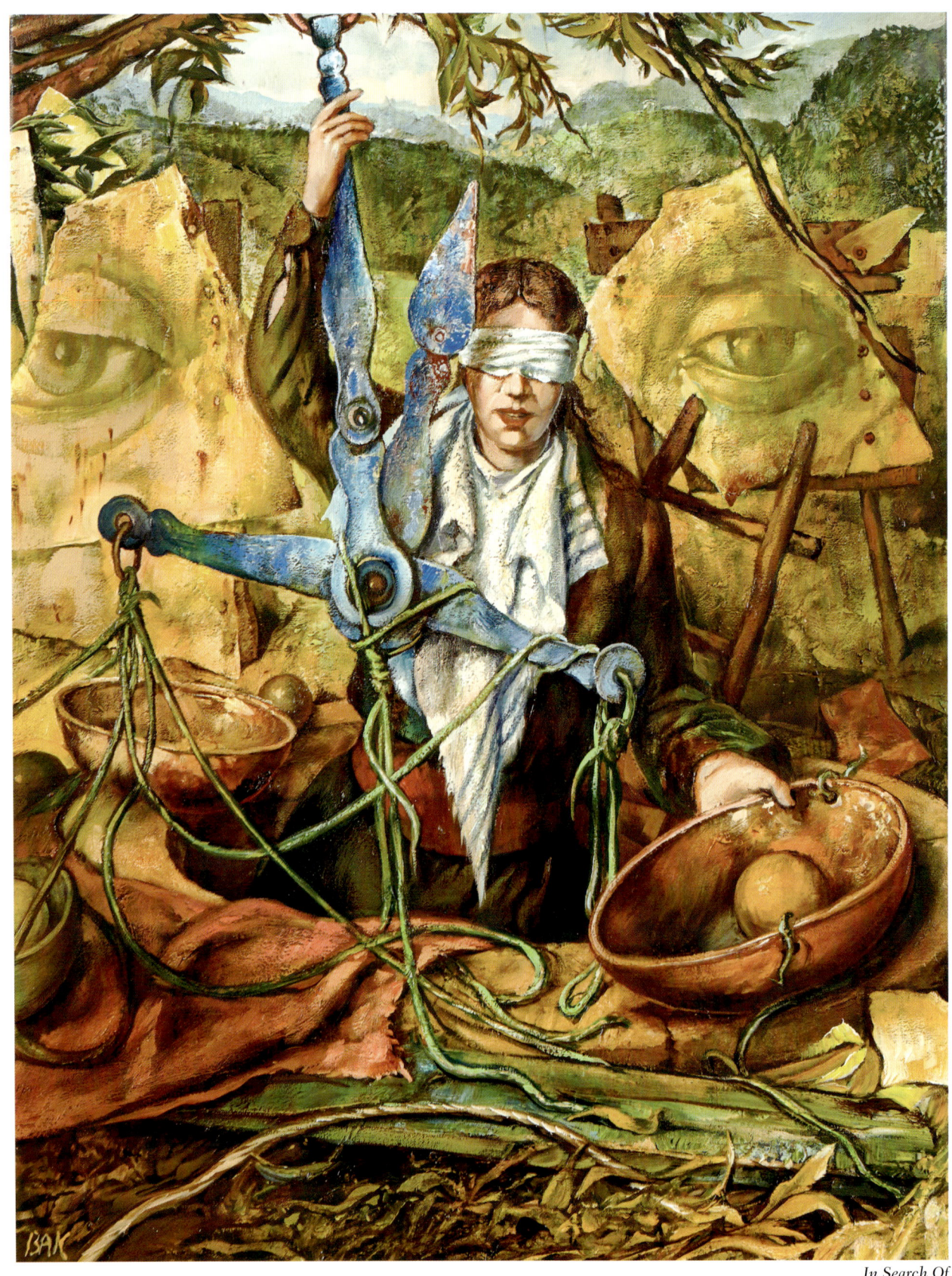

In Search Of
Oil on canvas
24 x 17.75"
BK1965

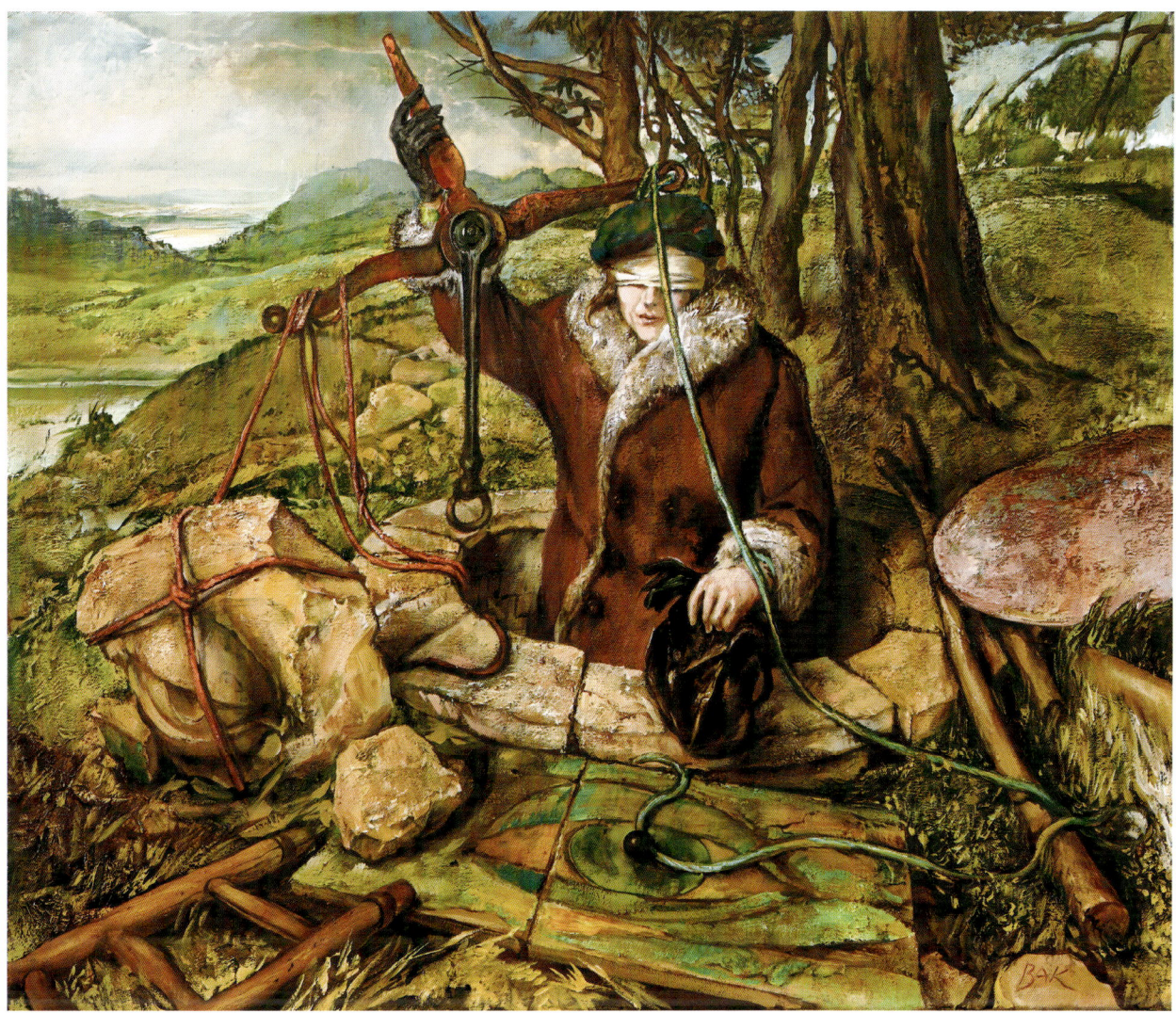

Emergence B
Oil on canvas
20 x 24"
BK1958

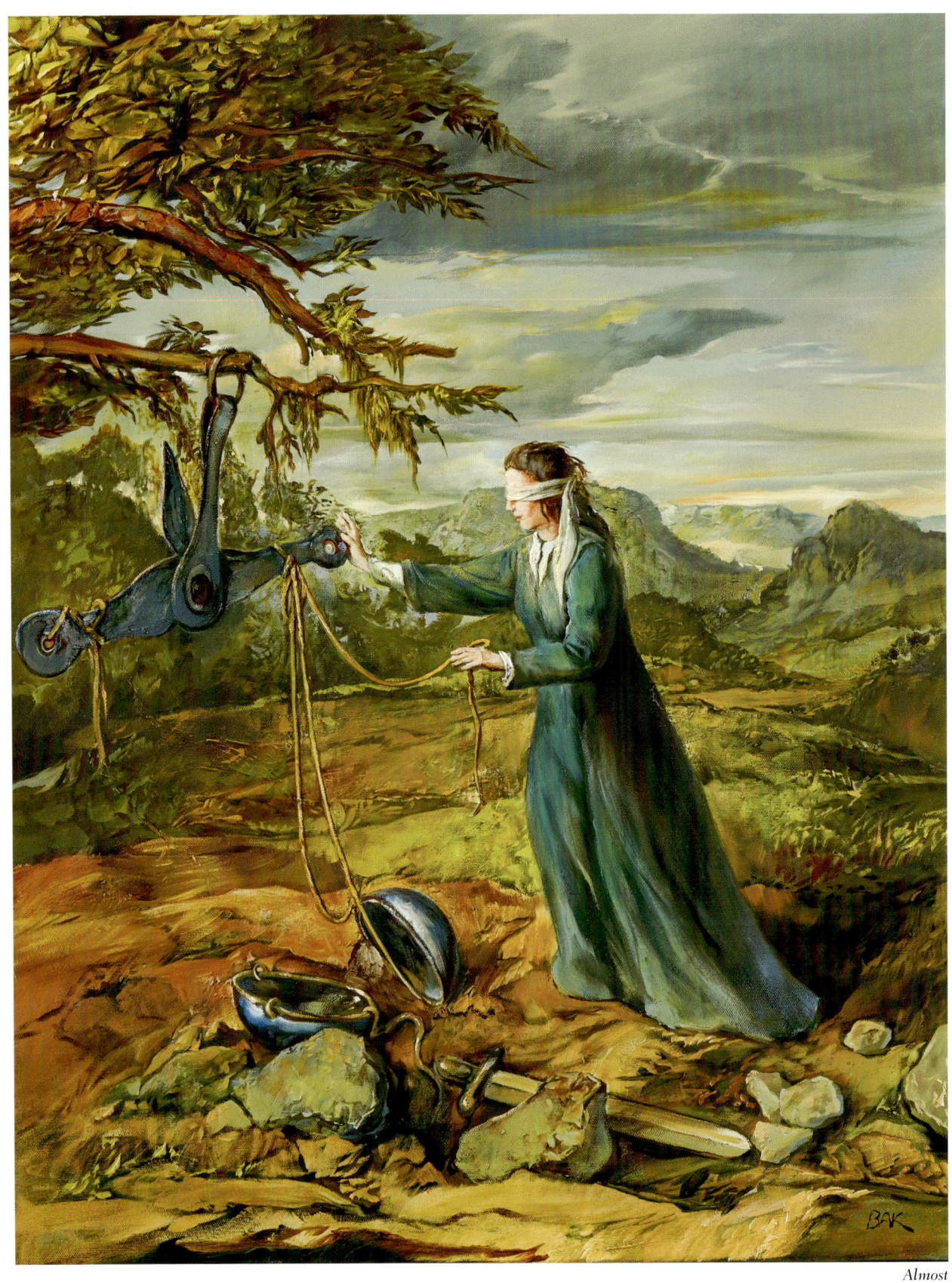

Almost
Oil on canvas
22 x 28"
BK1951

BIOGRAPHY

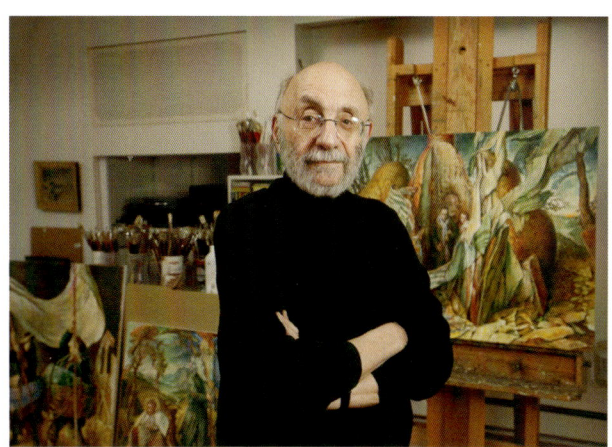
Samuel Bak

Samuel Bak was born in 1933 in Vilna, Poland, at a crucial moment in modern history. From 1940 to 1944, Vilna was under Soviet and then German occupation. Bak's artistic talent was first recognized during an exhibition of his work in the Ghetto of Vilna when he was nine years old. While he and his mother survived, his father and four grandparents all perished at the hands of the Nazis. At the end of World War II, he fled with his mother to the Landsberg Displaced Persons Camp, where he enrolled in painting lessons at the Blocherer School in Munich. In 1948, they immigrated to the newly established state of Israel. He studied at the Bezalel Art School in Jerusalem and completed his mandatory service in the Israeli army. In 1956, he went to Paris to continue his education at the École des Beaux Arts. He received a grant from the America-Israel Cultural Foundation to pursue his artistic studies. In 1959, he moved to Rome where his first exhibition of abstract paintings met with considerable success. In 1961, he was invited to exhibit at the "Carnegie International" in Pittsburg, followed by solo exhibitions at the Jerusalem and Tel Aviv Museums in 1963.

It was subsequent to these exhibitions that a major change in his art occurred. There was a distinct shift from abstract forms to a metaphysical figurative means of expression. Ultimately, this transformation crystallized into his present pictorial language. Bak's work weaves together personal history and Jewish history to articulate an iconography of his Holocaust experience. Across seven decades of artistic production, Samuel Bak has explored and reworked a set of metaphors, a visual grammar, and vocabulary that ultimately privileges questions. His art depicts a world destroyed, and yet provisionally pieced back together and preserves memory of the twentieth century ruination of Jewish life and culture by way of an artistic passion and precision that stubbornly announces the creativity of the human spirit.

Since 1959, the artist has had numerous exhibitions in major museums, galleries, and universities throughout Europe, Israel, and the United States including retrospectives at Yad Vashem Museum in Jerusalem, and the South African Jewish Museum in Cape Town. He has lived and worked in Tel Aviv, Paris, Rome, New York, and Lausanne. In 1993, he settled in Massachusetts and became an American citizen. Bak has been the subject of numerous articles, scholarly works, and twenty books; most notably a 400-page monograph entitled *Between Worlds.* In 2001, he published his touching memoir, *Painted in Words,* which has been translated into several languages. He has also been the subject of two documentary films and was the recipient of the 2002 German Herkomer Cultural Prize. Samuel Bak has received honorary doctorate degrees from the University of New Hampshire in Durham, Seton Hill University in Greenburg, Pennsylvania, and Massachusetts College of Art in Boston.

In 2017, The Samuel Bak Museum opened in the city of the artist's birth, on the first two floors of the Tolerance Center of the Vilna Gaon State Jewish Museum. In addition to fifty works already donated by the artist, the Museum will continue to accept works in the coming years and ultimately build a collection that spans the artist's career. The Museum honors Bak's life and art and is a testament to his commitment to educate current and future generations. Also in 2017, Samuel Bak was nominated by the Vilna Gaon State Jewish Museum, and subsequently named by the city's mayor, as an Honorary Citizen of Vilnius. He is only the 15th person to receive this honor, joining Ronald Reagan and Shimon Peres for their exceptional contributions to Lithuania.

Public Collections

Bard College, Annandale-on-Hudson, NY

Ben Uri Gallery, London, United Kingdom

Beth Israel Deaconess Medical Center, Brookline, MA

Boca Raton Museum of Art, Boca Raton, FL

Boston Public Library, Boston, MA

Constitutional Court of South Africa, Braamfontein, South Africa

Davis Museum and Cultural Center, Wellesley College, Wellesley, MA

DeCordova Museum, Lincoln, MA

Drew University, Madison, NJ

Dürer House, Nuremberg, Germany

Felix Nussbaum Haus, Osnabrück, Germany

Facing History and Ourselves, Boston, MA

Florida Holocaust Museum, Saint Petersburg, FL

Germanisches National Museum, Nuremberg, Germany

German Parliament, Bonn, Germany

Haifa University, Haifa, Israel

Hillel Foundation, Washington, DC

Hobart and William Smith College, Geneva, NY

Holocaust Memorial Center, Farmington Hills, MI

Holocaust Museum Houston, Houston, TX

Hood Museum of Art, Dartmouth College, Hanover, NH

Imperial War Museum, London, United Kingdom

Israel Museum, Jerusalem, Israel

Jewish Museum, New York, NY

Jüdisches Museum, Stadt Frankfurt am Main, Germany

Keene State College, Cohen Holocaust Center, Keene, NH

Kunstmuseum, Bamberg, Germany

McMullen Museum, Boston College, Chestnut Hill, MA

Municipality of Nuremberg, Nuremberg, Germany

Museum of Modern Art, San Francisco, CA

National Gallery of Canada, Ottawa, Canada

National Museum of Lithuania, Vilnius, Lithuania

Panorama Museum, Bad Frankenhausen, Germany

Philadelphia Museum of Art, Philadelphia, PA

Philips Exeter Academy, Exeter, NH

Rose Museum, Brandeis University, Waltham, MA

Royal Ontario Museum, Toronto, Canada

The Samuel Bak Museum, Vilnius, Lithuania

Sherwin Miller Museum of Jewish Art, Tulsa, OK

Simmons College, Boston, MA

Snite Museum of Art, Notre Dame University, South Bend, IN

South African Jewish Museum, Cape Town, South Africa

Springfield Museum of Fine Art, Springfield, MA

Swarthmore College, Swarthmore, PA

Tel Aviv Museum of Art, Tel Aviv, Israel

Tufts University, Medford, MA

Tweed Art Museum, University of Minnesota, Duluth, MN

UJA Federation of Greater Toronto, Canada

University of Scranton, Scranton, PA

University of Vermont, Burlington, VT

Wabash College, Crawfordsville, IN

Williams College Museum of Art, Williamstown, MA

Yad Vashem Museum, Jerusalem, Israel

Publications and Films

Samuel Bak, Paintings of the Last Decade, A. Kaufman and Paul T. Nagano. Aberbach, New York, 1974.

Samuel Bak, Monuments to Our Dreams, Rolf Kallenbach. Limes Verlag, Weisbaden & Munich, 1977.

Samuel Bak, The Past Continues, Samuel Bak and Paul T. Nagano. David R. Godine, Boston, 1988.

Chess as Metaphor in the Art of Samuel Bak, Jean Louis Cornuz. Pucker Art Publications, Boston & C.A. Olsommer, Montreux, 1991.

Ewiges Licht (Landsberg: A Memoir 1944-1948), Samuel Bak. Jewish Museum, Frankfurt, Germany, 1996.

Landscapes of Jewish Experience, Lawrence Langer. Pucker Art Publications, Boston & University Press of New England, Hanover, 1997.

Samuel Bak – Retrospective. Bad Frankenhausen Museum, Bad Frankenhausen, Germany, 1998.

The Game Continues: Chess in the Art of Samuel Bak, Pucker Art Publications, Boston & Indiana University Press, Bloomington, 2000.

In A Different Light: The Book of Genesis in the Art of Samuel Bak, Lawrence Langer. Pucker Art Publications, Boston & University of Washington Press, Seattle, 2001.

The Art of Speaking About the Unspeakable. TV Film by Rob Cooper and Pucker Art Publications, Boston, 2001.

Between Worlds: Paintings and Drawings by Samuel Bak from 1946-2001. Pucker Art Publications, Boston, 2002.

Painted in Words—A Memoir, Samuel Bak. Pucker Art Publications, Boston & Indiana University Press, Bloomington, 2002.

Samuel Bak: Painter of Questions. TV Film by Christa Singer, Toronto, Canada, 2003.

New Perceptions of Old Appearances in the Art of Samuel Bak, Lawrence Langer. Pucker Art Publications, Boston & Syracuse University Press, Syracuse, 2005.

Samuel Bak: Leben danach, Life Thereafter, Eva Atlan and Peter Junk. Felix Nussbaum Haus & Rasch, Verlag, Bramsche, Osnabrueck, Germany, 2006.

Return to Vilna in the Art of Samuel Bak, Lawrence Langer. Pucker Art Publications, Boston & Syracuse University Press, Syracuse, 2007.

Representing the Irreparable: The Shoah, the Bible, and the Art of Samuel Bak, Danna Nolan Fewell, Gary A. Phillips and Yvonne Sherwood, Eds. Pucker Art Publications, Boston, and Syracuse University Press, Syracuse, 2008.

Icon of Loss: The Haunting Child of Samuel Bak, Danna Nolan Fewell and Gary A. Phillips. Pucker Art Publications, Boston, and Syracuse University Press, Syracuse, 2009.

Adam & Eve in the Art of Samuel Bak, Lawrence L. Langer. Pucker Art Publications, Boston & Syracuse University Press, Syracuse, 2012.

Told & Foretold: The Cup in the Art of Samuel Bak, Lawrence L. Langer. Pucker Art Publications, Boston & Syracuse University Press, Syracuse, 2014.

From Generation to Generation: Paintings by Samuel Bak, Lawrence L. Langer. Pucker Art Publications, Boston & Syracuse University Press, Syracuse, 2016.

Just Is In the Art of Samuel Bak, Gary A. Phillips. Pucker Art Publications, Boston & Syracuse University Press, Syracuse, 2018.

AFTERWORD

As we approach the publication of our eighteenth book on the remarkable art of Samuel Bak, I am reminded what a privilege it is to work alongside him, to attempt to share and preserve his immense contribution to the world of art and thought, his profound considerations of the "human condition" in our day.

Bak's art is the definition of contemporary in that it allows us to confront the moral questions that grow out of the day to day lives of ourselves and others. Professor Gary Phillips has provided a remarkable text, exploring expectations and questions, inviting the reader/viewer to engage with the critical questions of our individual responsibilities to repair our broken world.

Rarely does art that is interested in the fundamental beauty of color, form, and texture also call us to confront the profound issues of humankind's inhumanity to others.

For this publication, we have included a "Reader's Guide" of ideas culled from the essay to encourage you to become included, to be an upstander instead of a bystander.

Great thanks to Sam and Josée for continuing to enrich our world with your vision and your unrelenting search for answers.

—*B. H. Pucker, Winter 2017*

BIBLIOGRAPHY

Adorno, Theodor W. *Aesthetic Theory.* Translated by Robert Hullot-Kentor. Minneapolis: University of Minnesota Press, 1997.

—. "Commitment." In *The Essential Frankfurt School Reader,* edited by Andrew Arato and Eike Gebhardt, 300–318. New York: Continuum, 1985.

—. "Metaphysics: Concepts and Problems." In *Can One Live After Auschwitz? A Philosophical Reader,* edited by Rolf Tiedemann. Translated by Rodney Livingstone and others, 427–469. Stanford: Stanford University Press, 2003.

—. *Minima Moralia: Reflections from Damaged Life.* Radical Thinkers Classics. Translated by E. F. N. Jeffcott. London: Verso, 2005.

—. *Negative Dialectics.* Translated by E. B. Ashton. New York: Continuum, 1992.

Bak, Samuel. *Painted in Words. A Memoir.* Boston: Pucker Art Publications, 2001.

Barber, Daniel Coluccieller. "Theodor Adorno." *In Religion and European Philosophy: Key Thinkers from Kant to Žižek.* Edited by Philip Goodchild and Hollis Phelps, 127–40. New York: Routledge, 2017.

Bernstein, J. M. *Adorno: Disenchantment and Ethics.* Modern European Philosophy. Cambridge: Cambridge University Press, 2001.

—. "Suffering Injustice: Misrecognition as Moral Injury in Critical Theory." *International Journal of Philosophical Studies* 13 (2005): 303–24.

Daube, David. "Eye for Eye." In *New Testament Judaism. Collected Works of David Daube,* edited by Calum Carmichael, 177–86. Vol. 2. Berkeley: University of California Press, 2000.

—. "Lex Talionis." In *Studies in Biblical Law,* 102–53. Cambridge: Cambridge University Press, 1947.

—. *New Testament and Rabbinic Judaism.* New York: Wipf and Stock, 1956.

Edgar, Andrew. "The Art of Useless Suffering." *Medicine, Health Care and Philosophy* 10 (2007): 395–405.

Fackenheim, Emil. *God's Presence in History: Jewish Affirmation and Philosophical Reflections.* New York: New York University Press, 1970.

Fewell, Danna Nolan, and Gary A. Phillips. "Bak's Impossible Memorials: Giving Face to the Children." In *Representing the Irreparable: The Shoah, the Bible and the Art of Samuel Bak,* edited by Danna Nolan Fewell, Gary A. Phillips, and Yvonne Sherwood, 92–113. Boston: Pucker Art Publication, 2008.

—. "From Bak to the Bible: Imagination, Interpretation, and Tikkun Olam." ARTS: The Arts in Religious and Theological Studies 20 (2009): 21–30.

—. *Icon of Loss: The Haunting Child of Samuel Bak.* Boston: Pucker Art Publication, 2009.

—. "Genesis, Genocide and the Art of Samuel Bak: "Unseamly" Reading After the Holocaust." In *Representing the Irreparable: The Shoah, the Bible and the Art of Samuel Bak,* edited by Danna Nolan Fewell, Gary A. Phillips, and Yvonne Sherwood, 75–91. Boston: Pucker Art Publication, 2008.

Freud, Sigmund. *Beyond the Pleasure Principle.* Standard Edition. Translated by James Strachey, Anna Freud, Alix Strachey, and Alan Tyson, 1–64. Vol. 24. London: Hogarth Press, 1920.

Frymer-Kensky, Tikva. "Tit for Tat." *Biblical Archeologist* 43 (1980): 230–34.

Gibbs, Robert. "Unjustifiable Suffering." In *Suffering Religion,* edited by Robert Gibbs and Elliott R. Wolfson, 13–35. New York: Routledge, 2002.

Hejinian, Lyn. *The Language of Inquiry.* Berkeley: University of California Press, 2000.

Hofmann, Klaus. "Poetry after Auschwitz—Adorno's Dictum." *German Life and Letters* 58 (2005): 182–94.

Horkheimer, Max, and Theodor W. Adorno. *Dialectic of Enlightenment. Philosophical Fragments,* edited by Gunzelin Schmid Noerr. Translated by Edmund Jephcott. Culture Memory in the Present. Stanford: Stanford University Press, 2002.

Jay, Martin. *Adorno.* Cambridge: Harvard University Press, 1984.

Langer, Lawrence L. "The Dilemma of Choice in the Deathcamps." In *Holocaust: Religious and Philosophical Implications,* edited by John K. Roth and Michael Berenbaum. New York: Paragon House, 1989.

—. *Holocaust Testimonies. The Ruin of Memory.* New Haven: Yale University Press, 1993.

—. *Using and Abusing the Holocaust.* Bloomington: Indiana University Press, 2006.

Langer, Lawrence L. and Samuel Bak. *Return to Vilna in the Art of Samuel Bak.* Boston: Pucker Art Publications, 2007.

Langmuir, Gavin I. *Toward a Definition of Antisemitism.* Berkeley: University of California Press, 1990.

Laub, Dori. "Bearing Witness or the Vicissitudes of Listening." In *Testimony: Crises of Witnessing in Literature,* Psychoanalysis, and History, edited by Shoshana Felman and Dori Laub, 57–74. New York and London: Routledge, 1992.

Laub, Dori, and Dan Podell. "Art and Trauma. *The International Journal of Psychoanalysis* 76 (1995): 991–1005.

Levi, Neil. *Modernist Form and the Myth of Jewification.* New York: Fordham University Press, 2014.

Levi, Primo. *Survival in Auschwitz.* Translated by Stuart Woolf. New York: Simon and Schuster, 1996.

Levinas, Emmanuel. "Useless Suffering." In *The Provocation of Levinas: Rethinking the Other,* edited by Robert Bernasconi and David Wood, 156–67. New York: Routledge, 1988.

Levitan, Eliat Gordon. "The Ghosts of Samuel Bak. Vilna Stories." Accessed May 30, 2017. http://www.eilatgordinlevitan.com/vilna/vilna_pages/vilna_stories_s_bak.html.

Moses Maimonides. *Laws of Wounds and Damages.* Available online: http://www.chabad.org/library/article_cdo/aid/1088908/jewish/Chovel-uMazzik-Chapter-One.htm. Accessed May 30, 2017.

Miller, William Ian. *Eye for an Eye.* Cambridge: Cambridge University Press, 2006.

Müller-Doohm, Stephan. *Adorno: A Biography.* Malden, MA: Polity Press, 2005.

Nosthoff, Anna-Verena. "Barbarism: Notes on the Thought of Theodor W. Adorno." *Critical Legal Thinking. Law and the Political.* Accessed May 30, 2017. http://criticallegalthinking.com/2014/10/15/ barbarism-notes-thought-theodor-w-adorno/.

Ostrove, Geoff. "Adorno, Auschwitz, and the New Categorical Imperative." *Perspectives on Global Development and Technology* 12 (2013): 298–309.

Parker, Theodore. "Of Justice and the Conscience." In *Ten Sermons of Religion,* 66–101. Boston: Crosby, Nichols and Company, 1853. Accessed May 30, 2017 https://archive.org/stream/tensermonsofreli00inpark/tensermonsofreli00inpark_djvu.txt.

Phillips, Gary A. "An Eye for an I: An Intertextual Reading of Matthew 5:38 and the Artwork of Samuel Bak." In The *Press of the Text: Biblical Studies in Honor of James W. Voelz,* edited by Andrew H. Bartlet, Jeffrey Kloha, and Paul R. Raabe, 179–199. Eugene: Pickwick Publications, 2017.

—. *"Icons of Just Is:* Justice, Suffering, and the Artwork of Samuel Bak." *Religions* 8/6 2017): 108. Accessed June 15, 2017. doi:10.3390/rel8060108.

Pols, Elizabeth. "Beyond Time: The Paintings of Samuel Bak." Paken Treger. *Magazine of the Yiddish Book Center.* Spring, 2010. Accessed May 30, 2017. http://www.yiddishbookcenter. org/language-literature-culture/pakn-treger/beyond-time-paintings-samuel-bak.

Pritchard, Elizabeth. "Bilderverbot Meets Body in Theodor W. Adorno's Inverse Theology." *The Harvard Theological Review* 95 (2002): 291–318.

Raskin, Richard. A Child at Gunpoint. *A Case Study in the Life of a Photo.* Aarhus: Aarhus University Press, 2004.

Resnik, Judith, and Dennis E. Curtis. "Images of Justice." *The Yale Law Journal* 96 (1987): 1727–72. Faculty Scholarship Series. Paper 917.Accessed May 30, 2017. http:// digitalcommons.law.yale.edu/fss_papers/917/.

Rosenzweig, Franz. *The Star of Redemption.* Translated by Barbara E. Galli. Madison: University of Wisconsin Press, 2005.

Roth, John K. *The Failures of Ethics. Confronting the Holocaust, Genocide and Other Mass Atrocities.* New York: Oxford University Press, 2015.

Rothberg, Michael. "After Adorno: Culture in the Wake of Catastrophe." *New German Critique* 72 (1997): 45–81.

Sachs, Carl B. "The Acknowledgement of Transcendence: Anti-theodicy in Adorno and Levinas." *Philosophy and Social Criticism* 37 (2011): 273–94.

Nahum Sarna. *Exodus.* The JPS Torah Commentary. Philadelphia: Jewish Publication Society, 1991.

Sartre, John-Paul. *What Is Literature and Other Essays.* Cambridge: Harvard University Press, 1988.

Thompson, James. *Twentieth-Century Theories of Art.* Ottawa: Carleton University Press, 1990.

Weaver, Dorothy Jean. "Transforming Nonresistance: From Lex Talionis to 'Do Not Resist the Evil One.' In *The Love of Enemy and Nonretaliation in the New Testament,* edited by Willard M. Swartley, 32–71. Louisville: Westminster John Knox Press, 1992.

READER'S GUIDE

Samuel Bak purposefully preserves ambiguity and poses questions in his art, reminding the viewer that ultimate responsibility for answers lies within themselves. Through the reiteration of certain passages in the text and the posing of questions inspired by it, this reader's guide accompanies you on a more nuanced and thought-provoking understanding of *Just Is.*

Passages to Contemplate

"Who and what, by implication, is missing from [these] pictures, no longer in sight, if not the Jews who were made to suffer uselessly?… Bak's unblinking talionic eyes stare back at us in search of answers to disturbing questions about *Just Is,* what we see, and, importantly, what we choose not to see." (page 15)

"How are the principles of retribution, restitution, and restoration possibly associated with lex talionis thinkable in view of the violence committed on [the scale of the Holocaust]? The weight of suffering Bak presents defies every measure of meaning and morality, the math too severe to account for the empirical reality." (page 17)

"Presenting Lady *Just Is* standing squarely amid, not above or removed from, the destruction, Bak asks if she, and we, are ready to stand upright before just is in this damaged world. As with much of Bak's representation of loss, we oscillate in a dialectical way between uncertainty and hope." (page 30)

"With eyes wide open and icons provisionally refashioned for the uncertain work ahead, Bak places the loss and repair of this suffering world, of *tikkun olam,* before our eyes and in our hands leaving us to decide what our next step will be." (page 33)

How does the beauty of Bak's paintings, which stands in jarring tension to the barbarity of their subject, help us to better understand suffering?

Have we, as human beings, failed to uphold justice and settled for what "just is"?

How do Bak's empty, broken, and violated scales bear witness to the impossibility of balancing unfailing cruelty with unfailing love? Which prevails?

Are we, as bystanders, implicated in the suffering injustice? Do we avert our eyes? What is required for us to confront the reality of injustice, take responsibility, and effect change?